cinema of actuality

asia-pacific: culture, politics, and society

Editors: Rey Chow, Michael Dutton, H. D. Harootunian, and Rosalind C. Morris

cinema of actuality

JAPANESE AVANT-GARDE FILMMAKING IN THE SEASON OF IMAGE POLITICS

yuriko furuhata

DUKE UNIVERSITY PRESS | DURHAM AND LONDON | 2013

Designed by Amy Ruth Buchanan
Typeset in Whitman by Tseng
Information Systems, Inc.

Library of Congress Cataloging-in-Publication Data
Furuhata, Yuriko, 1973–
Cinema of actuality : Japanese avant-garde
filmmaking in the season of image politics /
Yuriko Furuhata.
pages cm—(Asia-Pacific : culture, politics, and
society)
Includes bibliographical references and index.
ISBN 978-0-8223-5490-1 (cloth : alk. paper)
ISBN 978-0-8223-5504-5 (pbk. : alk. paper)
1. Motion pictures—Japan—History—20th
century. 2. Motion pictures—Political aspects—
Japan—History—20th century. I. Title. II. Series:
Asia-Pacific.
PN1993.5.J3F859 2013
791.430952—dc23
2013011687

contents

acknowledgments

It is incredible how writing a book could generate so many encounters. While there were difficult times—from locating obscure materials to being stuck in what seemed like a dead-end of research—now that the book is complete, happy moments prevail. The kernel of this project started out as a doctoral dissertation I wrote under the guidance of Réda Bensmaïa, Rey Chow, and Mary Ann Doane at Brown University. Their intellectual generosity and critical insight pushed me to think beyond disciplinary boundaries. As I began to explore the connection between media events and Japanese avant-garde filmmaking in earnest, the focus of the project shifted more toward media history. In the course of developing the project into a book, I benefited from encounters and conversations with a number of scholars and researchers. I would like to start by thanking a terrific group of friends and colleagues whose energy and intellectual rigor I admire. They have taken time to read drafts of my chapters and helped me develop my ideas: Thomas Lamarre, Masha Salazkina, Tess Takahashi, Alanna Thain, and Teresa Villa-Ignacio. Parts of the book were presented at conferences and delivered as talks where I received valuable feedback. I would like to thank in particular Aaron Gerow, Akira Mizuta Lippit, Mark Abé Nornes, Philip Rosen, and Miryam Sas for their enlightening comments and encouragement at various stages of this project.

In Montreal, I have found an amazing community of friends and colleagues at the Department of East Asian Studies and the World Cinemas Program at McGill University, as well as those at Concordia University and the Université de Montréal. From joyous 5 à 7 gatherings to exhilarating demos on the streets of Montreal to stimulating workshops and study groups, they cultivated my belief in our collective future. In addition to those whose names I have already mentioned, I want to give sincere thanks to Charles Acland, Alia Al-Saji, Brian Bergstrom, Erik Bordeleau, Luca Caminati, Michael Cowan, Kenneth Dean, Kay Dickinson, Victor Fan, Grace Fong, Adrienne Hurley, Erin Manning, Rosanna Maule, Brian Massumi, Livia Monnet, Derek Nystrom, Ara Osterweil, Matthew Penney, Elena Razlogova, Carrie Rentschler, Peter Rist, Catherine Russell, Johanne Sloan, Jonathan Sterne, Will Straw, Toshiya Ueno, Haidee Wasson, and Robin Yates.

In the course of completing this book, I discovered a convivial community of Japanese cinema and avant-garde art scholars, whose scholarship deeply informs my own work. Many thanks go to Roland Domenig, Sharon Hayashi, Gō Hirasawa, Shigeru Matsui, Anne McKnight, Michael Raine, and Julian Ross. In particular, I want to thank Gō for helping me connect with filmmakers, scholars, and activists in Japan. It was his pathbreaking research on *fūkeiron* that first inspired me to develop some of the chapters here. Likewise, I want to thank the following filmmakers for sharing their thoughts and allowing me to use images from their visual works: Adachi Masao, Kanai Katsu, Matsumoto Toshio, and the late Wakamatsu Kōji.

I count myself very fortunate to have met Ken Wissoker, my wonderful editor at Duke University Press. His constant assurance and strong support of my project made the entire process of producing the book enjoyable. Ken and the editorial staff—Elizabeth Ault and Jessica Ryan in particular—at Duke made me feel like I was on a ship with first-rate navigation. My sincere thanks also go to the two anonymous readers whose illuminating comments helped me fine-tune the manuscript. I would also like to extend my gratitude to Harry Harootunian and Rey Chow for inviting me to publish the book in their Asia-Pacific series. Special thanks also goes to Alain Chouinard, Valdis Silins, and Patrick DeDauw for copyediting the manuscript. I would also like to acknowledge the generous funding from the Fonds Québécois de Recherche sur la Société et la Culture (FQRSC), which allowed me to conduct additional research in Japan to complete this book.

Many others have helped me over the years, and some of them deserve to be thanked for sharing their thoughts and for just being there as good friends: David Bering-Porter, Roxanne Carter, Josh Guilford, Noriko Hinata, Franz Hofer, Ōko Ippōshi, Tomoko Komatsuzaki, Takashi Makino, Asako Miyoshi, Pooja Rangan, Julie Levin Russo, Braxton Soderman, Wen Lee Soo, Yuki Tanikawa, Jacob Weiss, and Michael Zryd.

I would also like to extend heartfelt thanks to my late grandmother, who steadfastly supported my decision to leave Japan to go to the United States, and to my fabulous mother, who inspired me to pursue my dreams without forgetting those who made them possible. From her I have inherited openness to the unknown and willingness to tread new territories. Equal thanks go to the rest of my family: my lovely sister and nephews for reminding me that academia is just one part of life, my father for passing on his love of books despite our disagreement over politics, and my amazing in-laws for making Montreal truly my second home.

The person who deserves my final thanks is Marc Steinberg. Without his patience to engage in countless hours of conversation over many breakfasts and his willingness to read numerous drafts, I am not sure I could have completed this book. In addition to appreciating Marc's intellectual support, I am grateful for the other times we spend together, forgetting our work and embracing moments of wonder. Without his presence, life would be lusterless.

Sections of chapter 1 appeared as my article "Audio-Visual Redundancy and Remediation in *Ninja bugeichō*," *Mechademia* 7 (2012): 249–62. Chapter 4 is a reworked and extended version of my article "Returning to Actuality: *Fūkeiron* and the Landscape Film," *Screen* 48.3 (autumn 2007): 345–62.

All translations from Japanese sources are mine unless otherwise noted.

introduction

In January 1968, the popular film magazine *Eiga Geijutsu* (Film art) published a dialogue—sensationally titled "Fascist or Revolutionary?"—between Oshima Nagisa, an acclaimed cinéaste and critic-representative of Japanese New Wave cinema, and Mishima Yukio, a renowned novelist who was to stage a failed coup d'état and ritual suicide as a spectacular media event two years later. The dialogue is intriguing not so much because it suggests a rare point of agreement between Oshima and Mishima, who are considered to stand at opposing ends of the spectrum of political activism (the antinationalist Left and the ultranationalist Right). Rather, the dialogue is fascinating because it highlights their shared interest in television and, more broadly, in the political effects of televisually induced media events. Oshima and Mishima concur that the New Left generation of Japanese student protesters are the children of television whose political actions are deeply conditioned by the ubiquitous presence of the news camera. Oshima calls this media-conscious form of student protest an "expressive act" akin to an artistic performance. Mishima criticizes this view by noting that the substitution of political action by the expressive act attests to the bleakness of the television age in which they all live. Oshima, in contrast, regards this blurring of the boundary between artistic performance and political action in a positive light, suggesting that the very meaning of politics and art should be rethought in light of this situation.[1]

Oshima and Mishima were not alone in remarking on the media consciousness of student protesters during the so-called season of politics (*seiji no kisetsu*) that erupted in the late 1960s and early 1970s. Various factions of student protesters allegedly chose the colors of their ubiquitous construction helmets (worn during protests) based on how they would look on color television.[2] Both the dialogue and this anecdote point to the increasing imbrication of politics and media in Japan, to which the rise and consolidation of television greatly contributed. The season of politics, which coincided with the golden era of leftist independent and avant-garde filmmaking practices, was, in effect, the season of *image* politics.

Oshima's call to redefine politics and art in light of the media-conscious student protesters also sheds light on a little-studied aspect of Japanese political avant-garde filmmaking in the 1960s: the tension between journalistic media and cinema that became visible against the backdrop of intensifying image politics. During the 1960s, the proximity between cinema and journalism gained wide attention from critics and filmmakers. Political avant-garde filmmakers started to approximate—or, more precisely, to appropriate—television and other journalistic media forms. This avant-gardist appropriation of journalism marks an important but overlooked tendency within postwar Japanese cinema. The timely appropriation of sensational news, high-profile media events, and other topical images widely circulating in the press by filmmakers such as Oshima Nagisa, Matsumoto Toshio, Wakamatsu Kōji, and Adachi Masao in the 1960s and early 1970s points to a collectively shared concern with journalistic actuality. For the sake of clarity, I will call this body of films the "cinema of actuality." The spectacular terrain of sensational newsmaking and media events in particular attracted these avant-garde filmmakers, but their appropriation of journalism was not a simple reversion back to cinema's early social function as a "visual newspaper."[3] Instead, the journalistic production of spectacular and sensational news became a complex site of calculated appropriations and critical experimentations in the 1960s, as these Japanese avant-garde filmmakers grappled with the intertwined questions of how to radicalize cinema in light of the escalating mediatization of politics and how to situate cinema within a rapidly changing media environment.[4] The appearance of the cinema of actuality was hence an extremely timely response to profound changes occurring in the Japanese media sphere.

Although these filmmakers belong to the generation of cinéastes who have been subsumed under the category of New Wave, not all of the so-called New Wave filmmakers contributed to the cinema of actuality.[5] Likewise, the filmmakers whose works I analyze in this book have affinities with underground and lesser-known experimental filmmakers, such as Jōnouchi Motoharu, Okabe Michio, and Kanai Katsu, who do not appear in most studies of the Japanese New Wave. I hence eschew the clichéd label *New Wave* in favor of the term *political avant-garde* in describing the filmmakers whose works form the cinema of actuality. The term *political avant-garde* acknowledges the permeability between commercial and underground forms of filmmaking—a permeability that is erased by the term *New Wave*.[6] Their common strategies of appropriating and recycling current, topical, and often sensational materials culled from the realm of journalism should also be read against the historical situation of the 1960s, a decade marked by a seemingly endless series of televised assassinations, hijackings, hostage crises, and mass street protests. My argument is that cinema—itself an apparatus of spectacle—became a testing ground for the reflexive critique of media spectacle precisely at this moment in Japan. Central to my analysis is the changing conception of cinema in relation to television and other image-based media; this change is registered by the rising intermedia consciousness among the filmmakers whose works form the cinema of actuality.

THE JOURNALISTIC TURN

The journalistic turn of political avant-garde filmmakers in the 1960s is exemplified by the increased discursive currency of a loan word: *akuchuaritii* (actuality). This term started to widely circulate in the Japanese discourses on film, photography, television, and literature during the late 1950s and became one of the key concepts used to discuss the political efficacy of art throughout the 1960s. The broad range of connotations (topicality, newsworthiness, currentness, contemporary relevance, and factuality) attached to the term *actuality* is integral to understanding why journalism became an object of critique for filmmakers concerned with the political efficacy of cinema. Another key term that entered the Japanese film-theoretical discourse during this period was *eizō* (image), which gained currency around the same time as the journalistic concept of actuality began to circulate among avant-garde circles. The term *eizō* was often invoked in order to articulate cinema's relation to television, the newly dominant medium that generated strong sensations of actuality. The concurrent proliferation of discourses on the image and actuality attests to a historical correlation between these two concepts as well as to the impact of television.

Not surprisingly, these intertwined discourses on the image and actuality arose when the Japanese film industry itself was undergoing a significant restructuration. Since the late 1950s, television had steadily eclipsed cinema as a prime source of entertainment, bringing about the fast decline of the vertically integrated Japanese film industry. The disintegration of the industry, as the narrative goes, in turn enabled small independent production companies to flourish in the 1960s. This decade thus came to be known as the golden age of independent cinema, a decade marked by an outburst of experimental and avant-garde film productions. The establishment in 1961 of the Art Theatre Guild (ATG)—a unique production, distribution, and exhibition company exclusively dedicated to the dissemination of art cinema—was emblematic of these institutional changes.[7] Almost all the filmmakers whose works are analyzed in this book exhibited their films at the Art Theatre Shinjuku Bunka or its underground counterpart, Theatre Scorpio (Sasori-za). Named after Kenneth Anger's experimental film *Scorpio Rising* (1964) by none other than Mishima, Theatre Scorpio was an epicenter of Japan's underground film culture and a hotspot for avant-garde theater, experimental music, and intermedia performances. Located below Shinjuku Bunka in Tokyo, this clandestine basement art space hosted lively discussions on politics and art, and fostered close collaborations among filmmakers, musicians, photographers, performance artists, and playwrights. A growing number of intermedial experiments that defied conventional boundaries between different media emerged directly from this social and cultural milieu.

This rough sketch of the sociocultural context of the 1960s that gave rise to the cinema of actuality, however, is perhaps not complete without a few additional remarks. One such element is the transfer of the principal production site of visual news from the film industry to the television industry. During the 1930s, newsreel theaters specializing in newsreels, short animations, and documentary films flourished in Japan. Major national newspaper companies, such as Asahi, Yomiuri, and Mainichi used to dominate the production of newsreels, with each running its own film production company regularly supplying newsreel theaters with their products. Major studios such as Shōchiku also began producing and marketing newsreels or visual newspapers (*me no shin-*

bun) as early as 1930.[8] In the 1950s and throughout the 1960s, the same newspaper companies shifted their focus and investment from film to television, while continuing to exert control over the journalistic sphere of news production.[9] Television gradually replaced newsreel theaters as the principal channel of disseminating visual news. The cinematic engagement with the sensation of actuality that emerged in the 1960s was, arguably, a response to this shift. Before the rise of television, cinema was a privileged medium for capturing the moment: it was *the* visual medium of actuality. Yet the rapid development of news shows on television, along with the postwar restructuring of the film industry with its emphasis on program pictures based on the star system, significantly weakened cinema's association with actuality. The journalistic turn of political avant-garde filmmaking during the 1960s came after this rupture, which severed cinema's affinity with news journalism. In this regard this journalistic turn was, partly, a gesture of *return* to the original fascination with the sensation of actuality that cinema used to impart in the early days.

A number of seminal theoretical texts on the mass media and television were also translated into Japanese during the 1960s. For instance, Daniel J. Boorstin's influential text, *The Image: Or What Happened to the American Dream?* (1962), appeared in translation in 1964, the year of the Tokyo Olympics, which boosted the nationwide sale of television sets. The following year the first translation of Walter Benjamin's texts appeared, including his essay "The Work of Art in the Age of Mechanical Reproduction," which came out in print three years prior to its English translation. Marshall McLuhan's 1964 bestseller, *Understanding Media: The Extension of Man*, was translated in 1967, accelerating the so-called McLuhan boom in Japan, and stirring passionate debates on the relation between contemporary art and mass media.[10] But if these newly translated texts found enthusiastic receptions from critics and artists in Japan, it is because these readers already were familiar with many of the theoretical issues articulated in these texts. Among my aims in this book is to present the theoretical and discursive context of debates around the image that preceded and accompanied the translations of such texts, and that prepared the way for their wide reception.

The focus on the discursive context points to another intervention I hope to make: to shed light on the important relationship between theory and practice among political avant-garde filmmakers of the time. There is an enduring misconception of Japanese film culture, namely the assumption that "the very notion of theory is alien to Japan; it is considered a property of Europe and the West," to invoke Noël Burch's memorable statement.[11] Even today, the term *theory* within film studies predominantly—and almost exclusively—refers to theoretical writings penned by European and North American critics and scholars, as is evident in the focus of numerous anthologies bearing the words "Film Theory" in their title. Yet there is irony in this exclusivity. For one, Japanese cinema played a significant role in the development of the film theory that emerged in the 1960s and the 1970s (also called 70s film theory or screen theory). Japanese cinema, as Mitsuhiro Yoshimoto notes, was instrumental at this formative stage of film studies as a discipline in North America. Some of the canonical texts of this film theory drew heavily on the work of Japanese filmmakers such as Ozu and Oshima.[12] The critical role Oshima's work played is especially visible in influential texts such as Stephen Heath's "Narrative Space" (1976).[13] In spite of such accrued interests in Japanese cinema in the 1970s, however, rich theoretical discussions on the cinema that Oshima and his contemporaries generated have not received due attention.[14]

Disproving Burch's claim before the fact, many of the avant-garde filmmakers at the time also thought of themselves as theorists. And their writings, published in numerous film journals (*Kiroku Eiga*, *Eiga Hyōron*, *Eiga Hihyō*, *Eizō Geijutsu*, and so on), were in close conversation with the filmmaking practices of the time. This is particularly true in the case of someone like Matsumoto, who spearheaded the experimental film and video art scene of the 1960s and 1970s. Matsumoto's first book, *Discovery of the Image: Avant-garde and Documentary* (*Eizō no hakken: Avangyarudo to dokyumentarii*, 1963) had a wide-reaching impact on his contemporaries, including Oshima, his greatest rival, and on the following generation of experimental filmmakers, such as Adachi, Jōnouchi, and others who congregated around the VAN Film Research Center (a filmmaking collective formed by former student filmmakers from Nihon University). Similarly, we cannot overlook the equally influential role played by an earlier generation of leftist intellectuals like Hanada Kiyoteru in inspiring the postwar generation of political avant-garde filmmakers. Matsumoto, Oshima, Adachi, and others took seriously Hanada's call to synthesize the avant-garde and documentary arts, and they also consciously inherited the activist notion of the "movement" (*undō*) that Hanada's cohort of avant-garde artists advocated in the 1950s. The activist edge of political avant-garde filmmaking that arose against the intense mediatization of student movements was further sharpened by the participation of activist-theorists like Matsuda Masao. Furthermore, the discursive attempt to theorize cinema in relation to politics at this time was paralleled by similar efforts in the adjacent field of photography. For instance, the work of the photographer-critic Nakahira Takuma—a co-founder of the influential photography group and magazine *Provoke*—should be read as a part of the dialogue with filmmakers and critics, such as Adachi and Matsuda. What unites the writings of these critics, filmmakers, and photographers is their shared concern with the actuality of the image and the political force of the mediatized spectacle.

THE POLITICS OF THE SPECTACLE

Indeed, this discursive milieu that brought together a number of intellectuals, filmmakers, and photographers was profoundly affected by the intensifying production of media spectacles that reconfigured the perception of politics as such. As Mishima and Oshima rightly recognized, student revolutionaries were children of the television age who learned to stage their political dissent for the camera. This deepening imbrication of politics and the media suggested that the image itself was fast becoming the very locus of political struggle. Nakahira's 1972 essay "The Document Called Illusion" ("Kiroku to iu gen'ei"), for instance, addresses the increasing dissolution of the distance between the mediatized spectacle and so-called reality: "A naïve belief that assumes photography to be a record of reality gets inverted in the mass media, which gives rise to the mass hallucination that whatever is photographed is real. But this also suggests another logical inversion: whatever is not recorded by photography or not broadcast on television is unreal."[15] The word *gen'ei* ("illusion" or "hallucination") used in the title of this essay is a direct reference to the word *image* used in the Japanese translation of Boorstin's book, *The Image: Or What Happened to the American Dream?*[16] Here, Nakahira follows Boorstin's observation that the very process of televisual mediation gives rise to "pseudo-events." For Nakahira, this causal inversion of mediation and event generates "a strange myth . . . whose logic confounds reality and its image."[17] This conflation of reality and its image, moreover, produces a new form of policing power. Once documented and broadcast on television, a simple snapshot of an ordinary house might start to look like a crime scene, and a passerby like a criminal. It is this imposition of moral judgment unleashed by the image and by newsmaking practice that Nakahira objects to.

Nakahira's critique of the manipulating power of the image forms the perfect obverse of Oshima's observation that the parameters of politics have greatly changed since the emergence of media-savvy student protesters, underlining the fact that the critique of the image was by no means uniform across the Left. Their complementary take on television and its power suggests how ambivalent the mediated appeal of the spectacle could be even for those on the Left who ostensibly share the same critical stance toward politics. The spectacle works not only in favor of one who benefits from the existing structure of domination, but also for those who contest it. For the camera-conscious protesters, the efficacy of direct action resides as much in the indirect process of its dissemination through the media as in the action itself. A clear distinction between directness and indirectness, or the immediacy of action and the mediatedness of its image, becomes untenable. In this Japanese version of the society of the spectacle, what we find is the fundamental ambivalence of the image.

If Nakahira's distrust of television comes close to Guy Debord's well-known critique of the spectacle, Oshima's call to reconceptualize politics in light of the spectacle reminds us of Jacques Rancière's recent critique of Debord's narrow definition of the spectacle as a source of disempowerment.[18] For Oshima, the deliberate act of setting up and staging the protest for the camera is nothing to be denigrated. Mishima, in the dialogue referred to above, assumes that there is an essential difference between a real political action and a theatrical or expressive act (with which he aligns student protests), and would thus seem to be in agreement with Nakahira's critique of the spectacle. Oshima, on the other hand, insists that such a distinction no longer holds. Here, Oshima might be envisioning the relation between politics and the spectacle in the manner comparable to Rancière, who overturns the Platonic prejudice implicit in Debord's negative view of the separation between the spectacle and the spectator.[19] Rancière's understanding of politics as something spectacular is a view that Oshima strongly espouses in his conversation with Mishima and in his filmmaking practice throughout the 1960s. For Oshima, the expressive act of student activists is often immediately political, and politics in turn is radically reconfigured through the dramatic act of staging the spectacle that attempts to dislocate and disrupt the existing police order.

As is evident in the disagreement between Oshima's and Nakahira's critique of television, however, the Japanese leftist discourse on politics and the spectacle in the 1960s and early 1970s is far from uniform: the spectacle is variably viewed as a polemical object of critique as well as a site of empowerment. In short, the problem with the image produced and relayed by television for these critics resides not in its spectacular appearance per se; rather it derives from the end to which it serves. This duality of the image as a means and a medium became, in effect, a recurrent problem for political avant-garde filmmakers. If the mediating function of the image in cinema and television received such intense scrutiny by political avant-garde filmmakers and critics in the 1960s, it is precisely because politics could no longer be thought apart from the fundamental ambivalence of the spectacle. This ambivalence marks the cinema of actuality and thus informs the tension between cinema and journalism.

In order to set up the main framework of analysis, I trace in chapter 1 the genealogy of the term *eizō* ("image") and examine its sudden proliferation in the wake of television. Beginning in the late 1950s, theoretical and popular discourse on cinema in Japan increasingly dealt with the question of cinema's specificity in relation to other forms of image-making media. The concept that played a crucial role here was *eizō*, a term that dominated the debates around image-making practice, and which designates a special class of images produced and mediated by a technological apparatus. This growing concern with the image, which took shape in various forms of image theories from the late 1950s and throughout the 1960s, also helped to revive discussions about cinema and its medium specificity. Through a close analysis of Matsumoto's and Oshima's intermedial experiments with still photography and the comic book, I lay the groundwork for the consideration of the cinema of actuality within a wider media-historical context.

The image is, of course, a topic that has received much attention in North America in recent years through the work of theorists such as W. J. T. Mitchell, Anne Friedberg, Jean-Luc Nancy, Georges Didi-Huberman, and Marie-José Mondzain. There has been a growing interest in the status of the image in contemporary societies among scholars of film studies, media studies, cultural studies, and art history, in part because of the growing prominence of digital media that radically reconfigured our understanding of the materiality of the image. However, this widely shared interest in the image has been marked by a curious tendency toward generalization that seems to leave out questions relating to its historical and cultural specificity. Scholars have too often used the word *image* to mean anything from the representation of an object in one's mind to a painting, a photograph, or a computer screen.[20] The shortcoming of this approach is that the image comes to encompass anything from an ancient cave painting to a photo displayed on a laptop, all while its implicit rootedness in Judeo-Christian epistemology remains unquestioned. Just as the term *theory* has been assumed to be an exclusive property of the West (Europe and North America), the term *image* in the disciplines of the humanities often presupposes its epistemological roots in this Western or Judeo-Christian tradition. My attempt to map out the genealogy of the term *eizō* is intended to provide an alternative framework of analysis grounded in the historical and cultural conditions of the postwar Japanese media environment.

Accompanying the discourse on the image I discuss in chapter 1 is an equally prominent concern with the concept of actuality. Extending the interrogation of cinema's relation to other media, in chapter 2 I historically situate the tension between cinema and journalism, and ask what was at stake in these cinematic experiments. In order to think through this question, I focus on the connection between theatricality and actuality. Tracing the tension between the documentary understanding of filmic actuality as factuality and the journalistic conception of actuality as topicality, I examine key debates in Japanese film theory surrounding this concept of actuality. These debates inform my analysis of Matsumoto's and Oshima's timely appropriation of high-profile media events and news in films such as *For the Damaged Right Eye* (1968), *Funeral Parade of Roses* (1969), *Death by Hanging* (1968), and *Diary of a Shinjuku Thief* (1969). Instead of simply reproducing the journalistic sensation of actuality, these films, which often directly appropriate and "remediate" topical media events, reveal the constitutive artifice at the heart of actuality, or what I call "artifactuality" (following Jacques Derrida).[21]

In chapter 3 I extend the investigation of artifactuality by highlighting the temporal difference between two economies of the image: journalism and cinema. The markedly experimental "Pink" or softcore films by Wakamatsu Kōji, which consciously and swiftly appropriate contemporary media events, provide a unique vantage point to analyze this difference. Wakamatsu's films from the 1960s and early 1970s play with a well-calculated timing of the cinematic appropriation of media events that generated an intense sensation of actuality. By situating Wakamatsu's practice within the larger political climate of the time, I explore how this mode of cinematic intervention was responding to the increasing mediatization of politics—both left wing *and* right wing—that television facilitated.

In chapter 4 I return to the relation between cinema and journalism, this time with an emphasis on the way in which this relation was problematized in the film discourse of the *fūkeiron* ("theory of landscape" or "landscape theory") and its attendant filmic works: *A.K.A. Serial Killer* (1969), an experimental documentary film shot by Adachi, and *The Man Who Left His Will on Film* (1970), an experimental narrative film shot by Oshima. These two films and the concomitant discourse of fūkeiron added a new dimension to Japanese film theory, as they approached the image of landscape in terms of state power, and governmental control over urban space in particular. By drawing attention to the formal similarity between the actuality films of early cinema and these two landscape films, I show how the formal strategy of focusing on empty landscapes helped these filmmakers to develop a new framework for analyzing the policing power of the state.

In chapter 5 I investigate a case in which the cinema of actuality directly confronted television. In this chapter I closely analyze Wakamatsu and Adachi's singular propaganda news film, *The Red Army/PFLP: Declaration of World War* (1971), which opens with remediated news footage of airplane hijackings. Comparing *The Red Army/PFLP*'s use of televisual news and images of the landscape to the remarkably similar work *Here and Elsewhere* (1974), a film shot by Jean-Luc Godard, Jean-Pierre Gorin, and Anne-Marie Miéville, I examine how these films complicate the ideal of militant cinema. Emphasis is placed on the tension between the alleged directness of a militant action, such as hijacking, and the alleged indirectness of the cinematic mediation of such an action.

In the conclusion I map out the eventual decline of the cinema of actuality in relation to two epochal events of the 1970s: the World's Fair in Osaka (Expo 70) held in 1970 and the hostage crisis known as the Asama Sansō Incident in 1972. By tracing the structural transformation in the governmental control over urban space, the policing of the contiguity between street politics and cinema, the rise of video art, and the increasing retreat of image-making practices into enclosed spaces of exhibition, I situate the end of the season of image politics in a wider historical context.

In sum, I take as my point of departure the presupposition that Japanese avant-garde cinema of the 1960s and early 1970s must be situated firmly within its theoretical and its medial contexts. It is thus to the discourse of the image and the burgeoning intermedia practice that I now turn.

one

intermedial experiments and the rise of the eizō discourse

On 25 February 1967, Oshima Nagisa's experimental film *Band of Ninja* (*Ninja bugeichō*) premiered at the Art Theatre Guild's main theater, Shinjuku Bunka in Tokyo.[1] Based on the comic writer Shirato Sanpei's 1959–62 *manga* (a Japanese term for "comic book") of the same title, the film *Band of Ninja* is a meticulously filmed and edited version of the original manga, sitting somewhat uncomfortably between comic book and animation. The film strikes one as odd not only because it is entirely composed of motionless drawings, but also because these drawings bear the marks of original sketch lines. The drawings contain parts of word bubbles and graphically rendered onomatopoeias (which are so prevalent in Japanese manga) as well as the speed lines used to designate the movements of characters or things. Arguably, the very visibility of these sketch lines, word bubbles, onomatopoeias, and speed lines contribute to the incipient "intermedial" look of this film. Made in 1967, the year when one of the first events bearing the word *intermedia* (*intaamedia*) in its title took place in Japan,[2] Oshima's formal experiment in *Band of Ninja* offers a useful vantage point from which to consider a shifting conception of cinema amid a growing number of border-crossing experiments undertaken by avant-garde filmmakers, musicians, performance artists, and graphic designers in the late 1960s.

The term *intermedia* is often evoked in relation to the confluence of Japanese and North American performance-based arts, exemplified by the eponymous activities of Fluxus in the 1960s. Coined by the Fluxus artist Dick Higgins in 1966, the term quickly entered the vocabulary of Japanese music, film, and performance discourses, forming a close semantic network with related terms.[3] As Tone Yasunao, a musician and another Fluxus member, explains, unlike neighboring terms such as *happening* and *event*, the use of the term *intermedia* was initially associated with an underground film movement.[4] By the early 1970s, however, its connection to cinema was no longer apparent. The following definition of *intermedia*—offered by Ichiyanagi Toshi, an avant-garde composer who worked closely with Fluxus members, in the 1972 article "Encyclopedia of Contemporary Situations of Cinema"—is suggestive in this regard.

> There are many auteurs whose works exude an intermedial style or attitude, though it is hard to name those who are specializing only in intermedia. For instance, we can include filmmakers who are engaged in the practice of expanded cinema, multiprojection, and environmental cinema, musicians who work on aleatoric music, live electronic music, theater work, and so-called events, or visual artists who do happenings, light art, kinetic art, and light shows. In one way or another all of these people are working in the field of intermedia.[5]

This inclusive sense of intermedia, which encompasses various mediums and platforms, emphasizes its eventfulness and multiplicity of style. Cinema is in no way privileged. Instead, intermedia came to refer more broadly to various kinds of artistic experiments that aim to facilitate mutual transformations of the multiple media involved in a single work, a process through which generic expectations and aesthetic conventions accompanying a particular medium are overturned or challenged. This gradual decentering of cinema as a primary site of intermedial artistic experiments is reminiscent of a similar process that had taken place a few years earlier when the word *eizō* (image) entered the discursive milieu of Japanese film theory and media criticism. Examining this process prior to the introduction of the intermedial discourse is crucial, because it allows us to see how the boundary of cinema started to shift, as the technologically produced image became a theoretical problem in its own right.

The aim of foregrounding the concept of eizō, a term that designates a class of images produced and mediated by a technological apparatus, is twofold. First, it helps situate increasing efforts by Japanese avant-garde filmmakers to appropriate and directly incorporate noncinematic media into films within the larger historical, cultural, and theoretical milieu of the 1960s. Second, the concept of eizō helps better explain how the incipient intermedial practice developed within the field of avant-garde filmmaking interacted with the emergent theoretical discourse on the image. At stake in the interaction between practice and theory is a familiar question of medium specificity, which the concept of the image helped to revive and subsequently undermine.

The rise of television in the 1950s also played no small part in this process. But while television was an obvious catalyst in reviving general interest in the notion of medium specificity, it was by no means at the center of "image theories" (*eizō ron*) that flourished in the late 1950s and the 1960s; cinema continued to occupy the privileged point of reference. However, in spite of the seeming centrality of cinema in the growing discourse on the image, cinema eventually lost its claim to singularity. This subtle shift in the privileging of cinema is reflected in the discourse. The fact that the technologically produced image was a common property shared by other media forms, such as television and photography, made it particularly difficult to maintain cinema's specificity based on this concept, even though earlier proponents of image theories tried to do so. The most symptomatic—and in some ways foundational—case in which this tension unfolded was the "debate on the image" (*eizō ronsō*), a series of articles published in 1958–60. In this debate we find a curious conflation of the image and cinema, as if the former simply functions as a synecdoche for the latter; as if the image is a part that defines the whole of cinema. However, the hierarchical relationship between the two was eventually overturned, as cinema became one species of the larger genus of image-based media. It is this reclassification of cinema and its connection to intermedial experiments that I want to investigate in this chapter.

One filmmaker and theorist who played a particularly important role in shaping the discourse on the image and contributed to the gradual decentering of cinema was Matsumoto Toshio. It is not surprising that Matsumoto, who was an active contributor to Japanese film theory throughout the 1960s, became heavily involved in two of the most representative intermedia events of the decade: the symposium "EXPOSE·1968: Say Something, Search Now" ("EXPOSE·1968: Nanika ittekure, ima sagasu"), which took place at the Sōgetsu Art Center in April 1968, and "Cross-Talk/Intermedia," an international art event sponsored by the American Cultural Center in February 1969. Matsumoto's theorization of avant-garde documentary filmmaking and his own experiment with the still-image medium of photography thus provide an especially useful context with which to interpret Oshima's comparable experiment with the still-image medium of the comic book.

AUDIOVISUAL REDUNDANCY IN *BAND OF NINJA*

Perhaps the slightly out-of-place look of *Band of Ninja* explains why this is the most rarely discussed film by Oshima, one that tends to be ignored by film scholars and critics.[6] After all, Oshima is known for his innovative narrative filmmaking, but not for animation. The film's meticulous appropriation of Shirato's original drawings has led some critics to claim that *Band of Ninja* is his "most anti-auteurist" work.[7] And yet for all the film's oddities and peculiarities, and despite its general neglect by film scholars in the past, Oshima felt it to be one of his major accomplishments. Oshima compares his undertaking of this project to Eisenstein's ultimately unrealized project of creating a cinematic version of Marx's *Capital*. Much like making Marx's *Capital*, argues Oshima, "making a filmic version of Shirato's *Band of Ninja* was considered to be impossible."[8] But the direct filming of the original manga panels allowed him to realize this project, a success which led him to proclaim: "Everything can be made into cinema."[9]

While we may simply take Oshima's statement as a self-congratulatory remark, we can also probe its underlying assumption. For instance, what does it mean to say that there is nothing that cannot be made into cinema? Implicit in this statement is a presupposition that cinema has the capacity to absorb and subsume other media forms, including the heterogeneous medium of the comic book. Combined with the intermedial look of the film, this positioning of cinema as a metamedium coincides with a key transitional moment in the history of Japanese film discourse, a moment marked by the rise of the image as a theoretical problem.

Oshima envisioned making a filmic version of Shirato's *Band of Ninja* as early as 1962, when the scriptwriter Sasaki Mamoru first brought the comic to his attention. However, it was only after Oshima made an experimental short film, *Diary of Yunbogi* (*Yunbogi no nikki*, 1965), entirely composed of rephotographed snapshots, that he realized the feasibility of turning Shirato's comic into an actual film. A brief memo published in 1966, the year Oshima started to film *Band of Ninja*, notes that he had discovered a radically new, "unparalleled" method of making a film.[10]

What he calls an unparalleled method refers to a double process of mediation that Jay David Bolter and Richard Grusin have elsewhere called *remediation*. According to Bolter and Grusin, all historically new forms of media were developed by appropriating and absorbing the formal traits of earlier media, and, conversely, older media appropriate newer media in order to refashion themselves, even if these processes are not always acknowledged.[11] What Oshima does in the production of *Band of Ninja* is to make this process of remediation explicit to the point that the presence of the appropriated medium of the comic book becomes conspicuous and visible.

Instead of *adapting* the comic book and redrawing its images in order to make an animated version of Shirato's work, Oshima directly films and remediates the original drawings. This cinematic remediation of the comic book, which Oshima claims to have pioneered in *Band of Ninja*, is produced by simply photographing each panel of the original comic book in succession. However, the inventiveness of Oshima's *Band of Ninja* lies in its refusal to be animation. Strictly speaking, none of the figures that appear in this film are animated. There is no attempt to create an illusion of movement *through* the drawings themselves. Instead, any motion that appears on-screen remains extrinsic to the drawings. The impression of movement one perceives in viewing this film derives solely from camera movement (mostly from the pan). This is why Noël Burch calls *Band of Ninja* "an exercise in dynamizing still pictures."[12] Oshima also occasionally crops and reframes Shirato's motionless drawings in *Band of Ninja*. But precisely because it is the camerawork that adds a semblance of movement to otherwise motionless images, the film constantly draws the spectator's attention to the material gap between the filmic images and the images that serve as its profilmic objects. This material gap also surfaces through the film's preservation of audiovisual redundancies.

A brief comparison between Oshima's remediation of the comic book and the standard practice of animation would be useful. One thing to keep in mind while making this comparison is the fact that by the mid-1960s the style of limited animation had become solidified primarily through the works of television animators, such as Tezuka Osamu and his production team.[13] In spite of the similar emphasis placed on the stillness of the image in television animation (or *anime*), however, there is a notable difference between Oshima's cinematic experiment in *Band of Ninja* and the conventional style of limited animation that was used on television: Oshima refuses to redraw manga panels onto cels or to draw in-between frames to supplement missing motions. Instead, he opts for the direct filming of Shirato's original drawings frame-by-frame, using not a professional animation stand, but a makeshift device. Oshima and his crew placed the original drawings against the wall in the living room at his home, and filmed over 10,000 images drawn with paper and ink. Since they were not filming transparent cels, they had to use high-key lighting and overexposure to emphasize the whiteness of the paper and to reduce smudges, extraneous pencil lines, and uneven brushstrokes.[14] Nevertheless, the finished film is far from devoid of these elements. Tactile textures of paper, ink, and pencil not only come through in Oshima's remediated version, but semiotic markers of the comic book medium (word bubbles, speed lines, onomatopoeias) are also prevalent on-screen. The presence of these visual elements—highly irregular from the perspective of the mainstream practice of animation at the time—contributes to the intermedial look of the film. The animation style of *Band of Ninja* is quite unusual in this regard.

For instance, Oshima does not try to compensate for the lack of movement in the original drawings by adding extra drawings. Instead of concealing this lack of movement, he highlights it. He does this in ways that significantly deviate from the standard practice of animation. The standard practice of animation involves, initially, drawing "key frames" that serve as a reference point for onscreen movements, and subsequently filling in the movements by drawing "in-between" frames. Since it is the "in-betweens" that generate the sense of movement in animation, we might analogize the use of still images in *Band of Ninja* as the creation of an animated film solely through a sequence of key frames. The resulting effect is a curious one. The film forces us to direct our attention to the jarring gap or dissonance between two media: cinema and the comic book. What is at stake here is hence not the complete absorption of one medium by another, but their coexistence.

The coexistence of the two media appears deliberate considering that Oshima invented a neologism, *feature film–comic book* (*chōhen firumu gekiga*), to advertise *Band of Ninja*. The moniker is suggestive of Oshima's desire to differentiate his work from the television animation of the time. Bringing the words *film* and *comic book* together, this neologism explicitly draws attention to the intermedial quality of the film. Oshima's choice of the word *gekiga* also indicates his desire to further distance the film from televised animation series, most of which were adaptations of manga catering to children. The word *gekiga* refers to a particular genre of manga or comics that targets a young adult readership. When it first emerged in the late 1950s, its promoters presented the genre as a more grown-up alternative to the lighthearted current of mainstream manga.[15] Unlike mainstream manga, which avoided elements considered inappropriate for children, gekiga emphasized dramatic (and often violent) actions, contained complex plot structures, and included nudity. Shirato Sanpei was a leading gekiga artist who brought popularity to the genre. His work often focused on socially marginalized characters and their struggles against oppression, and attracted high-school and university students hungry for comics with serious and subversive themes. In Oshima's words, Shirato's work offered "an alternative model of activism and philosophy" to the Left-leaning students.[16] The term *feature film–comic book*, which Oshima used in the promotional materials, including trailers and a published script, invokes this countercultural positioning of Shirato's comics.

The timeliness of Oshima's filming *Band of Ninja* in the mid-1960s must also be noted. Oshima first used the method of remediation in his earlier experimental short, *Diary of Yunbogi* (*Yunbogi no nikki*, 1965), which bears an uncanny resemblance to Matsumoto Toshio's experimental short, *The Song of Stone* (*Ishi no uta*, 1963), a work composed entirely of rephotographed still photographs. But before comparing Oshima and Matsumoto, it is worth examining how the form of *Band of Ninja* differs from the mainstream television animation of the period. The television animation series *Fujimaru of the Wind* (*Shōnen ninja Kaze no Fujimaru*) serves as a salient point of comparison. *Fujimaru of the Wind* was aired on the NET channel (Nihon kyōiku terebi) between June 1964 and August 1965, and it was also based on Shirato's comic book, originally titled *Ninja Whirlwind* (*Ninja senpū*). The major production company Toei Animation adapted it to make a year-long animated television series. Oshima's *Band of Ninja* is in many ways antithetical to *Fujimaru of the Wind*, despite the fact that both are based on the work of the same author, Shirato Sanpei. The difference derives not only from their venues of exhibition (movie theater and network television) and from their formats (nonserial and serial), but also, and more importantly, from the ways in which *Band of Ninja* plays up the structure of redundancy between the original manga and its filmic version, while *Fujimaru of the Wind* strives to eliminate it.

The crucial difference between *Band of Ninja* and *Fujimaru of the*

Wind indeed lies in the former's emphasis on audiovisual redundancies. *Band of Ninja* contains extraneous replications that are usually minimized in animation works that adapt comic books. The first and perhaps the most obvious element of this is the film's inclusion of word bubbles and written onomatopoeias. For instance, we often *read* onomatopoeias written on the margins of the panel (depicting sword fights and battle scenes, for example), as we *hear* sound effects corresponding to these onomatopoeias. This creates a distinct sense of redundancy (figures 1.1 and 1.2). The film's inclusion of such graphic onomatopoeias ends up heightening the materiality of the original comic-book medium instead of concealing it.

Partial preservations of word bubbles similarly function to create visual effects of redundancy in the film. While the voice-over substitutes the written speech of the characters, we often see the remnants of word bubbles above or next to drawn characters. In the standard practice of television animation, as in the case of *Fujimaru of the Wind*, such graphic remnants of the original drawings are eliminated at the stage of redrawing them onto cels so that there are no redundancies between the soundtrack and the image-track. Word bubbles and graphic onomatopoeias, if left, would draw too much attention to the two-dimensionality of the image, counteracting illusions of depth and motion. Placing moving characters or objects next to static word bubbles and onomatopoeias would create a visual dissonance. Word bubbles and onomatopoeias are, in short, semiotic signs that presuppose the motionless surface of the comic book, and would not function well within the moving image.

Indeed, at the most basic level, onomatopoeias and word bubbles are visual substitutes that compensate for the lack of sound and speech. To use one of Yomota Inuhiko's apt expressions, an onomatopoeia inscribed on the page of a comic book is "a sound that is turned into graphism."[17] In this regard, graphic renditions of sound and speech function similarly to intertitles in silent cinema. They are semiotic codes that doubly signify the silent and motionless medium of the comic book. Given the specific functions of onomatopoeias and word bubbles, it is not surprising that the standard practice of television animation in the 1960s eliminated these graphic elements and replaced them with voice-overs and sound effects. What differentiated anime from manga, or animation from the comic book, was not only the inclusion of movement but also the inclusion of sound. A similar argument can be made with regard to

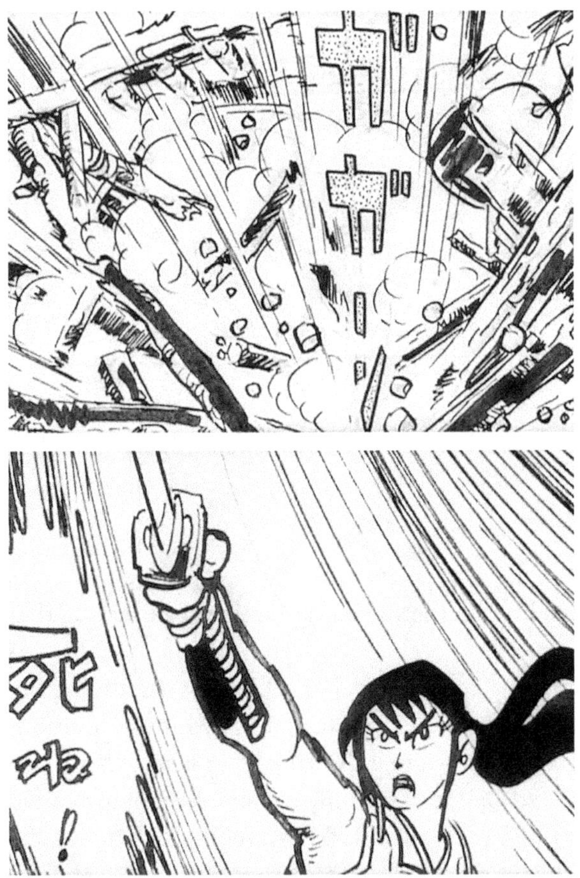

1.1. Graphic onomatopoeia. Still from *Band of Ninja* (1967), dir. Oshima Nagisa.

1.2. Word bubble ("Die!"). Still from *Band of Ninja* (1967), dir. Oshima Nagisa.

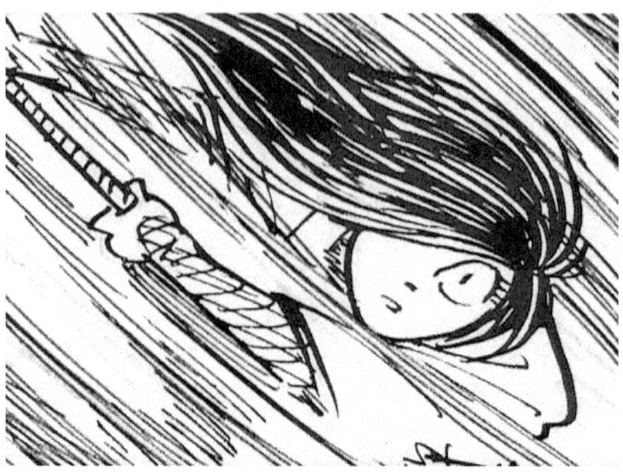

1.3. Speed lines. Still from *Band of Ninja* (1967), dir. Oshima Nagisa.

the elimination of speed lines in the standard practice of animation that adapts comic books.

Speed lines function as a conventional graphic code signifying the speed or velocity of a moving object or character within the motionless panel of comics. Shirato's original drawings for *Band of Ninja* are filled with speed lines, and Oshima faithfully preserves them instead of erasing and replacing them with animated movements. Set in the sixteenth century, the original comic of *Band of Ninja* narrates a series of epic conflicts between peasants, samurai feudal lords, and anonymous ninjas. Scenes of violent sword fights, horseback battles, and spectacular executions abound. For instance, in a scene depicting a pivotal duel between the ninja character Hotarubi and the samurai character Jūtarō, the speed lines literally fill the space within a panel. The filmic version of *Band of Ninja* retains these lines as it cuts between tightly framed close-ups that depict the swift sword of Hotarubi mercilessly amputating Jūtarō's left arm (figure 1.3).[18] The resulting impressions of velocity and conflict emanate from graphic densities and compositions, rather than from the actual movements of characters and objects.

Oshima's *Band of Ninja* thus preserves semiotic codes of sound and movement that are specific to the still and silent medium of the comic book while adding camera movement, voice-overs, and sound effects *over* the speed lines, word bubbles, and onomatopoeias. The addition of camera movement and sound appears functionally redundant as the movement and sound are already visually signified by the semiotic codes of the comic book. But this redundancy effectively draws our attention to the second-order image making that takes images created in another medium as its profilmic objects. The structure of redundancy here heightens the material difference between the two media—cinema and the comic book—rather than mask it, and confers on the film an incipient intermedial look.

The sense of intermediality generated by *Band of Ninja* is indicative of a particular historical circumstance to which this work belongs. This context includes the preceding filmic and theoretical works of Matsumoto Toshio, the concurrent discourse on the image, and the rise of television as a troubling double of cinema. The formal experiment Oshima undertook in *Band of Ninja* is not an isolated event, but in fact partakes in larger cultural, medial, and discursive transformations taking place in the 1960s. The most important of these transformations is the tension between cinema's claim to medium specificity and its subordination to the general category of "image-based media" (*eizō media*). This tension characterizes the very process of remediation that came to be associated with an "avant-garde documentary" mode of filmmaking.

PARALLEL EXPERIMENTS WITH STILL-IMAGE MEDIA

According to Oshima, his sudden inspiration for his "unparalleled" method of directly filming comic book panels came after he made *Diary of Yunbogi*. Like *Band of Ninja*, *Diary of Yunbogi* is composed entirely of still images, though the medium involved is photography rather than the comic book. Oshima used snapshots of Korean street children, which he took during a trip to South Korea while making the television documentary *A Monument of Youth* (*Seishun no hi*, 1964). On his return from Korea, Oshima rephotographed the snapshots with a movie camera, and added poetic voice-overs.[19] Released in 1965, the year when the Treaty of Basic Relations between Japan and the Republic of Korea (South Korea) was ratified, *Diary of Yunbogi* was meant to be a timely critique of Japan's involvement in Cold War politics and its wartime responsibility toward Korea.[20]

But beneath this apparent political commentary is another factor that marks the timeliness of *Diary of Yunbogi*—the film's absolute reliance on the still image. In spite of Oshima's claim of methodological novelty, he was not the first to make a film based entirely on still images; *Diary of Yunbogi* actually followed similar experiments undertaken by his contemporaries. The most obvious example is Chris Marker's *La Jetée* (1962), an experimental "photo-roman" that is composed of a series of montages of rephotographed photograms.[21] The similarity between the formal structures of *Diary of Yunbogi* and *La Jetée* is hard to overlook. Oshima himself lists Marker's *La Jetée* as a source of his methodological inspiration: "I knew that we could make a film using just a montage of still photographs, most likely because of *La Jetée*."[22]

Oshima, like many other filmmakers at the time, attended the Festival of the Avant-Garde Cinema of the World (Sekai Zen'ei Eigasai) hosted by the Sōgetsu Art Center in February 1966. The festival showcased the canonical works of prewar and postwar avant-garde cinema from Europe and North America. In the 7 March edition of the newspaper *Nihon dokusho shinbun*, Oshima published a short essay summarizing his impression of the festival: "To be honest, the only films which made me feel that I could not compete with them were Luis Buñuel's *Un chien andalou* and Chris Marker's *La Jetée*. The rest of the films were inferior to my work."[23] While this remark may suggest that Marker had a direct influence on Oshima, it would be too hasty to simply conclude that *La Jetée* was the sole precursor to *Diary of Yunbogi*. There was also Agnès Varda's *Salut les cubains* (1962–63), a film composed entirely of 1,800 photographs she took in Cuba. Even closer to home is Matsumoto Toshio's experimental short documentary, *The Song of Stone* (1963).

The Song of Stone is a 16 mm film shot for the documentary channel of TBS television. Composed entirely of rephotographed snapshots of Japanese stonecutters at a quarry in Shikoko taken by the *LIFE* cameraman Ernest Satow, *The Song of Stone* is an ambitious work that deviates from the conventional practice of both film and television documentaries of the time. Matsumoto used the technique of stop-motion animation to rephotograph hundreds of snapshots Satow had already taken at the quarry. Matsumoto then edited them in-camera, frequently using dissolves and superimpositions to lend the impression of movement to otherwise immobile images. For the soundtrack, Matsumoto asked an experimental composer, Akiyama Kuniharu (a member of the avant-garde group Jikken Kōbō, or Experimental Workshop), to use the sounds directly recorded at the quarry to compose a musique concrète piece. While the film was completed in less than ten days, and barely one hour before it went on air, its experimental edge—still rare in the field of documentary filmmaking at the time—clearly reflected Matsumoto's view of the "avant-garde documentary film" (*zen'ei kiroku eiga*), a mode of filmmaking that he started to theorize in 1958.

Not surprisingly, *The Song of Stone* opened to conflicting responses from audiences in Japan and abroad.[24] Among its ardent supporters were Marker and the film historian George Sadoul. Marker saw *The Song of Stone* when he visited Japan in 1964. Apparently impressed with Matsumoto's work, Marker sent him a copy of *La Jetée* after he returned to France. When *The Song of Stone* was invited to the Tours Film Festival, in 1964, Sadoul wrote a favorable review in *Les Lettres Françaises*.[25] Given the close-knit community of Japanese avant-garde filmmakers and critics at the time, it is hard to believe that Oshima knew nothing of Matsumoto's innovative use of still photographs in *The Song of Stone*. If Oshima fails to mention this work, we may surmise, it is because he wanted to imply that *he* was the first to make films out of still images, at least in Japan. Considering Oshima's well-known rivalry with Matsumoto, his silence over the latter's work is understandable. Matsumoto, on his part, acknowledged the similarity between their works, listing *The Song of Stone* and *Diary of Yunbogi* (as well as *La Jetée*) as exemplary cases of radical experiments with stillness in a 1967 essay.[26] However, more important than the formal similarities in Oshima's and Matsumoto's films is the historical timing of their experiments.

By the early 1960s, Matsumoto had already established himself as an intellectual filmmaker and critic with a Marxist flair. Not only did Matsumoto's ferocious critique of the war responsibility of documentary filmmakers parallel Oshima's attack on the "pseudo-subjectivity" of commercial filmmakers, but also his idea of the "avant-garde documentary film" was extremely influential, leading Oshima to call Matsumoto a veritable "opinion leader" of his generation.[27] Their comradeship and rivalry go back a long way, before they started to direct films. In 1957, Oshima and Matsumoto joined a study group, Eiga to Hihyō no Kai (Association for Film and Criticism), organized by aspiring young filmmakers, critics, and scriptwriters. The group was directly modeled after preceding postwar artist collectives such as Yoru no Kai (The Night Association), which the Marxist avant-garde critic Hanada Kiyoteru founded with the artist Okamoto Tarō.[28] Among the members of the group were notable filmmakers and critics, such as Hani Susumu, Yoshida Kijū, Tamura Takashi, Satō Tadao, and Sato Jūshin. Intellectual activities of groups such as Eiga to Hihyō no Kai also led to the publication of a short-lived film journal, *Eiga Hihyō I* (1957–59).[29] In addition to the young critics and filmmakers associated with Eiga to Hihyō no Kai, an older generation of leftist intellectuals, including Hanada, frequently contributed to the journal.

Around the same time as *Eiga Hihyō I* was launched, Matsumoto and others involved in the field of nonfiction filmmaking started to radicalize documentary film criticism, often with the aid of contemporary avant-garde literary and art criticism. Matsumoto's critical writings published in the journal *Kiroku Eiga* (Documentary film, 1958–64), in particular, played a decisive role in shifting the ground of Japanese documentary discourse.[30] His theorization of documentary as a properly avant-garde method of reflexively interrogating reality significantly changed the meaning of the word *documentary*, and had a wide-reaching impact not only on the immediate circle of documentary filmmakers, but also on filmmakers like Oshima who were working within the studio system at the time.[31]

Matsumoto and Oshima had much in common. In spite of institutional differences—Matsumoto working for a nonfiction documentary production company and Oshima working for a commercial studio—they held a similar political commitment to the Left.[32] As their investment in the mass protest against the renewal of the U.S.-Japan Security Treaty (ANPO) in 1960 suggests, Oshima and Matsumoto shared the same political perspective. By the early 1960s, they had both become known as outspoken critics of Japanese cinema who mercilessly criticized conservative filmmakers seeking to maintain the status quo, as well as leftist filmmakers working under the aegis of the Communist Party.[33]

In July 1963, Oshima published *Postwar Cinema: Destructions and Creations* (*Sengo eiga: Hakai to sōzō*), the first collection of his essays. Just five months later, Matsumoto published *Discovery of the Image: Avant-Garde and Documentary* (*Eizō no hakken: Avangyarudo to dokyumentarii*).[34] Together, these two books marked an important turning point in the history of film theory in Japan. For both Oshima and Matsumoto belonged to a new generation of filmmakers who actively theorized cinema with the aim of generating a new cinematic "movement." According to Matsuda Masao, "The fact that Matsumoto's *Discovery of the Image* was published by the same press only half a year after Oshima's

Postwar Cinema was an epoch-making event. For they were both critics who emerged out of a film movement or the space 'inside' it, notwithstanding their different provenances in fiction and documentary filmmaking."[35]

Oshima expresses this sense of belonging to the same community of activist-filmmakers in his 1963 essay "The Subject and the Situation of Postwar Japanese Cinema." Noteworthy in this essay is his use of the pronoun *we*, which indicates his sense of belonging to a community of filmmakers and critics who worked together to revolutionize cinema from within.

> We tried to interject the fundamental question "What is Cinema?" into the space of Japanese cinema in order to break away from the traditional methods of filmmaking, establish our own methods, and create cinema that we all believed in. Now, I hastily used the word *we*. Perhaps I should clarify who the "we" are by naming each member of the group, and by specifying what kind of movement we were generating. But I prefer not to do so. From my point of view, this "we" roughly refers to my fellow assistant directors with whom I started writing scripts at the Shōchiku Studio, and to critics, documentary filmmakers, assistant directors from other studios, and activists from ciné-clubs, all of whom I met through my participation in the group Eiga to Hihyō no Kai and its journal, *Eiga Hihyō*.[36]

As Oshima makes quite clear, the "we" here includes those who participated in Eiga to Hihyō no Kai, including Matsumoto.

This shared sense of commitment to revolutionize Japanese cinema pushed Matsumoto and Oshima to expand the horizon of filmmaking by experimenting with noncinematic media in films like *The Song of Stone*, *Diary of Yunbogi*, and *Band of Ninja*. Matsumoto and Oshima gradually parted ways—often exchanging heated rebuttals, critiquing each other's work or political commitment—but Oshima never stopped acknowledging the initial inspiration he received from Matsumoto's earlier theoretical work. Referring to Matsumoto's seminal essay "On the Method of the Avant-Garde Documentary Film," Oshima notes, "I cannot forget the shock I felt when I read his essay for the first time."[37] What was the argument of this essay that gave Oshima such a shock? Answering this question will bring us closer to the problematic of the image, which became a core issue in film theory.

Matsumoto's "On the Method of the Avant-Garde Documentary Film" ("Zen'ei kiroku eiga no hōhō ni tsuite") was published in the inaugural issue of the film journal *Kiroku Eiga* (Documentary film), in 1958. Matsumoto appropriated Hanada Kiyoteru's idea of a dialectical synthesis of the avant-garde and the documentary mode of interrogating reality. Matsumoto called this new method of filmmaking "avant-garde documentary."[38] In developing his theory of this method, Matsumoto closely followed Hanada's proposition that one must synthesize the documentary approach to the external social reality with the historical avant-garde—or more precisely, the surrealist—approach to the internal psychic reality. Matsumoto's emphasis on the "irrational" dimensions of the unconscious as an object of investigation for documentary filmmakers was novel, and provoked negative responses from the readers and contributors of *Kiroku Eiga*, many of whom held an instrumental view of nonfiction filmmaking as an empirical mode of knowledge production.

Breaking away from this instrumental view of documentary, Matsumoto introduced a new vocabulary and set of concepts to theorize documentary as first and foremost a method of challenging habituated modes of perception. In his insistence on breaking down perceptual habits, Matsumoto's conceptualization of documentary echoes the Russian formalist Viktor Shklovsky's understanding of art as a technique of defamiliarization (and Matsumoto's emphasis on the importance of chance encounters also bears the influence of the work of André Breton). But the basic tenet of Matsumoto's theory of the avant-garde documentary is indebted to Hanada's earlier theorization of the avant-garde in the 1950s. Many of the keywords Matsumoto uses in this essay—such as, for example, *irrational*, *internal realism*, *dialectical synthesis*, *negation of negation*, *actuality*—are used by Hanada in his seminal essays on the avant-garde arts.

Yet this does not mean that Hanada was the only theorist who influenced Matsumoto. For instance, one senses the influence of Okamoto Tarō, a painter, artist, and critic who studied with Marcel Mauss and befriended Georges Bataille in Paris in the 1930s, and with whom Hanada founded a legendary art collective, Yoru no Kai, in the 1940s. There was also an influential, preceding work by Takiguchi Shūzō, a poet and critic who introduced surrealism to Japan. Takiguchi's seminal introduction of contemporary European art movements, *Kindai geijutsu* (Modern art, 1938), published under the supervision of the Marxist philosopher Tosaka Jun during the war, shaped Hanada's development as an avant-garde literary critic, and Takiguchi himself left a considerable impact on Matsumoto.[39]

In a short essay published in 1963, Matsumoto sums up his intellectual debt to Takiguchi and Hanada.

> When I first encountered Takiguchi's seminal work—*Modern Art*—in the spring of 1951, I felt like I was hit by a thunderbolt. *Modern Art* discussed various art movements of the twentieth century since cubism with a principal focus on surrealism. I was studying art at the time, and the book opened my eyes to the essence of "thought" and "spirit" that generated and undergirded avant-garde art. Until the publication of Hanada Kiyoteru's *Avant-Garde Art* in 1954, Takiguchi's *Modern Art* was the only excellent guidebook for thinking about artistic revolution.[40]

Inheriting the modernist view of art from these critics, Matsumoto embraced cinema's potential to disrupt habituated modes of perceiving everyday reality and applied it to documentary.[41] In a number of essays published in the late 1950s and early 1960s, Matsumoto rejected a style of documentary realism, which privileged the factuality of the referent over the plasticity of the image. The camera, in his view, could not simply be a tool that transparently mediated between the profilmic reality and its image; instead, the camera had to become a conscious means of interrogating perceptual habits. Matsumoto's privileging of the defamiliarizing capacity of the camera is evident in passages like the following: "The most urgent task for us documentarists today is to break away from the methodological impasse of the Griersonian model of filmmaking, which overestimates our faculty of cognition; we need to liberate the meaning of the term *document* from the shackles of naturalism as soon as possible."[42] What Matsumoto calls avant-garde documentary filmmaking is a practice that actively negates the documentary's claim to factuality and objectivity based on the indexical function of the camera. Against the recognizability of the image, Matsumoto prefers the opacity of the image, which bears traces of the unconscious. The avant-garde documentary filmmaker, in his view, must "distrust the *visible*, external world that appears objective, and delve into the *invisible*, internal world of his own subjectivity."[43]

In "Record of the Hidden World" (1960), Matsumoto further develops the dialectic of visibility and invisibility. Again following the framework set by Hanada in his book *Avangyarudo geijutsu* (Avant-garde art, 1954), Matsumoto defines documentary as a critical method of interrogating the unconscious realm of social and psychic realities.[44] Extending Hanada's argument on the unconscious, Matsumoto introduces the Freudian concept of the uncanny (*unheimlich*) in order to articulate the dialectic of visibility and invisibility.[45] He writes, for instance, "I want to make a point of Freud's perspective on the uncanny, since he sees the essence of the uncanny as something hidden coming to the surface and this process is related to the irrational workings of the mind. I believe that this perspective must be the premise of avant-garde documentary arts."[46] By using the notion of the uncanny, Matsumoto positions the method of avant-garde documentary as a dialectical means of visualizing what remains invisible to and "hidden" from consciousness.

In developing his idea of the avant-garde documentary through the Freudian notion of the uncanny, Matsumoto tries to bring together the insights of Marxism and psychoanalysis.[47] Although rather schematic in his interpretation of Marx and Freud, Matsumoto argues that the unconscious mechanism of repression that gives rise to the experience of the uncanny must be understood as a result of the systemic alienation of individuals in capitalist society.[48] He thus draws a causal relationship between the unconscious mechanism of repression and the socioeconomic structure of capitalism that alienates individuals from their own labor—and desire. The experience of the uncanny functions as a symptom of the psychic and social structures of repression and concealment. For while the individual unconscious structurally corresponds to the social unconscious, they work together to conceal the real workings of capitalism. In this manner, Matsumoto interprets the Freudian understanding of psychic disturbance through the Marxist framework of alienation. The individual experience of the uncanny is subsequently explained as a secondary *effect* of ideological distortions already at work in capitalist society.

Matsumoto's logic again follows the preceding interpretation of psychoanalysis provided by Hanada, who argued for the historical-materialist understanding of the unconscious in his book, *Avant-Garde Art*. Taking Marx's dictum "It is not the consciousness of men that determines their existence, but their social existence that determines their consciousness," Hanada applied it to the psychoanalytic understanding of the unconscious.[49] Hanada's argument was that, like consciousness, the unconscious of the individual is directly determined by the external material conditions of social existence.[50] Matsumoto applies this view to the cinematic experience of the uncanny. The uncanny experience provided by cinema can be used to analyze the external material conditions of capitalist society, since the uncanny is a symptom of the collective forgetting of these conditions. While Matsumoto does not use the word *ideology*, the recurring metaphor of "unveiling" and his comparison of the veil to what he calls "everyday consciousness" suggests that what he has in mind is the ideological displacement of the real material conditions of social existence. It is precisely this veiled state of consciousness and the mode of seeing associated with it that Matsumoto thinks his method of avant-garde documentary can interrogate.

Matsumoto's introduction of the unconscious into Japanese documentary discourse was groundbreaking, though as Abé Mark Nornes suggests this insight was not taken up by other Japanese theorists.[51] Perhaps what makes Matsumoto's theorization of the uncanny difficult to follow is the way he combines different theoretical frameworks in order to make essentially the same point. Psychoanalysis is just one of several frameworks that he appropriates to articulate cinema's political potential for defamiliarization. For instance, the 1958 essay "Method and the Image" ("Hōhō to imeeji"), published in the film journal *Eiga Hihyō*, invokes a similar logic of unveiling the stereotyped or habituated everyday mode of seeing. While it is this essay that Matsumoto quotes at length in his 1960 essay on the uncanny, the main framework of analysis here is neither Freudian psychoanalysis nor Marxist critique of ideology: it is Jean-Paul Sartre's existential phenomenology.

Matsumoto draws his critique of everyday consciousness from Sartre's fictionalized meditation on the encounter with brute existence that is devoid of meaning in the novel *Nausea*. Focusing on the celebrated passage from *Nausea* where the protagonist Roquentin experiences a sudden nausea as he stares at the root of a chestnut tree, Matsumoto writes,

> At this moment the root of the chestnut tree lost the "meaning" as root, and appeared as a naked "thing." Furthermore, the unique structure and movement of this "thing" corresponded to a certain situation hidden deep inside the mind, and thus this hidden situation rose to the surface of his consciousness and took the objective

form of this "thing." Roquentin felt nausea when he saw the image of a raw lump [in the root of the chestnut tree] because he discovered the fundamental absurdity of existence in this image.[52]

Matsumoto then argues that surrealists had already appropriated the disturbing encounter with a "thing" unhinged from the network of signification, and tried to induce such encounters through their artworks. Of particular importance is the fact that Matsumoto discovers an artistic method of disrupting everyday consciousness in the experience of encountering the bare existence of things described by Sartre and compares it to the surrealist method of chance encounter. In the 1960 essay, Matsumoto appropriates the Freudian notion of the uncanny to articulate his methodological interest in cinema's potential to induce an unexpected experience, which in turn suspends control of everyday consciousness. The Sartrean understanding of the "thing" offers him a similar opportunity to articulate cinema's potential to disrupt habituated modes of perception and to call consciousness itself into question. However, instead of further pursuing this philosophical interrogation of consciousness, Matsumoto turns to psychoanalysis and Marxism to historicize the unconscious in relation to something more specific: capitalism.

Around 1960, his emphasis thus shifts from the cinematic exploration of the ahistorical, ontological existence of the "thing" to the historically determined condition of alienation under capitalism. The real existence hidden beneath the façade of everyday consciousness is no longer approached through the existential perspective, but through the historical-materialist perspective.

> If we were to understand the question of "the hidden world" as strictly belonging to the inner problem of the mind, that would be one-sided and indeed inverted. For the hidden distortions of the inside are ultimately determined by and reflect the hidden distortions of the outside. If we speak more precisely in the materialist manner, the inside is an extension of the outside; there is nothing that absolutely separates the two. Indeed, the condition of alienation is first and foremost that which exists in the outside world. . . . The closer we get to the essence or the real existence of the overall structure of this outside world, the more *uncanny* it becomes.[53]

This passage sums up Matsumoto's effort to synthesize psychoanalysis and existentialism through the mediation of Marxism in order to arrive at an idiosyncratic theory of defamiliarization ("unveiling of everyday consciousness").

Importantly, Matsumoto's investment in the process of defamiliarization is already evident in "On the Method of the Avant-Garde Documentary Film." While this essay, which predates both "Method and the Image" and "Record of the Hidden World," does not explicitly engage with Freud or Marx, it anticipates Matsumoto's later theorization of the defamiliarizing potential of cinema. This essay also warrants attention for additional reasons: first, it is here that Matsumoto initially articulates his idea of the dialectical synthesis of avant-garde and documentary as a method, an idea that inspired Oshima; and second, and more important, the essay provides a theoretical ground for his cinematic experiments. The method of avant-garde documentary filmmaking Matsumoto proposes hinges on the process of remediation, which anticipates his own as well as Oshima's formal experiments with still images in works such as *The Song of Stone* and *Band of Ninja*. We find the first clear indication of his interest in intermedial experiments in this essay, which occupies a singular place in the history of Japanese film theory.

ON THE METHOD OF THE AVANT-GARDE DOCUMENTARY FILM

Central to Matsumoto's theorization of an avant-garde documentary method is Alain Resnais's treatment of Pablo Picasso's painting *Guernica* in his short documentary film, also titled *Guernica* (1950). What Matsumoto discovers in the film *Guernica* is a reflexive process of reworking an existent work in another medium, a process by which the original becomes thoroughly defamiliarized. Matsumoto thus finds the model of his avant-garde documentary method in Resnais's remediation of Picasso's painting. In Resnais's *Guernica*, he notes, the camera constantly crops, fragments, and pans over immobile objects (mostly paintings but also newspaper headlines and sculptures). The techniques of superimposition and dissolve, which characterize Matsumoto's *The Song of Stone*, are frequently used in the film *Guernica*.[54] Through his reading of *Guernica*, Matsumoto is able to develop his idea of avant-garde documentary filmmaking around the process of double mediation or remediation. Resnais's documentary inspires him because it is a filmic work based on the meticulous remediation of a painting.

According to Matsumoto, Resnais's refusal to reproduce Picasso's painting in full view indicates his wish to become a visionary, a seer who refuses to take what is visible and self-evident. Instead of simply using the camera to record and reproduce Picasso's painting in its entirety, Resnais uses the camera to fragment it. The camera mediates the painting and transforms it. Resnais's readiness to inflict violence on the original painting, in Matsumoto's view, is an indication of his desire to see beyond what is already visible: "While Alain Resnais takes Picasso's *Guernica* as his object, he does not depend on the strength of this material alone. Of course, the image presented in each shot is always some part of Picasso's painting. Yet what these images embody is no longer Picasso's painting; they embody the 'Picasso seen by Resnais' or the 'Resnais seeing Picasso.' . . . Here, the naïve idea of documentation has already been negated."[55] Matsumoto thus locates the significance of the film *Guernica* in Resnais's willingness to sacrifice the integrity of the original painting in order to foreground the cinematic process of mediation. For him, the decision to undermine the organic unity of the painting indicates a shift away from prioritizing profilmic reality to prioritizing the process of mediation itself as an object of documentation.

For Matsumoto, Resnais's decision not to present the original painting in a full view also shows his determination to break away from the traditional view of artwork as an organic unity. "If Resnais's intention was to cinematically reproduce or re-present the tableau that stood in front of him," writes Matsumoto, "he would have tried to include at least one shot that revealed the tableau in its entirety by using a pan or any other means."[56] Matsumoto concludes that Resnais's gesture, his refusal to display Picasso's painting in full view, is an indication of his will "to *see* Picasso's painting, but not to simply *show* it."[57] This interrogative mode of seeing translates into a reflexive mediation of the painting, and the camera records this reflexive process of mediation. The resulting effects of fragmentation and disorientation refute the camera's capacity to simply reproduce reality.

The emphasis on fragmentation and disorientation is echoed in Matsumoto's own filmmaking practice. From *Security Treaty* (ANPO *jōyaku*, 1960) to *Nishijin* (1961) and *The Song of Stone* (1963), Matsumoto's early documentary works are likewise characterized by a refusal to display in full the object of investigation. *Nishijin*, for instance, refuses to provide any establishing shots. The film is filled with extreme close-ups of the machine, the weaver's body parts, and the architecture of the town. Matsumoto deliberately works against the expectation of a recognizable and lucid image, which we habitually bring to the genre of documentary.

Matsumoto's analysis of Resnais's *Guernica* is equally applicable to *The Song of Stone*. While the original intention of TBS television was to produce a standard documentary program introducing Satow's photojournalistic career, Matsumoto basically took this opportunity to create an experimental work based on the remediation of Satow's photographs. In so doing, he boldly sacrificed the integrity of the original photographs.[58] For Matsumoto, the unfaithful remediation of the original was necessary in order to see beyond the surface of the documentary photographs, and to present the process of mediation itself as the basis of his avant-garde documentary film.

Matsumoto's treatment of Satow's photographs through constant cropping, rotation, solarization, zoom, and superimposition is indeed strikingly similar to Resnais's treatment of Picasso's painting in the film *Guernica*. Matsumoto's own analysis of *The Song of Stone* also suggests a clear continuity between this film and his reading of *Guernica*. The motif of stonecutting, argues Matsumoto, allegorizes the very process of appropriating and transforming the still-image medium of photography into the moving image medium of cinema. Just as Matsumoto animates Satow's photographs, the stonecutters bring life to inanimate stones. Immobile stones and still photographs are doubly distant from cinema, a medium customarily associated with life-like movement. But these still objects can be animated through artistic labor: "As I continued to look at Satow's photographs, certain imagery started to take shape in my mind. The inspiration came from the episode in which stonecutters described the process of chiseling and polishing the stones cut from the mountain as a process of pouring energy into stones as if these stones themselves came to life."[59] *The Song of Stone* thus doubles the animating process of breathing life into inanimate objects by mimicking the very process documented by Satow's camera. The technique of stop-motion animation is more than appropriate in this regard. Matsumoto's *The Song of Stone* is a work of animation that foregrounds the cinematic process of remediating photography.

Writing around the same time as Matsumoto, André Bazin made a comparable analysis of Resnais's *Guernica*. Their arguments are quite similar, albeit with different conclusions. A brief comparison will help me expand on Matsumoto's theorization of avant-garde documentary filmmaking. In the well-known essay entitled "Painting and Cinema," Bazin praises Resnais's effort to offer new perspectives on the work of Picasso or on the work of Van Gogh by inflicting certain violence onto the original paintings.

> Films of paintings are not animation films. What is paradoxical about them is that they use an already completed work sufficient unto itself. But it is precisely because it substitutes for the painting a work one degree removed from it, proceeding from something already aesthetically formulated, that it throws a new light on the original. It is perhaps to the extent that the film *is* a complete work and as such, seems therefore to betray the painting most, that it renders it in reality the greater service.[60]

The seeming "betrayal" of the original artwork is necessary, since "[it] is in pulling the work apart, in breaking up its component parts, in making an assault on its very essence that the film compels it to deliver up some of its hidden powers."[61] In short, it is through the betrayal and the destruction of the original painting that a work of cinematic remediation, such as Resnais's *Guernica*, can make visible what remained invisible in the original, and thus do "the greater service" than do the films that attempt to faithfully reproduce it.

The key phrase here is "a work one degree removed from [the original]." It is this sense of removal or distance from the original that the cinematic practice of remediation generates. The goal of filmmaking lies in going beyond the visible surface of reality. On this point Bazin and Matsumoto are in agreement. For them cinema is more than an indexical medium that faithfully records traces of reality; it is a visionary medium that reveals what remains inaccessible beneath the surface of visibility.

But the relevance of Resnais's treatment of Picasso's painting for Matsumoto's theory of the avant-garde documentary does not end here. Although Matsumoto falls short of articulating this point, the significance of Resnais's experiment in the context of his theory lies in the fact that Resnais's camera remediates an artistic work of visual representation already composed and completed by a medium other than cinema. This is where the question of intermediality comes in. The camera no longer documents physical reality, but images produced and completed in another medium. What is at stake here is the process of mediation through which images—rather than reality—become profilmic objects of the documentary gaze. Documentary filmmaking becomes *a second-order image making*—the production of an image out of another image. Second-order image making entails both a fragmentation and preservation of the original work, which in turn produces an effect of intermediality. While the notion of intermediality often implies the dissolution of the strict boundary between heterogeneous media or artistic genres, it can also be used to describe a work that deliberately draws attention to the material and formal differences between two (or more) media that coexist on the same plane or space.

When understood in this light, one can see a connection among Resnais's *Guernica*, Matsumoto's *The Song of Stone*, and Oshima's *Diary of Yunbogi* and *Band of Ninja*. All are works of remediation that deliberately draw attention to a gap between the cinematic medium and non-cinematic media—whether painting, still photography, or the comic book. In all these cases, the finished work is one degree removed from the original work. This sense of removal at once highlights the differences between the media and their coexistence. It was precisely the coexistence of heterogeneous media that the discourse on the image addressed.

THE DISCOURSE ON THE IMAGE AND THE CONCEPT OF EIZŌ

In the 1950s and 1960s, the conception of cinema as the hegemonic medium of the moving image was greatly challenged. The rise of television—the newest moving-image medium—was its main catalyst, but it was not the sole culprit. On the one hand, the desire to reinvent cinema shared by filmmakers, including Matsumoto and Oshima, manifested itself in their direct remediation of still-image media. However, Matsumoto and Oshima were by no means the first to use this technique. Takiguchi Shūzō, for instance, was involved in an experimental art film project that remediated woodblock prints made by the Edo period artist Katsushika Hokusai in the early 1950s. Takiguchi and others associated with Bijutsu Eiga Kenkyūkai (a research group on art film) started to film Hokusai's prints in 1951. They experienced financial difficulties and had to sell the project to another production company led by young filmmakers. The new director who took over the task of supervising the project was Teshigahara Hiroshi, a filmmaker who frequented Hanada's circle of avant-garde artists and who founded the

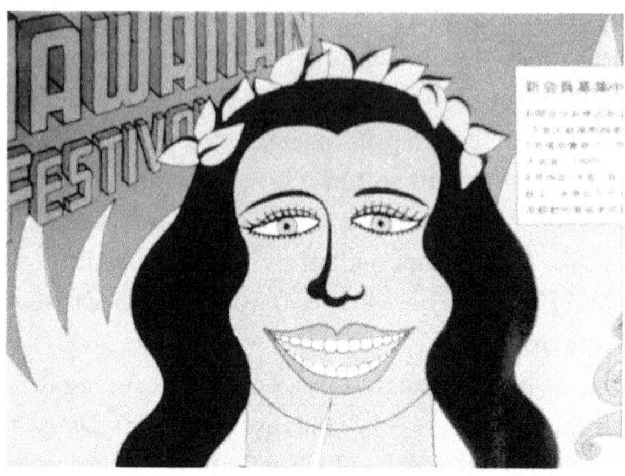

1.4. An advertisement poster designed by Yokoo Tadanori. Still from *Anthology No. 1* (1964), dir. Yokoo Tadanori.

Sōgetsu Art Center in 1958. Using only the footage already shot by Takiguchi's group, Teshigahara completed the film *Hokusai* in 1953. Takiguchi's published script suggests that he wanted to add the sensation of movement to Hokusai's prints by using close-ups and pans.[62] His decision to film Hokusai's prints in an analytical manner anticipates Matsumoto's remediation of Satow's photographs in *The Song of Stone*.

Although experimental filmmaking based on the technique of remediation was already taking place in the 1950s, the 1960s was the decade when it became widely used. If documentary was one field in which this technique took firm hold, experimental animation was another. A number of experimental animation films made by graphic designers who ventured into the field of animation, such as Yokoo Tadanori and Uno Akira, also used this technique. Yokoo's experimental short *Anthology No. 1* (1964), presented at the first animation festival held at the Sōgetsu Art Center, in September 1964, is an exemplary work that simply remediates posters and illustrations he had designed and created before.[63] As the camera moves across the surface of posters and pages from books, we see portions of graphic images, captions, and texts (figure 1.4). Yokoo's other animation films—*Kiss Kiss Kiss* (1964) and *Kachi kachi yama meoto no sujimichi* (1965)—are again based on a remediation of his own illustrations and graphic designs. Sidestepping generic conventions of animation filmmaking, Yokoo emphasizes the absence of movement and the materiality of print media; the resulting effects are surprisingly similar to those of *The Song of the Stone*, *Diary of Yunbogi*, and *Band of Ninja*.

While these pioneering experiments were unfolding in the fields of documentary and animation, something else was taking place. The term *eizō* began to gain currency in film theory and media criticism in the late 1950s. Although it is often translated as "the moving image," the precise meaning of *eizō* is not easy to translate or even to define. The eizō refers to a particular kind of image created and mediated by technological means, including cinema, television, photography, and computer imaging. Hence, images created by hand, as in the case of painting or drawing, are not eizō. However, precisely because eizō refers to all types of technological media that can make images, its referent is much broader than the moving image. Furthermore, because it presupposes the mediation by technological or mechanical apparatus, eizō does not refer to pictorial, mental, literary, or theological notions of the image.

As recent works on the history of the concept of the image suggest, in the Christian-influenced Western tradition this concept is intimately tied to theological notions of incarnation, idolatry, and the sacred. The word *image* is etymologically linked to the Latin words *imago* and *imitari*, signifying the ideas of likeness, imitation, and copy. This mimetic understanding of the image in Western culture carries subtle but insistent theological connotations. According to Marie-José Mondzain, the contemporary understanding of the power of visual images is rooted in the idea that "it is God who sets the example, *and it is he whom one imitates*."[64] Even if it is not immediately religious, "the image is always sacred," contends Jean-Luc Nancy.[65] In his analysis of the rhetoric of the image, Roland Barthes also asserts that "the image is re-presentation, which is to say ultimately resurrection."[66] These connotations (imitation, the sacred, resurrection, etc.) are fundamental to the dominant visual paradigm of Western art and art history. As Georges Didi-Huberman puts it, this is so because the theology of the image in Christianity based on the rift between the visible and the visual, or what manifestly shows itself and what is virtually present, has conditioned the very basis of aesthetics in the West.[67] In contrast, the Japanese concept of eizō does not carry these connotations, even if it arguably belongs to the modern regime of visuality influenced by Western aesthetics. The visual paradigm in question here has much narrower historical and epistemological parameters, which are firmly rooted in the modern technological era of visuality. More precisely, the rise of eizō as a key concept runs parallel to the postwar transformation of the media environment in Japan. Given this specificity, it is necessary to outline a brief genealogy of this concept.

The word *eizō* was long used to describe the phenomenal realm in philosophy and science, but its connotation changed in the 1950s. Before the 1950s, it was customary to write this word with the character signifying shadow or silhouette (otherwise read as *kage*). Between the 1950s and 1960s, the homonymic word *eizō* written with the character signifying the optical processes of reflection and projection (otherwise read as *utsusu*) became dominant and gradually replaced the old transcription using the character for shadow. While in the immediate postwar years both versions were still used interchangeably to refer to the cinematic image, by the end of the 1950s the use of the new transcription with the connotation of the mechanical projection and reflection had become the standard. Not surprisingly, this graphic change occurred just when television gained prominence.

The proliferation of eizō in film theory and media criticism during this period thus suggests two things: first, that the technologically produced image became an important topic of analysis; and second, that the rise of television spurred this turn toward the image. This turn to the image prompted by television was accompanied by a renewed interest in the question of medium specificity. It is often the case that the emergence of a new medium revitalizes debates on the uniqueness of each medium. This was true in the case of television in Japan. But the problem was that the concept of eizō undermined—or at least complicated—the very idea of medium specificity, as it was applicable to a broad range of images generated by optical media and apparatuses, including photography, cinema, television, video, slide projectors, and computers. Consequently, two intertwined tendencies emerged in Japanese film theory and media criticism: one emphasized the specificities of each image-based medium; the other emphasized the commonality among different image-based media. Taken as a whole, the discourse on the image in the 1950s and 1960s generated this radical reorientation in conceptualizing the medium.

The sudden proliferation of eizō in the late 1950s and throughout the 1960s can be glimpsed by the sheer number of journals and books bearing this particular word in their titles. Among them we find Matsumoto's book *Eizō no hakken* (Discovery of the image, 1963). Matsumoto claims that he was indeed the first writer to use the word *eizō* in the book title.[68] But this does not mean that other writers did not discuss this concept. On the contrary, eizō became an object of intense theorization around 1958–60, mainly through the publications of critics, filmmakers, and writers who contributed to what is known as the "debate on the image" (*eizō ronsō*). This debate involved prominent figures such as the avant-garde writer Abé Kōbō, the literary scholar Sasaki Kiichi, the film scholar Okada Susumu, and the documentary filmmaker Hani Susumu.[69] Around this time a number of essays and books discussing the differences and similarities between various image-based media began to appear in leading film and art journals including *Kiroku Eiga* (Documentary film) and *Gendai Geijutsu* (Contemporary art). Among such publications, the short-lived journal *Gendai Geijutsu* was particularly instrumental in generating a comparative analysis of media. Founded by the members of Kiroku Geijutsu no Kai (Association of Documentary Arts), which took up Hanada and his cohort's idea of synthesizing different art forms and genres, the journal offered a discursive space where a diverse group of critics and artists engaged in different media (e.g., photography, film, television, painting, literature) could collaborate, debate, and exchange ideas.

From the discursive milieu that encouraged the comparative analysis of media emerged a number of publications that highlighted the question of the image: *Hekiga kara terebimade: Eiga no atarashii ronri* (From cave painting to television: A new logic of cinema, 1959) and *Gendai eizō ron* (A contemporary theory of the image, 1965) by Okada Susumu; *Kamera to maiku: Gendai geijutsu no hōhō* (Camera and microphone: The method of contemporary art, 1960) by Hani Susumu; *Sabaku no shisō* (A thought of the desert, 1965) by Abé Kōbō; *Eizō to wa nanika* (What is an image?, 1966), an anthology of essays written by Okada, Matsumoto, and others; *Shashin geijutsuron* (A theory of photographic art, 1967) by Shigemori Kōan; and *Gendai eiga jiten* (Contemporary encyclopedia of cinema, 1967), edited by Okada Susumu, Sasaki Kiichi, Satō Tadao, and Hani Susumu. To this list, we can also add Matsumoto's books, *Eizō no hakken* as well as *Hyōgen no sekai* (The world of expression, 1967), both of which deal with the questions of medium specificity and the image. Furthermore, in 1964 a new journal, *Eizō Geijutsu* (Image arts) was launched. The publication of this journal accompanied the establishment of another artist collective, Eizō Geijutsu no Kai (the Association of Image Arts), spearheaded by Matsumoto and the documentary filmmaker and critic Noda Shinkichi.

The manifesto published in the inaugural issue of *Eizō Geijutsu* gives a sense of the centrality of the concept of the image and its implied intermediality.

> We are hereby founding an organ of the art movement, Eizō Geijutsu no Kai, by gathering the auteurs and technicians who aim to critically transform the image arts [*eizō geijutsu*]. The unbound possibilities of the image arts, cinema and television in particular, are a treasure house of creativity. The image arts are the adolescence of art. Here we have dazzling possibilities of dialectically synthesizing and sublating various genres of art forms that came before. We, as modern artists, bet on this rich horizon of the future.[70]

As suggested by this manifesto, the decisive use of the word *eizō* is linked to the idea of synthesizing various arts and media. Of relevance here is also the fact that this broad approach to image-based media as a whole became dominant in Japanese film discourse in the mid-1960s, overshadowing a more narrowly conceived approach to cinema that treated the medium in isolation.

While the activities of groups such as Kiroku Geijutsu no Kai and Eizō Geijutsu no Kai in the 1960s had a more wide-reaching impact, the discursive shift toward the multiplicity of image-based media rather than the singularity of cinema was arguably already underway in the 1950s. An early proponent of the comparative approach to cinema was Imamura Taihei, a film theorist known for his classic studies of animation and documentary. Two years before the publication of the journal *Eizō Geijutsu*, Imamura launched a similarly titled film journal, *Eizō Bunka* (Image culture). This journal was a reincarnation of an earlier film journal, *Eiga Bunka* (Film culture), which Imamura edited with prominent intellectuals such as Hanada and Nakai Masakazu in the early 1950s. The manifesto published in the inaugural issue of the journal *Eiga Bunka* in 1950 anticipates the discourse on the image in the 1960s: "We hope to gain knowledge of the substance of the image culture [*eizō bunka*] by considering all new phenomena generated by cinema, and by researching everything that cinema contributes to the development of society. In doing so, we hope to understand the essence of the twentieth-century society that gave birth to this image culture. It is for these reasons that we gathered together here to publish a strictly theoretical journal, *Eiga Bunka*."[71] Here, cinema is envisioned as one aspect of what Imamura and others call the eizō bunka. In spite of the seeming centrality of cinema—clearly signaled by the title of the journal—this manifesto indicates their desire to connect cinema to its wider media environment.

While anyone claiming to be at the origins of a particular discourse should be regarded with suspicion, Imamura argues that it was his cohort of intellectuals who first started to use the term *eizō* to theorize cinema in the 1940s.[72] In the 1940s, it was still written with the character for "shadow," suggesting the central importance of the medium of cinema. In the 1950s, Imamura and others associated with *Eiga Bunka* started using the term *eizō* written with the character for "reflection" or "projection," and extended its application from cinema to television.[73] The increased attention to television was clearly one of the underlying conditions that facilitated the semantic transformation of the word *eizō* itself. As Imamura notes in his essay "The Continuity between Cinema and Television: The Origin of New Problems of the Image" (1963), a comparative approach to the study of cinema *and* television based on the shared properties of the image was becoming an important current in the early 1960s.[74]

A few other writers and critics have also taken credit for popularizing the word *eizō* as a critical term. Matsumoto makes this claim: "While the concept of 'image' has become thoroughly generalized by entering everyday parlance, it was not yet used widely in the late 1950s. There were only a handful of us—including Okada Susumu, Hani Susumu and myself—who made frequent use of this term on purpose."[75] Similarly, Okada opens his essay "The Logic of Image and the Logic of Language" (1958) with the following remark: "The word *eizō* has recently become thoroughly fashionable, though I may be blamed for spreading the use of this ambiguous term."[76] Despite the term's ambiguity, Okada continues, its use allows him to rethink the specificity of cinema anew. If the notion of the image has attracted such wide attention, "it is because, today, the function of the image seems to be ignored in cinema."[77] Okada's argument is that Japanese cinema has forgotten the aesthetic value of the image in its pursuit of narrative. This critique of story-driven filmmaking is not limited to Okada, but is shared by many who were involved in avant-garde art collectives, such as Kiroku Geijutsu no Kai. The call to rethink the primacy of the image has indeed accompanied many debates and discussions on the medium specificity of cinema.

THE DEBATE ON THE IMAGE

In his essay "The Meaning of the Image in Cinema: A Perspective on the Cinematic Language" (1958), Okada asserts that the medium specificity of cinema lies in the image and that cinematic images function as an independent form of language. While his assertions of cinema's autonomy and its status as a unique language system were not necessarily new—he admitted that the idea of the "cinematic language" was an old one, already discussed by Balázs, Eisenstein, and Pudovkin—his argument became a point of contention and criticism in the "debate on the image," a series of published discussions on the semiotic functions of the image and language. The debate was sparked originally by a need to rethink montage in light of the newly introduced idea of *caméra-stylo* by the French filmmaker and critic Alexandre Astruc. Both Okada and Hani Susumu emphasized the autonomy of one shot supported by the integrity of its image, and argued that the view of storytelling that privileges montage, and hence the relation between shots, needed to be abandoned.[78] As Hani writes in his essay "Why Do We Insist on the Image?," their emphasis on the integrity of one shot stemmed from a desire to reinvent cinema at a particular historical moment, when television had started to displace its cultural importance. Hani finds his inspiration in the work of postwar filmmakers, such as Astruc, Bresson, Kawalerowicz, and Antonioni, all of whom he regards as inventors of a new language of cinema.[79] Underlying Okada's and Hani's arguments is an investment in the poetic and affective forces of the cinematic image, which is why some of their opponents compared their positions to the proponents of *photogénie*.

However, precisely because Okada insisted on rethinking this photogénic understanding of the image in terms of an autonomous language system, he invited fierce criticism from writers and critics such as Abé Kōbō and Masaki Kyōsuke. It is worth noting that all of the participants in this debate belonged to the aforementioned art collective, Kiroku Geijutsu no Kai, founded by writers, literary critics, painters, photographers, and filmmakers close to the avant-garde circle of Hanada. The debate on the image was unfolding at exactly the same time as Matsumoto and Oshima were participating in Eiga to Hihyō no Kai—another group bearing the influence of Hanada.

Schematically put, Abé and Masaki shifted the focus of the debate from the image to language by reframing the protosemiotic understanding of cinematic images as signifiers. Against Okada who asserted that the new understanding of cinema *as* language must shake off its assumption that it is a second-order language inferior to verbal or written language, Abé, for instance, suggested that the linguistic analogy is misleading, not because the image is outside the influence of language, but precisely because our perception of any image is mediated by language. According to Abé, our cognitive faculty hinges on our ability to organize sensory stimuli into a coherent whole, and this organizational process is always already mediated by language. In short, language is what offers a fundamental order to our perceptual and cognitive syntax, with which we constantly but unconsciously navigate through our everyday activities.[80]

Unlike Okada, Abé thus maintained the view that one cannot separate the signifying functions of the cinematic image from verbal language. For the imperceptible operation of language structures our perception of the image to the point that "even the silent 8 mm film that records a simple movement of an insect without the help of an intertitle or a *benshi* [narrator]" is already trapped in the signifying grid.[81] If we do not consider the intermediary function of language, we see only beams of lights and shadows flickering on the screen. Abé hence opposed Okada's view that cinema could instantiate a purely visual mode of communication, in which images speak *like* words and transmit thoughts and ideas without the mediation of language. Therefore, while Abé maintained his view that film and visual-media theorists could not afford to ignore the constitutive role of language in human perception, he equally insisted that filmmakers must explore the maximum potential of the cinematic image to destabilize spectators' perceptual habits. Abé's essay "A Script for an Experimental Film," published in 1960, advanced this line of argument: "The reason I took an oppositional stance toward [Hani Susumu and Okada Susumu], who advocate for the image media, is that I wanted to show that I took these images more seriously than they did. They contend that images can construct the world of abstraction just as language constructs it. But this is not possible. In fact, the power and strength of the image resides in *not speaking* like language."[82]

Abé's ultimate refusal to reduce the image to its signifying function (on the premise of preserving the defamiliarizing force of the image) ironically dovetailed with his opponent Okada's call for respecting the image. Their disagreement regarding the analogy of language notwithstanding, we can observe a common thread running through this debate. Namely, the comparison of language and image was animated first by a concern about the specificity of cinema, then by a desire to articulate the relations between one medium (language) and another (cinema, photography, etc.). Abé's and Okada's focus on signification as an essential component of the medium specificity of cinema suggests a protosemiotic approach to cinema. As Christian Metz keenly observed in his essay "The Cinema: Language or Language System?" (1964), concern with language was not limited to Japan, but was equally present in France during the 1950s and 1960s: "When approaching the cinema from the linguistic point of view, it is difficult to avoid shuttling back and forth between two positions: the cinema as a language; the cinema as infinitely different from verbal language. Perhaps it is impossible to extricate oneself from this dilemma with impunity."[83] In this sense, the debate on the image in many ways paralleled contemporaneous debates held by theorists such as Gilbert Cohen-Séat and others associated with *filmologie* (with which Metz was associated).[84] Given the fact that Okada was the one who introduced the work of French theorists, including that of André Bazin and Edgar Morin, the resonance between Japanese discourse on the image and French film theory is not surprising.[85]

However, what is more important than this intriguing connection between Japanese and French film theories is the significance the debate on the image has had in the wider discursive context of Japan. The underlying question for the participants of this debate was how to speak about the medium specificity of cinema, and the image and language became two central frameworks by which to articulate this specificity. What this indicates is that by the beginning of the 1960s the question of the specificity of the cinematic medium was permeating Japanese film theory, and the concept of the image (eizō), which had steadily gained currency since the 1950s, played *an enabling role* in thinking through this question. Furthermore, the turn to medium specificity was spurred by the arrival of television, a troubling double of cinema, whose defining feature was also the moving image. The resurgent interest in the specificity of the cinematic medium was, therefore, a rather symptomatic response to the relativized position of cinema, which had lost its hegemonic claim as the sole medium of the moving image.

In light of this situation, the publication of the aptly titled anthology *What Is an Image?* (1966) merits our attention. Prominent critics and theorists of cinema, photography, and television, including Okada and

Matsumoto, as well as Sasaki Kiichi and Wada Ben, contributed to this anthology. The essays collected in *What Is an Image?* cover a wide range of topics, from the medium specificity of cinema to the relation between language and image, to the characteristics of still photography, as well as the semiotic analysis of image-based modes of communication. The broad scope of the book suggests that there is no consensus among its contributors regarding the central question ("What is an image?").[86] By 1966, the image had become a broadly shared problematic for filmmakers, critics, and visual artists. It is precisely within this intellectual context that we must place Matsumoto's and Oshima's intermedial experiments with photography and the comic book. When isolated from the concurrent discursive events (such as the debate on the image and the publication of *What Is an Image?*), the historical significance of their experiments is lost. Without an understanding of the larger epistemic shift toward the problematic of the image, their experiments appear merely formal. But their experiments with remediation—a form of second-order image making—were also a response to concurrent theoretical debates on medium specificity and the image. Considered together, filmmaking practice and the discourse on the image point to an underlying conflict between the desire to reaffirm cinema's specificity as a moving-image medium and the desire to break down the boundaries between image-based media.

In this regard, Okada's eventual conversion from film scholar to media scholar is emblematic. While he was a principal defendant of cinema's singularity during the debate on the image, his work gradually veered toward the opposite end. The following passage from *A Contemporary Theory of the Image* (1965) encapsulates his now relativized view of cinema: "The 'image' [eizō] today is no longer an exclusive property of cinema. It is a common cellular element of both cinema and television, and therefore we must try to understand the quality of this common element instead of distinguishing cinema and television on the basis of their outward appearance."[87] As if to echo Okada's sentiment, Oshima also argued that television "liberated" the image from its confinement to the dark space of the movie theater. With the arrival of television, "the image multiplied and diversified."[88] With hindsight we can see the acute relevance of Oshima's remark on the multiplication and diversification of the image to the rapidly changing mediascape of the 1960s.

Indeed, in the years between two international expositions—Expo

67 in Montreal and Expo 70 in Osaka, during which a number of spectacular intermedia events were organized and executed—the use of multiprojection and nonrectangular screens became notably prevalent. Often combined with live performance and live music or the use of slide projectors, the cinematic projection of prerecorded images at these events never stood in isolation. Take, for instance, the illuminating case of the five-day symposium "EXPOSE·1968," an intermedia event which preceded Expo 70. Conceived by the editorial members of the graphic-design journal *Dezain Hihyō* (Design review), and organized by Awazu Kiyoshi, Hariu Ichirō, Kawazoe Noboru, Matsumoto Toshio, Nakahara Yūsuke, and Tōno Yoshiaki, this symposium generated impressively diverse and heterogeneous types of "images." Many of the images projected or transmitted defied the conventional boundaries associated with discrete media. As if to underscore the structure of multiplicity, Matsumoto's multiprojection film *For the Damaged Right Eye* (*Tsuburekakatta migime no tame ni*, 1968), which nonsequentially juxtaposes images of student protesters, sports, the Vietnam War, underground gay culture, advertisements, and so on, was presented as a work of "cinema mosaic."[89] The curious usage of this phrase suggests Matsumoto's awareness of Marshall McLuhan's media theory—the key word *mosaic*, which McLuhan used to define newspaper and television, was by then well-known in Japan. But the metaphor of mosaic also suggests Matsumoto's interest in the aesthetics of the newspaper and television.[90] Additionally, it indicates his desire to foreground the coexistence of heterogeneous image types in the same work, something he had been interested in since his theorization of the avant-garde documentary method and his analysis of *Guernica*. Fittingly, many of the images appearing in *For the Damaged Right Eye* are direct remediation from other media such as television commercials, graphic designs, comics, and newspapers (figure 1.5).

This interest in the structure of multiplicity and an expanded conception of cinema led Matsumoto to generate more technologically involved projection projects. *Projection for an Icon* (*Ikon no tame no purojekushon*, 1969), which used twenty gigantic balloons, five film projectors, and numerous light sources, is a work he made for the "Cross-Talk/Intermedia" event. As indicated by a photographic record of the event, published in *Bijutsu Techō*, the balloons, floating just above the ground and colliding with one another, served as a surface onto which

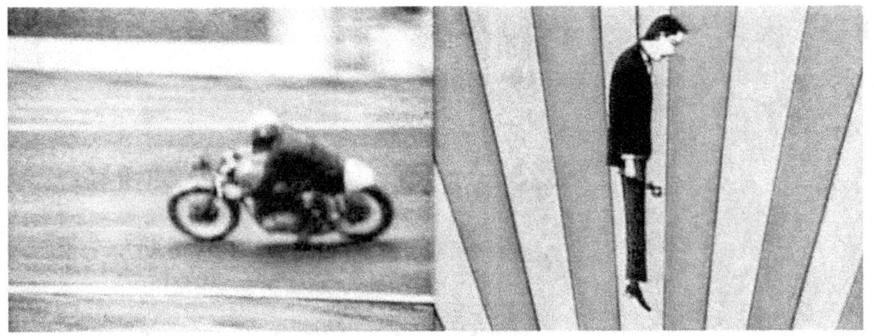

1.5. Sports news on television (left screen) and Yokoo Tadanori's graphic illustration (right screen). Still from *For the Damaged Right Eye* (1968), dir. Matsumoto Toshio.

Matsumoto projected images (figure 1.6). He also created *Space Projection Ako* (*Supeesu purojekushon Ako*, 1970), a three-dimensional installation-projection work made for Expo 70, by using sculptures attached to the projection surface. In these later projects, which expanded the conception of cinema and meshed it with the emergent trend of "environmental art" (*kankyō geijutsu*), Matsumoto literally multiplied, diversified, and crossbred various image-based media. Clearly, Matsumoto's attempts for expanded cinema works came in the wake of similar efforts undertaken by North American experimental filmmakers and artists, most notably Stan Vanderbeek, whom Matsumoto visited in 1968 and whom he regarded as the "representative filmmaker of expanded cinema."[91] Vanderbeek was in turn invited to participate in the "Cross-Talk/Intermedia" event along with avant-garde composers like Roger Reynolds, Gordon Mumma, Robert Ashley, and Salvatore Martirano. It was also in 1969 that Matsumoto incorporated his first video artwork, *Magnetic Scramble*, into his first feature-length film, *Funeral Parade of Roses* (*Bara no sōretsu*, 1969). He used a magnetic coil to distort television images showing student protesters, an attempt that recalls an earlier experiment with television by Nam June Paik. A trajectory of Matsumoto's intermedial endeavors in the 1960s thus suggests his continual engagement with techniques of remediation and his exploration of multiple types of image-based media. In some cases, the specificity of the cinematic medium comes to the fore, and in other cases it recedes into a background as one of many platforms for the image. There is a

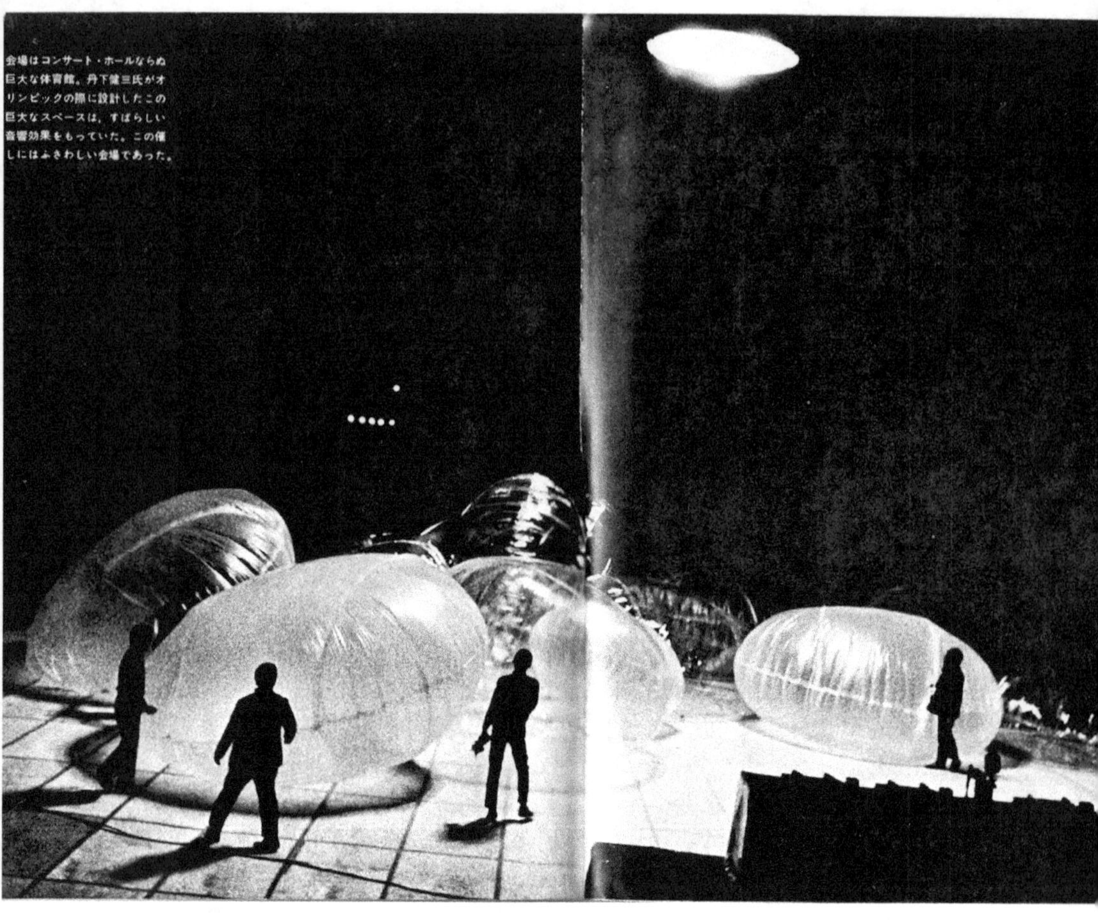

1.6. Matsumoto Toshio's *Projection for an Icon* (1969) at the "Cross-Talk/Intermedia" symposium. In *Bijutsu Techō* (April 1969), 103.

sense of oscillation between specificity and generality of the image in Matsumoto's work from this period.

Much of what is presented as "image theory" in the 1960s is also marked by the dialectic of specificity and generality. On the one hand is an attempt to encompass multiple platforms of media under the umbrella category of the image; on the other is an attempt to separate each medium on the basis of its specificity. If the image, which became the dominant problematic during this decade, brought on this oscillation, it is because there was an urgent need to theorize newer media such as television, video, and the computer. The 1960s is, as often pointed out, the time when the existing boundaries of media and artistic genres were finally dismantled. This decade witnessed the rise of anti-art movements, led by groups such as Neo-Dada Organizers and Hi-Red Center, and of the "happening" performance groups, such as Zero Dimension; the emergence of the *angura* (underground) theater movement, led by charismatic figures such as Terayama Shūji and Kara Jūrō; and the proliferation of student filmmaking, led by experimental groups such as VAN Film Research Center. Undoubtedly, the activities of these underground groups and the intermedial experiments undertaken by more established artists frequenting places such as the Sōgetsu Art Center facilitated the dismantling of media boundaries. Nevertheless, if we focused solely on these practices, we would miss the historical importance of the concurrent discourse on the image. This is why I have offered a close analysis of this discourse in relation to the technique of remediation and the question of intermediality in this chapter.

Throughout the 1960s, Oshima continued to use the technique of remediation in films such as *Death by Hanging* (*Kōshikei*, 1968) and *Boy* (*Shōnen*, 1969), and he played with the structure of redundancy in the exact repetition of the opening sequence in *Three Resurrected Drunkards* (*Kaette kita yopparai*, 1968). His experiment with the comic book medium in *Band of Ninja* is also echoed in his use of redundant graphic intertitles in *Diary of a Shinjuku Thief* (*Shinjuku dorobō nikki*, 1968). In addition to intermediality, all these works from the late 1960s exhibit a strong investment in relaying the ephemerality of news and the journalistic sense of actuality. Similarly, Matsumoto's work from the late 1960s also exhibits a great concern with cinema's relation to the news media, especially television, even though he gradually moved away from this type of engagement, focusing more on video and installation works. In spite of the different paths Oshima and Matsumoto would take in the 1970s, their films from the late 1960s are marked by their shared investment in the journalistic domain of actuality and the intermedial appropriation of non-cinematic media, bearing witness to the concurrent theorization of the image in film theory.

two

cinema, event, and artifactuality

At midnight on 21 February 1968, a handful of filmmakers and critics were driving down a highway from Shinjuku to Sumatakyō, a rural hot-spring town where an ethnic Korean man named Kim Hiro (a.k.a. Kin Kirō) was causing a hostage crisis. Among the people in the car were Oshima Nagisa, Wakamatsu Kōji, Adachi Masao, and Matsuda Masao, all of whom had the desire to be present at the site alongside news reporters and television crews in what had quickly turned into a media event. This hostage crisis was a salient case of what would later be called "theatrical crime" (*gekijōgata hanzai*), a type of criminal act aiming for media coverage in order to publicize a certain cause. It was also a politically charged crime, in which the hostage-taker demanded an apology from a policeman for his racist comments about, and racial profiling of, ethnic Koreans. The unprecedented apology was indeed broadcast on national television the day after Kim started the hostage crisis. The police cordoned off the surrounding area and Oshima and the other filmmakers who rushed to Sumatakyō in order to support Kim were unable to reach the inn where Kim and his nine hostages hid behind a makeshift barricade.[1]

In April 1968, Matsumoto made his multiprojection film, *For the Damaged Right Eye*, for the five-day symposium "EXPOSE·1968" at the Sōgetsu Art Center. For this film Matsumoto appropriated several clips from television news and press photographs reporting on Kim Hiro's hostage crisis, including an iconic shot of Kim holding a rifle and peeking through the window of the Fujimi Inn intercut with a shot of a news helicopter.

Two months after the screening of *For the Damaged Right Eye*, Oshima visited the Cannes Film Festival, which was canceled amid the May '68 uprising. On returning from France, Oshima held a press conference, announcing his plan to make a new film, entitled *Diary of a Shinjuku Thief*. Four days after the press conference Oshima began shooting the film. The first scene he filmed was the outbreak of a riot that took place in front of Shinjuku Station. Filmed at night with a black-and-white stock, this documentary sequence captures the unstaged moment when a young man, stepping out of an agitated crowd, suddenly throws a stone into a police box adjacent to the station, shattering its window.

According to Oshima, this small riot prefigured a much larger event to come: the legendary Shinjuku Riot of 21 October 1968. On this International Anti-War Day, thousands of demonstrators who had gathered to protest the Japanese government's support of the Vietnam War violently clashed with riot police. In an eerie reverberation of the brutal suppression of demonstrators on International Workers' Day in 1952, the government mobilized the police force and applied the riot law—Article 106 of the Penal Code—to arrest hundreds of protesters.[2] Shot during the summer of 1968, *Diary of a Shinjuku Thief* captures the eventful atmosphere of Shinjuku, an epicenter of underground art and political activism. When the film opened in February 1969 at the Shinjuku Bunka (the main theater of the Art Theatre Guild), its journalistic reference to the events of 1968 was far from lost on its audience. On the contrary, it was hailed for its journalistic quality of "actuality."[3]

In September 1969, seven months after *Diary of a Shinjuku Thief* premiered at the Art Theatre Shinjuku Bunka, Matsumoto's first feature film, *Funeral Parade of Roses*, opened at the same theater. Focusing on a contemporary tale of incest between father and son interpreted through the Greek tragedy of *Oedipus Rex*, the film continues Matsumoto's exploration of the burgeoning underground gay culture in Tokyo, which he started with *For the Damaged Right Eye*. More important than the thematic continuity, however, is Matsumoto's commitment to capturing a sense of the immediate present in both works. It is precisely this commitment to the present that brings together Matsumoto's *Funeral Parade of Roses* and Oshima's *Diary of a Shinjuku Thief*.

While Oshima and Matsumoto were not the only filmmakers to

exhibit this journalistic sensibility toward the present in their filmmaking, their works from the turbulent years of 1968 and 1969 in many ways crystallize the ambivalent *proximity* between cinema and journalism. This proximity manifests itself through the incessant appropriation and remediation of journalistic materials, an experimental practice that gains visible momentum within Japanese political avant-garde filmmaking in the late 1960s. The works are exemplary in how they visualize this proximity and go beyond the merely formal appropriation of found footage, by sustaining tight referential connections to contemporary media events and news.

Even a cursory glance at Japanese independent filmmaking practice in the late 1960s shows how pervasive it was to mix fiction and nonfiction and appropriate topical journalistic materials or well-known media events. A number of ATG-funded films exhibit this tendency, albeit to different degrees: Imamura Shōhei's *A Man Vanishes* (*Ningen jōhatsu*, 1967), Yoshida Kijū's *Eros Plus Massacre* (*Erosu + gyakusatsu*, 1969) and *Heroic Purgatory* (*Rengoku eroika*, 1970), and Oshima's *Death by Hanging* (*Kōshikei*, 1968) and *Boy* (*Shōnen*, 1969). Similarly, we find frequent appropriations of journalistic materials in the contemporaneous work of filmmakers, such as Wakamatsu Kōji's *Violated Angels* (*Okasareta byakui*, 1967), *The Season of Terror* (*Teroru no kisetsu*, 1969), *Go, Go, Second Time Virgin* (*Yuke yuke nidome no shojo*, 1969), and *Sex Jack* (*Seizoku*, 1970); Jōnouchi Motoharu's *Gewaltopia Trailer* (*Gebarutopia yokokuhen*, 1969); Kanai Katsu's *The Deserted Archipelago* (*Mujin rettō*, 1969); and Terayama Shūji's *Emperor Tomato Ketchup* (*Tomato kechappu kōtei*, 1971). Exhibiting a strong concern with the immediate social and political conditions of the 1960s, many of the filmmakers who worked outside the studio system started to either incorporate unscripted "documentary" sequences into their films or directly remediate topical journalistic materials. However, the works of Oshima and Matsumoto pushed this practice to a new level by using cinematic artifice to expose the constitutive theatricality of journalism itself.

Extending my interrogation of cinema's relation to other image-based media, I now focus on cinema's growing proximity to journalistic media, in particular to television. In order to think through this question, I interweave a discourse on actuality with an analysis of exemplary filmic works. First, I trace an intellectual genealogy of the concept of "actuality" (*akuchuaritii*) in Japan through two discursive frameworks:

theoretical debates on the definition of documentary film and the relevance of the Marxist philosopher Tosaka Jun's theorization of journalism for these debates. I then analyze how the films of Matsumoto and Oshima—in particular, *For the Damaged Right Eye*, *Diary of a Shinjuku Thief*, and *Funeral Parade of Roses*—respond to this problematic of actuality in the late 1960s. Their responses lead to a timely interrogation of the journalistic production of the actuality effect, or the production of what (following Derrida) I call "artifactuality." These films expose the presence of theatrical artifice at the very heart of journalistic actuality. The filmic exposition of theatricality within the journalistic sphere in turn allows me to situate the journalistic turn among political avant-garde filmmakers like Oshima and Matsumoto within the larger context of the intense mediatization of politics in the late 1960s.

Importantly, all three films that I analyze in this chapter highlight theatrical performance, and two of the most celebrated *angura* (underground) troupes of the time make appearances in the films: the Situation Theater (Jōkyō Gekijō) in *Diary of a Shinjuku Thief* and Zero Dimension (Zero Jigen) in *Funeral Parade of Roses*. While it is easy to read their appearances as a reflection of Oshima and Matsumoto's interest in the underground theater movement, there is, in fact, something more to the question of theatricality. If, as Rancière suggests, "there is no theater without a spectator," perhaps the reverse is also true: any dramatic performances that "place bodies in action before an assembled audience" might be called theatrical in a broad sense.[4] Theatricality so defined can thus extend to any relation between the staged performance and an assembled spectator, mediated or unmediated by the camera, and inside or outside the theater.

While media events such as the theatrical crime of Kim Hiro's hostage crisis were unfolding in front of the television camera, filmmakers were appropriating and remediating these news events, often juxtaposing them with documentary footage of angura performances. Together these phenomena point to a strange affinity between two forms of spectacle: media events and theatrical performances. This affinity is the very locus of politics, or more precisely, the political dimension of the journalistic sensation of actuality, which Oshima's and Matsumoto's films prompt us to consider.

TRACING THE DISCURSIVE VECTOR OF "ACTUALITY"

Why did Oshima append the documentary footage of the July 1968 riot at Shinjuku Station in *Diary of a Shinjuku Thief*? Why did Matsumoto end *Funeral Parade of Roses* with shots in which a crowd of passersby circles around the protagonist, Eddy, who walks out of an apartment with a bloody knife after he stabs his own eyes? How do we understand Oshima and his fellow filmmakers' desire to be present at the site of Kim Hiro's hostage crisis? How do we interpret the inclusion of the news coverage of Kim's crime alongside other topical news items and events of 1968 in *For the Damaged Right Eye*? In order to answer all of these questions, we must consider two overlapping understandings of actuality: journalistic actuality and documentary actuality.

The general concern with actuality in its journalistic sense traversed different fields of artistic practice in the 1950s and 1960s. The loan word *akuchuaritii* (actuality) had become a buzzword among leftist critics, writers, filmmakers, and artists by the end of the 1960s. While critics and artists, often associated with avant-garde collectives such as Yoru no Kai and Kiroku Geijutsu no Kai, frequently used this term in the 1950s in order to express their commitment to critical art that directly addressed or indirectly invoked contemporary social and political situations, the term soon gained wider circulation. Essays and articles bearing titles such as "The Challenge of Actuality," "The Actuality of Documentary Art," "The Actuality of Nonreality," "What Is Actuality?," and "The Reality of Postwar Literature: Is Actuality Possible?" popped up in leading literary, art, and film journals such as *Shin Nihon Bungaku*, *Bijutsu Hihyō*, and *Kiroku Eiga* during the late 1950s and early 1960s.[5] The most emblematic debate over the journalistic capacity of art to engage with the immediate social and political situations of the present erupted in the form of the "debate over pure literature" in 1961. Certainly, the idea of critical engagement with the present had been popular since the end of the war (the influence of Sartre's work is apparent here), and the Japanese surrealists had previously used *akuchuaritii* to articulate their poetic exploration of reality in the 1930s.[6] However, it was really during the late 1950s and early 1960s when this particular term gained wider currency among leftist intellectuals and artists who debated the political potential of art.[7]

Tracing the genealogical trajectory of this term may appear trivial at first, but it helps us understand the significance of the growing proximity between cinema and journalism that became visible during the 1960s. Just as the increased currency of the term *eizō* (image) during this period points to a fundamental shift in the conceptualization of cinema's relation to other media, the widespread use of the term *akuchuaritii* during this same period sheds light on the peculiarly journalistic quality of avant-garde and experimental films produced in the 1960s.

The term *akuchuaritii* was popularized through the work of avant-garde literary critics and artists who gathered around Hanada. Interestingly, it is in the work of Hanada that we can see a clear convergence of two differing conceptions of actuality, one that focuses on the journalistic sense of topicality, relevance, and immediacy, and one that focuses on the documentary sense of factuality, nonfiction, and authenticity. The first sense of actuality puts an emphasis on its temporal vector, while the second highlights its existential vector, though both hold a referential relation to the present. Actuality is a concept that highlights one's temporal and existential relation to present-day reality, and for this reason it became important for intellectuals like Hanada who wished to bring criticism to bear on immediate social and political situations.

Establishing a critical relation to the present was a task that many politically conscious intellectuals faced, and not only in Japan. Indeed, European intellectuals from Sartre and Adorno to Benjamin, Foucault, and Derrida addressed this issue, often framing it directly in terms of actuality. In Japan, one of the key figures who engaged in the sustained critique of the present was Tosaka Jun, a Marxist philosopher who was arrested for his unreserved criticism of Japan's militarism and died in prison at the end of the World War II. Tosaka was not alone in his investment in actuality. Japanese surrealists contemporary to Tosaka, for instance, also mobilized akuchuaritii in their exploration of surreality.[8] Yet Tosaka's journalistic conception of actuality as the essential attribute of the news media is what informs Hanada's writings on cinema and avant-garde art in the postwar period.

It is hence useful to examine Tosaka's theorization of actuality before turning to Hanada's discussion of avant-garde and documentary filmmaking. Hanada's definition of actuality as a temporal quality will, in turn, shed light on the mounting tension between cinema and journalism, which manifests itself in the eventful years of 1968 and 1969.

PHILOSOPHY AND THE JOURNALISTIC CONCEPTION OF ACTUALITY

In order to understand Tosaka's avowed interest in actuality, we might first look to his critique of the institutionalized discipline of philosophy. Writing in the 1930s against the rise of fascism in Japan, he fervently argues that the discipline of philosophy must begin to integrate the critical perspective of journalism, an antidote to philosophers' tendency to avert their gaze from the current political situation and retreat into the safe haven of ideational abstraction. According to Tosaka, academicism and journalism form two principal ideological apparatuses, which must be dialectically synthesized to produce a viable platform from which to critique existing political and economic conditions.[9] Placing a strong emphasis on philosophy's need to be "actual" and relevant to the present, Tosaka redefines philosophy as a practice of *timely criticism situated in the present*.[10]

Like his European Marxist contemporary Theodor Adorno, Tosaka's interest in historically situated philosophical criticism is accompanied by distrust of the transcendental idealist disposition of phenomenology that was in vogue at the time. "All branches of phenomenology remain ahistorical," writes Tosaka in his *On Japanese Ideology* (1935).[11] In a similar vein Tosaka criticizes Heidegger's philological approach to phenomenology: "Of course nothing is wrong with the existence of philology as a discipline, but the *actuality* of the present world cannot become an object of philological inquiries."[12] Here he deliberately uses *akuchuaritii* to underscore his point. As his earlier works on newspaper journalism and literature make clear, actuality for Tosaka encompasses both the temporal immediacy and practicality that characterize journalism. Tosaka's critique of phenomenology and philology and his affirmation of journalism complement one another. Neither phenomenology nor philology offers a philosophical mode of critique that allows political engagement with present-day reality.

According to Tosaka, the dialectical synthesis of philosophy and journalism in turn becomes possible when critics take their historical relationship to present-day social and political reality as the very condition of their criticism. In Tosaka's work, the concept of actuality is hence used in conjunction with terms, such as *quotidian*, *practical*, *current*, and *topical*.[13] Pointing out Tosaka's Marxist preoccupation with the temporality of the present, Harry Harootunian comments on the concept of actuality and its temporal specificity: "To envisage the current situation—the now—philosophically opened the way to evaluating and even judging those 'journalistic phenomena' that concentrate on daily eventfulness (*jijisei*) and to explaining why, therefore, they are necessarily a problem of actuality for both literature and philosophy. Hence, the problem of everydayness was intensely bonded to the question of the 'situation' (*jikyoku*), implying, of course, the recognition of a specific temporality."[14] Tosaka's theorization of the everyday and his concern with its temporality ("the now") naturally led him to invest in the study of mass media, in particular the newspaper. It is in his analysis of newspaper journalism that we find the most elaborate discussion of the temporally grounded concept of actuality.

In the 1920s and 1930s, many intellectuals turned to the modern technologies of mass communication in order to theorize their ideological and political efficacy. As the historian of journalism Wada Yōichi points out, the academic study of journalism in Japan flourished at the beginning of the 1930s, and Tosaka was one of the first among his contemporaries to analyze the medium of the newspaper from the standpoint of philosophy. Noteworthy here is the influence of the German *Zeitungswissenschaft* (newspaper studies) on this generation of Japanese intellectuals and media critics, Tosaka included.[15] This explains why many of Tosaka's bibliographical references on newspaper journalism are German sources, and also clarifies why Tosaka uses the German word *Aktualität* interchangeably with the English word *actuality* and the Japanese loanword *akuchuaritii* in his work.

Tosaka was indeed among the first generation of Japanese media theorists who paid serious attention to the temporal concept of *Aktualität*, which occupies an important place in the work of his European contemporaries, especially Walter Benjamin.[16] Like Tosaka, Benjamin contrasted the temporality of actuality to that of eternity. As Esther Leslie suggests, Benjamin invoked Aktualität in order to articulate the need "to enmesh critique in precise social observations and to be responsive to the urgencies and apprehensions of the moment, to be topical."[17] Similarly, Tosaka placed Aktualität at the center of his theorization of materialist philosophy. In so doing, he brought together the journalistic concept of Aktualität (timeliness and contemporary relevance) and the materialist concept of Wirklichkeit (the actually existent reality) in order to express his conviction that the philosopher-critic must engage with temporally present and materially existent reality.[18] Actuality understood in this context conveys the Marxist view of a philosopher-critic's timely engagement with present-day reality. Hanada's frequent use of the term *akuchuaritii* in his discussion of the avant-garde and documentary arts bears the traces of Tosaka's earlier theorization of actuality. And it was through Hanada's writings that the term regained popularity in the 1950s, making its way into the parlance of film and media criticism, often generating heated discussions around the precise meaning of the term itself.[19]

Most likely, the attraction to the term *akuchuaritii* felt by Hanada and his cohort derives from their search for an alternative to the term *riariti* (reality). The term *reality* conjured the ghosts of philosophical idealism and socialist realism, from which these avant-garde critics and artists wished to step away. Not surprisingly, those who proposed to redefine documentary as an avant-garde method of critically engaging with present-day reality were the ones who appealed the most to the concept of actuality. The term *actuality* thus started to circulate first among critics, filmmakers, and artists close to Hanada who shared this commitment to the dialectical synthesis of avant-garde and documentary arts.

One exemplary group which spearheaded the project of redefining documentary as an avant-garde method was Kiroku Geijutsu no Kai. Kiroku Geijutsu no Kai brought together notable intellectual and artistic figures such as Hanada, Abé, Teshigahara, Sasaki, and Haryū. The initial impetus for its creation came from their monthly group discussion of film, which was serially published in the Marxist literary journal *Shin Nihon Bungaku* (New Japanese literature). Officially launched in May 1956, the association was known, from the very beginning, for its support of a diverse community of artists and critics who dared to break down the boundaries between artistic genres and various media. While it inherited the utopian vision of earlier postwar avant-garde collectives such as Yoru no Kai, what distinguished Kiroku Geijutsu no Kai was its emphasis on documentary. As its manifesto, published in 1957, specifies, its mission was to redefine documentary as an artistic methodology applicable to both nonfictional and fictional works of art.[20]

The younger generation of filmmakers, including Matsumoto and Oshima, who joined a study group Eiga to Hihyō no Kai (which was loosely connected to Kiroku Geijutsu no Kai) responded to the call to rethink and reinvent documentary as a new artistic method. The widespread use of techniques such as on-location shooting, improvisation, and the insertion of unscripted documentary sequences during the 1960s—many of which are also defining features of what has been called New Wave cinema—coincided with the rise of documentary as a theoretical problem.[21] At the discursive level, this effort to redefine documentary as an artistic method appeared as the interrogation of actuality in cinema. In order to better understand how the question of actuality intersected with the political avant-garde filmmaking of this period, let us now turn to Hanada's reinterpretation of documentary.

ACTUALITY VERSUS REALITY

In the early 1950s, Hanada contested the well-known film critic Tsumura Hideo's interpretation of the British strain of documentary theory.[22] In an essay on the British documentary filmmaker and theorist Paul Rotha, Tsumura argues that Rotha deliberately used the word *actuality* instead of *reality* in his definition of documentary film as the "creative dramatization of actuality," a definition borrowed from John Grierson. Tsumura claims that "Rotha does not use the expression 'dramatization of reality'; instead, he says 'dramatization of actuality.'"[23] While the distinction between reality and actuality was in fact not present in the work of Rotha who interchangeably used *reality* and *actuality* in his definition of documentary, Tsumura's (mis)reading inadvertently produced a philosophically inflected interpretation of documentary.[24] In his interpretation of Rotha, Tsumura distinguished the philosophical categories of reality and actuality, and argued that the conceptual difference between reality and actuality could be better understood if translated from English into German: *Realität* and *Wirklichkeit*.[25]

As Tsumura rightly points out, the term *Realität* in German philosophy refers to the ahistorical, metaphysical realm of "truth" or "essence." By contrast, the term *Wirklichkeit* often signifies reality in the sense of historical, material, or physical "existence." Marx, for instance, used the term *Wirklichkeit* to discuss his materialist understanding of reality in *Theses on Feuerbach* (1845). The intellectual history surrounding these two German words is quite complicated, as Heidegger's interpretation of Kant suggests.[26] It is not my intention here to recount the philosophical debates pertaining to the difference between *Realität* and *Wirklichkeit*. Nonetheless, it is important to acknowledge this distinction, since Tsumura's philosophical interpretation became a focal point of Hanada's critique in his subsequent discussion of documentary.

When Hanada challenged Tsumura's interpretation of Rotha's theory in the 1950s, he brought back a journalistic way of defining actuality in relation to cinema. For Hanada, the difference between reality and actuality was not only existential, but also, and most importantly, temporal—an interpretation likely influenced by his reading of Tosaka.[27] In his discussion of documentary film theory and its usefulness for avant-garde art, Hanada highlighted the journalistic understanding of actuality as timeliness, topicality, and relevance. These journalistic connotations are more explicit in the German word *Aktualität* or the French word *actualité* (a term used interchangeably with the English word *actuality* by Japanese avant-garde critics). By shifting the ground of debate from reality to actuality, Hanada thus reformulated documentary as a journalistic method of engaging with the present.[28]

According to Hanada, the present is also defined by chance or contingency, the potential for an utterly unpredictable change in the future. It is this understanding of the present as contingency that the concept of actuality serves. Hanada writes, "We can think of actuality as contingency. Reality is what dialectically synthesizes possibility and necessity, but contingency is the middle term that mediates the two."[29] Present-day reality is thus characterized by contingency and its dependency on chance, and the element of contingency mediates between the past (necessity) and the future (possibility). The emphasis on chance led Hanada to argue further that a new method of documentary filmmaking that respects actuality must incorporate the surrealist embrace of chance encounters. The *new* kind of documentary, in his view, needed to dialectically sublate the achievements of the historical avant-garde from the 1920s.

Hanada developed the idea of the dialectical synthesis of the avant-garde and the documentary in a series of essays published in the mid-1950s, and gave a new name to this dialectical method in 1958: *sur-documentarism*. He coined this term in an essay he published in the February issue of the film journal *Eiga Hihyō*.[30] The particular timing of this essay, which again takes up Rotha's definition of documentary as the creative dramatization of actuality, is worth noting. It came out two years after the launch of Kiroku Geijutsu no Kai, and in the same year that two other epochal essays on similar topics were published: Matsumoto's "On the Method of Avant-garde Documentary Film," published in the May issue of the film journal *Kiroku Eiga*; and Abé Kōbō's "In Support of the New Documentarism," published in the July issue of the literary journal *Shisō*.

Matsumoto's theorization of avant-garde documentary filmmaking articulated in his 1958 essay was deeply indebted to the preceding work of Hanada. It is hence not surprising that here we find an argument that exactly echoes Hanada's view of sur-documentarism. For instance, citing a passage from Arthur Rimbaud's *La lettre du voyant*, Matsumoto writes: "What we the documentarists need today is Rimbaud's spirit of becoming a seer (*voyant*). We must substantialize this spirit, which will transform contingency and actuality into necessity and reality."[31] His emphasis on the present as a site of contingent encounters and transformations further echoes Hanada's point: "We must make conscious or objectivize what has been ignored [by documentary filmmakers]—the unconscious, irrational elements that generate complex psychic movements within us—in a manner corresponding to the constantly changing, actual, and new reality."[32] The task of an avant-garde documentary filmmaker becomes interrogative, penetrating not simply into the visible realm of social reality, but also into the invisible realm of the social unconscious. In order to differentiate the avant-garde documentary method from the standard practice of documentary filmmaking, Matsumoto emphasizes the importance of contingency and chance encounters, which enable the filmmaker to serendipitously escape his conscious—and thus expectant—apprehension of reality. Actuality is aligned with this element of surprise.

This desire for actuality in art, which propelled Matsumoto, Abé, and Hanada to argue for the reinvention of documentary, was also shared by other critics. Take, for instance, the 1961 roundtable discussion on "Documentary Film and Fiction Film." Matsumoto and his fellow documentary filmmakers Hani Susumu, Noda Shinkichi, and Teshigahara Hiroshi (who started his filmmaking career in the documentary field before he collaborated with Abé on films such as *The Pitfall* and *Woman of the Dunes*) were the main participants of this event. Matsumoto praised Hani's films for "attempting to grasp the actuality or contingency inherent in documentary." Hani, in turn, suggested how the question of actuality must be sought in relation to "the journalistic quality inherent in the documentary method."[33] Time and time again, we find similar concern with documentary's relation to actuality in a number of essays, interviews, and discussions published throughout the 1960s. A strong sense of the affinity between the practice of documentary filmmaking and that of journalism marks them all.

Aside from the genealogy of the term *akuchuaritii* and Hanada's influence on its postwar usage, what else might account for the widely shared interest in the affinity between cinema and journalism among these filmmakers? Was there any other reason for this collective obsession with actuality at this particular historical moment? One way to answer these questions is to relate the turn to actuality to the rise of image theories. Cinema at this time was facing a fundamental change in status: it was becoming just one possible incarnation of the image-making media. When the general category of image-making media (all of which share the common attribute of eizō) absorbed cinema, cinema's distinctiveness as a medium became threatened. The discourse on the image enabled filmmakers and critics to articulate the similarities as well as the differences between cinematic images and the images produced by other forms of media. The growing interest in actuality, a concept that highlights the proximity between cinema and journalism, is another manifestation of the shifting conception of cinema. To put it differently, the concurrent rise of these questions—the question of the image and that of actuality—are reflective of the changing media environment in the 1960s.

Like the concept of the image (discussed in the previous chapter), the definition of actuality that developed during this period was not singular. Rather, a polysemic understanding of actuality emerged, which can be summarized as (1) the contingency of unscripted actions and events in documentary practice; (2) journalistic topicality or newsworthiness; and (3) the critical relevance of a work in relation to present-day social and political situations. These overlapping connotations point to a significant crossover between the filmmaking and journalistic practices of this period, taking place primarily in the realm of television. The avant-garde filmmakers' desire to record and report on the immediate social reality—that is, to make films that directly addressed the present—was also shared by television programmers, especially by those who worked on news and documentary programs.

The proximity between cinema and journalism became a focal point of discussions precisely around the time when television began to threaten cinema with its strong appeal to actuality. A new critical understanding of actuality emerged just when the relation between documentary filmmaking and documentary programming on television became more intimate. The problem of television indeed appears to be the main impetus that spurred these critical debates on documentary and actuality, as it was the quintessential medium deemed most capable of evoking the *sensation of actuality*.

THE SENSATION OF ACTUALITY

In his classic work on crowd psychology, Gabriel Tarde discusses a mechanism behind what he calls the "sensation of actuality." It derives from the virtual assurance that one belongs to the greater community of the audience that receives journalistic information. Importantly, the sensation of urgency, topicality, or timeliness associated with this information hinges on its mass reception and, moreover, on the presumed simultaneity of this reception.[34] Writing on the cusp of the twentieth century, Tarde naturally focuses on the print medium of the newspaper, though his observations are equally useful in understanding the way in which television produces a similar sensation of actuality. Tarde describes a hypothetical situation in which a person is reading a newspaper with great pleasure; the events recounted and the information in the pages of the newspaper grip this hypothetical reader. When he finishes reading, he realizes that the newspaper is completely out of date. Whether it is from yesterday or last month does not matter. He feels disgusted. Where does this disgust originate, asks Tarde, which we feel at the moment when we discover that the newspaper we are reading is out of date? According to Tarde, it does not originate from our awareness that the information contained in the newspaper is simply old. Instead, it originates in the sense of exclusion, a feeling of being left out of the public sphere composed of the reading masses. The sensation of actuality hence is inseparable from an anonymous collectivity.

One aspect crucial to the sensation of actuality is the expiration of information deemed new. In other words, this sensation depends closely on its relation to journalistic periodicity. The first goal of news-oriented journalism is to deliver information about the latest events. It does not report on things that are perfectly foreseeable and calculable, since its commodity value hinges on novelty. To use Benjamin's expression: "The value of information does not survive the moment in which it was new."[35] What defines the obsoleteness of information in its journalistic sense is, therefore, its status of being out-of-date. The sensation of actuality is supported by its very expirability. Each outburst of this sensation is momentary, lasting only until the next installment of information arrives. The possibility—and threat—of expiration is thus constitutive of information. For this reason, saying that something is "dated" in the journalistic context has implications that are twofold: it means both bearing a date and having undergone the erosion of time (and thereby becoming obsolete). In his discussion of newspaper journalism, Tosaka suggests that the entire practice of journalism is in fact predicated on two complementary but opposing imperatives: *timeliness* and *periodicity*.[36] Since the speed of reporting news affects the temporal validity of the news, the periodic structure of journalism dictates how long the sensation of actuality can last: "The faster the reporting of news becomes, the sooner the expiration dates of the reported news as news."[37] The logic of expiration, which is a by-product of journalistic periodicity, underscores the very production of the sensation of actuality.

Television (and now the Internet) intensifies and accelerates the production of the sensation of actuality by its appeal to immediacy, presentness, and simultaneous mass receptivity. The affective impact of television and its production of the actuality effect—the sensation of actuality—are not limited to its purportedly "live" programs, though the ideology of liveness certainly enhances their efficacy.[38] The temporal spectrum of felt actuality is wider than the limited spectrum of liveness, as it can be produced by different journalistic media including newspaper, magazine, radio, television, or the Internet, each of which operates at a different pace. The intensity of the actuality effect also fluctuates depending on the mode of address enacted by a particular genre or medium. Nonetheless, the successful production of the sensation of actuality does hinge on the magnitude and the speed of its reception, and during the 1960s, television was its quintessential conduit. What is more, the sensation of actuality intensifies when television organizes time around a crisis event.

As Mary Ann Doane argues, information, crisis, and catastrophe are the three dominant modalities that help television structure its temporality and manage the affect and attention of the viewer. While the order of information generates a sense of the continuous flow of time—it appears as steady and ubiquitous—the crisis and the catastrophe both condense and compress time, disrupting the continuous flow of information and amplifying a sense of rupture. According to Doane, the catastrophe (often associated with death) appears to be intimately linked to technological failure as much as to natural disaster. It is hence linked to suddenness, a dramatic "overturn" of the event: "Catastrophe is on the cusp of the dramatic and the referential and this is, indeed, part of its fascination."[39] As the most intensified form of crisis, the catastrophe is a type of event that appears "subject-less," happening "all at once." In contrast, the crisis implies a human subject, an agency behind the dramatic event. As Doane argues, "For that reason, crises are most frequently political — a hijacking, an assassination, the takeover of an embassy, a political coup, or the taking of hostages." The crisis understood in this manner is fundamentally durational: "It demands resolution within a limited period of time."[40]

The hostage situation created by Kim Hiro from 21 February to 24 February 1968 attests to the televisual order of the crisis. The crisis in its ordinary sense may have started on the evening of 20 February, at the moment Kim shot to death two members of a *yakuza* group and called the local police station to inform them of his crime. But the crisis in its televisual sense started when Kim answered a phone call made to the inn by one of the television presenters. This phone conversation, between Kim and an anchorperson of the news program *Kijima Norio Morning Show*, was broadcast live on television on the morning of 21 February. This was the beginning of the Kim Hiro Incident as *media event*, over the course of which television stations and newspapers competed to get in touch with Kim, eagerly collaborating with him to develop this hostage crisis into an exemplary case of "theatrical crime" in which the criminal became a dramatist and an actor, scripting, staging, and performing the event.[41]

The first scene Kim staged was an interview with a local newspaper reporter and a reporter from NHK, the national television network, during which he demanded the network's help in eliciting a public apology from a policeman who had made racist comments about ethnic Koreans. On afternoon television, the chief of the local police station directly appealed to Kim and urged him to surrender. Kim, for his part, continued to take interviews with reporters from national newspapers and network television stations. On the morning of 21 February, the policeman who had offended Kim apologized for his prejudicial statements against ethnic Koreans. The morning news program on NHK also reported on Kim's diary, which he passed on to the network himself. This crisis-as-media event was finally resolved when policemen disguised as reporters arrested Kim on the morning of 24 February.

One thing that this hostage crisis made quite clear was the centrality of the agency of the human subjects and, moreover, that of the social actors who willingly performed for the camera. Not only did the criminal himself consciously act for the camera, but so, too, did policemen, reporters, and some of the victims. Gathering momentum with Kim's

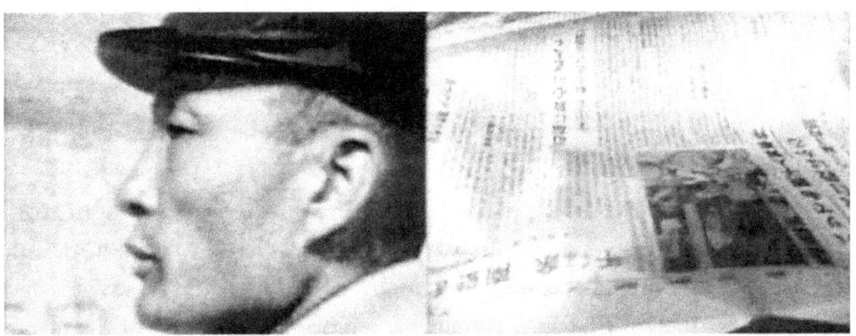

2.1. Kim Hiro (left screen) and the newspaper used as a prop during the happening-style event at Shinjuku Station (right screen). Still from *For the Damaged Right Eye* (1968), dir. Matsumoto Toshio.

sentimental diary and his interviews with reporters, the event unfolded like a theatrical drama, a spectacle that gripped the attention of countless television viewers from the moment the unscripted conversation between Kim and the morning television show host was broadcast live. Now, if television helps to transform a crisis into a media event, and in so doing enhances the sensation of actuality, what kind of intervention can cinema make when it appropriates such a media event? Appropriation of journalistic materials abounds in films of the 1960s, most notably in the avant-garde works of Japanese filmmakers who pushed the boundary of cinema from within. Made less than two months after Kim's hostage crisis, Matsumoto's experimental news film, *For the Damaged Right Eye*, offers a case in point.

The first image of Kim that appears in the multiple-projection film *For the Damaged Right Eye* is juxtaposed with a black-and-white sequence, which documents a happening-style art performance involving newspapers staged at Shinjuku Station. On one screen is a close-up of Kim's face, while on the other screen is a close-up of the newspaper held by one of the performers (figure 2.1). While we continue to see this theatrical happening, in which a crowd of passersby is shown to be watching several men dressed in business suits being tied with rope to columns and covered with newspapers, the other screen shows a rapid montage of television advertisements, art posters, press photographs reporting on Vietnam, sports news, and documentary footage of marching riot police, in addition to the television footage of Kim's hostage crisis. The film voraciously samples, mixes, and remediates various journalistic sources, including the television footage of Kim's interview and his subsequent arrest.

The multiple-screen format of the film was meant to mimic the visual layout of a newspaper. In a newspaper, heterogeneous information coexists on the same page and is thus, as Matsumoto himself says, suited to represent "the nonlinear time-space of the present from which entangled relations of newsworthy events and politics jump out at once."[42] The film attempts to visually evoke the spatial layout of a newspaper that emphasizes the simultaneous occurrence of disparate events. Matsumoto thought the visual analogy of the multiple-screen format to the newspaper was fit to capture the sensation of simultaneity and document the mosaic appearance of reality during the volatile year of 1968. As implied by Matsumoto's use of the McLuhanesque terms "nonlinear" and "mosaic," another medium of comparison here is television.[43] While the spatial juxtaposition of multiple screens resembles the frontal layout of a newspaper, the film is also strongly evocative of the televisual economy of information that generates a seemingly endless sense of flow. The film's lack of a coherent narrative and the continuous stream of image and sound fragments sampled from various television programs, print advertisements, and newspapers create an impression that information here "is not chained to a particular organization of the signifier or a specific style of address."[44] *For the Damaged Right Eye* is a film that is profoundly journalistic, topical, and of the moment.

Similarly, in his 1969 film *The Deserted Archipelago*, Kanai Katsu appropriates the Kim Hiro Incident in order to foreground the endless consumption of news as information. The incident is referenced twice in the film. The iconic image of Kim first appears indirectly as an unnamed character who engages in a shootout with a rifle-yielding nun. He is dressed with a hunting cap and a jacket, reminiscent of Kim himself. The second reference to the Kim Hiro Incident appears in the scene where an ordinary-looking couple is eating dinner in a room covered with newspapers (figure 2.2). On the soundtrack we hear the voice of Kim himself giving a press interview. As the voice of Kim plays in the background, the husband pastes a newspaper onto the wall and proclaims, "Our most important task today is to beautifully paste newspapers on the wall." In both *For the Damaged Right Eye* and *The Deserted Archipelago*, the Kim Hiro Incident functions as a locus of formal experimentation. Crucially, it is also the use of the newspaper as a visual

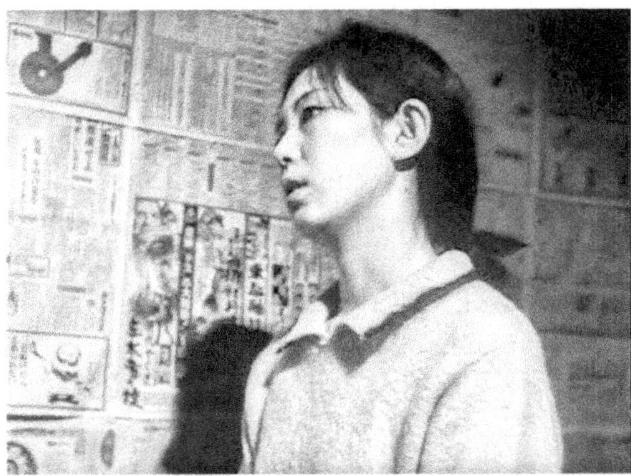

2.2. The set is covered with newspapers. Still from *The Deserted Archipelago* (1969), dir. Kanai Katsu.

motif that plays an important role in enabling this experimentation. The newspaper is a key motif that also structures Oshima's 1968 film *Death by Hanging*, to which I turn shortly.

As the documentary footage of the happening-like performance involving newspapers in *For the Damaged Right Eye* indicates, the motif of the newspaper bridges the journalistic realm of the Kim Hiro Incident as a sensational media event and the theatrical realm of the street performance. The journalistic logic of actuality is thus closely aligned with the apparently "fictional" element. Juxtaposed against the remediated television footage of the Kim Hiro Incident, this performance sequence underscores the theatrical nature of the purported crisis as reported in the news media. During the course of the performance, we see some of the participants tied to a column covered in newspapers. The performers are themselves subsequently wrapped in newspapers; the media literally "covers" this entire event. Moreover, the event itself would seem to stage one of the key modalities of television—crisis—insofar as the tying up of performers imitates the hostage crisis (subsequently) invoked on the adjacent screen by the images of hostage-taker Kim.

The connection between theatrical performance and crisis mediated by television and newspaper would seem to point to something that journalism is unwilling to admit: that the crisis itself plays out as drama, and that its factuality is always enmeshed with its artifice. The crisis as an "actual" event reported by journalism is as manufactured as theater—and is thus not so different from a scripted performance by artists. Here, the boundary between the nonfictional event (such as Kim's hostage crisis) and the fictional event (such as this happening) breaks down. What the film's multiprojection format (which Matsumoto analogizes to the layout of the newspaper, which displays an assemblage of information at once) effectively reveals is a fundamental affinity between actuality and artifice. The affinity or inseparability between actuality and artifice is, to use the expression of Jacques Derrida, "artifactuality."

THE PRODUCTION OF "ARTIFACTUALITY"

By this portmanteau word, *artifactuality*, Derrida is referring to the fabricated nature of events deemed actual, current, and newsworthy: "The first trait is that actuality is, precisely, *made* [faite]: in order to know what it's made of, one needs nonetheless to know that it is made."[45] Through the concept of artifactuality, Derrida highlights the fabricated nature of actuality as filtered through journalistic media. Our perception of the present—that is, our perception of what is happening in the world now—hinges on a plethora of information we receive from the media. Actuality is hence "not given but actively produced, sifted, invested, performatively interpreted by numerous apparatuses which are *factitious* or *artificial*, hierarchizing and selective, always in the service of forces and interests to which 'subjects' and agents . . . are never sensitive enough."[46] The term *artifice* here does not necessarily imply deception, but it points to the constructed nature of actuality. The sensation of actuality that the media generates daily relies heavily on the process of fabrication, and there is indeed no actuality apart from this artifice.

What is crucial to note here is again the presence of the human subject, the agency behind the fabrication or creation of events that appear actual, timely, and newsworthy. This is why the artifactuality of the televisual mode of the crisis is much more pronounced than the artifactuality of the catastrophe. The crisis does not simply happen; it is *made*. Kim Hiro's hostage crisis in 1968 was exemplary in this sense, as it revealed the artifactual nature of the event. During the course of this crisis, not only the media personnel but also the hostage-taker, the hostages, and even the viewers collaborated to make the crisis into a media event. It required a collective agency, a shared desire to manufacture and to take part in the media event. When Oshima, Wakamatsu, Adachi, and five others drove down from a bar in Shinjuku to the town of Sumatakyō where Kim was staging his theater of crisis, were they not partaking, albeit indirectly, in the collective production of the media event? If this is the case, how might this experience have inflected their filmmaking practice? In order to answer these questions, it is necessary to further examine how they regarded this event.

In his recollection of the Kim Hiro hostage crisis, Oshima describes the long drive they took that night: "We wanted to support him. We felt, if there were even one person who is fighting, we would go and back him up. Unfortunately, we were stopped [by the police] before we reached our destination. But because we were stopped, we did not become criminals. . . . The shock I received from going down to Sumatakyō was huge, because it made me realize that there are individuals who take up guns, sit face to face [with the state] and start a guerrilla war."[47] The tone of admiration is evident in Oshima's recollection of the hostage crisis, and those around Oshima appeared to have shared his affirmative response to it.

Here, it is useful to consider the general intellectual environment of the late 1960s, during which the work of postcolonial theorists, revolutionaries, and civil-rights activists, from Frantz Fanon to Che Guevara and Stokely Carmichael, were introduced to Japan and avidly studied by Left-leaning artists and critics. One of the members who drove down to Sumatakyō with Oshima was Matsuda Masao, an influential film critic and renowned political activist who performed the role of the district attorney's secretary in Oshima's *Death by Hanging*, a film released on 3 February 1968. Matsuda also famously introduced the work of Fanon to Oshima. "I remember asking Matsuda to give lectures on Frantz Fanon in early 1968. At the time the idea he introduced—political issues surrounding ethnic minorities and minority groups will move the world—was refreshing," recalls Oshima.[48] Matsuda's debut essay was an analysis of Gillo Pontecorvo's film *The Battle of Algiers* (*La battaglia di Algeri*, 1966). Not surprisingly, Matsuda was among those who advocated for the revolutionary struggles of the "Third World," a concept that Oshima found particularly attractive at the time. Oshima notes, "I felt that the revolution that involves not only Japan but also the Third World was possible. The term *Third World* was delightful—I felt the light was shining upon us when I realized that the Third World exists."[49] While we should be cautious of the danger of romanticizing the Third World, by the same token we cannot ignore the impact Third Worldism—and the contemporary relevance of the Third World as a collective "project," in the words of Vijay Prashad—had on Japanese filmmakers and intellectuals circa 1968.[50]

Indeed, the rise of Third Worldism in Japan is just one side of the historical awareness of the "present" which they perceived, experienced, and wished to act on. Around 1968, this historical awareness was often expressed by the term *global synchronicity* (*sekai dōjisei*). This sense of synchronicity or simultaneity underscores the experimental narrative structure of *Diary of a Shinjuku Thief*, which opens with a memorable montage of intertitles indicating the time in different cities (e.g., New York, Paris, Moscow, Beijing, Saigon, and Tokyo). Similarly, *For the Damaged Right Eye* visualizes synchronicity through its use of multiple screens. Furthermore, it is this same sense of simultaneity that Wakamatsu and Adachi's propaganda-news film *The Red Army/PFLP: Declaration of World War* (1971) aims to impart by linking the armed struggle of the Popular Front for the Liberation of Palestine with the activism of the Japanese Red Army. The turn toward the problematic of actuality (which entailed raising pressing questions regarding cinema's appropriation of the journalistic attributes of topicality, timeliness, and immediacy) was further accelerated by the collective desire to partake in the contemporary revolutionary struggles that swept through Asia, Latin America, Africa, and the Middle East in the 1960s. This rhetoric of revolution greatly influenced political avant-garde filmmaking practices in Japan, and the practices of filmmaking and political activism were both sustained by the utopian belief in the simultaneity of world revolution. History will change, not gradually, but in compressed time, like that of the crisis. Accordingly, we often see the analogy between crisis and revolution—two modes of temporality based on rupture expressed by the concept of the *event*.

Perhaps it is not surprising, then, that the focal point of Matsuda's recollection of the midnight drive he took with Oshima, Wakamatsu, Adachi, and others on 21 February is the question of revolutionary violence. Matsuda's essay "The Root of Terror Inside Me," published a few weeks after the hostage crisis, is noteworthy for this reason. Recalling the moment when they realized that they could not enter the cordoned off area and stood four kilometers away from the inn, Matsuda writes,

> Why did we come here? Perhaps the short "journey" we took to arrive here itself is our goal, though we thought we were being driven by our dark, inexorable passion. We hold a discussion in the empty schoolyard enveloped by the loud noise of helicopters. Surprisingly, there are quite a few of us who express the opinion that we should encourage Kim to pursue his political struggle in court or in prison, since his demand has already been met in some way. No, that's not right. Instead I emphasize that the more pressing issue we face is to support Kim's battle unconditionally—a battle for which he staked his life—and to fight alongside him, perhaps even to witness his "death" with our own eyes. Yet, as I argue these points, I start to feel empty, though I don't know why. Even when everyone reaches an agreement, we may all feel somehow empty, futile. Why? It was "violence" that mediated Kim's action, by which he cut off the chain of discrimination and seized the whole world in that instant. Are we then supposed to stand on his side and participate in his "violence"?[51]

For Matsuda, the answer remains ambivalent. On the one hand, he sees Kim's action through the lens of counter-violence as theorized by Fanon and applauds Kim's willingness to use violence as a means of political resistance. On the other hand, he is hesitant to join Kim as he acknowledges that he does not have the same "right" to make the counter-violence his own. Kim's action clearly fascinates Matsuda, but his fascination is inflected by his refusal to forget his own privilege as a Japanese for whom this rhetoric of counter-violence is not available.[52] Matsuda's view seemed to have struck a chord with Oshima who was searching for an appropriate language to express his own critique of the Japanese state and its colonial legacy.

BETWEEN ARTIFACTUALITY AND THEATRICAL ARTIFICE

It is hence more than fitting that Matsuda and Adachi, who drove down to Sumatakyō with Oshima, also collaborated with him and appeared in *Death by Hanging*, an acclaimed narrative film that engages heavily with another famous media event: the Komatsugawa Incident of 1958. This widely covered incident was itself an uncanny precursor to Kim's hostage crisis.[53] Recalling the moment when he heard the news about Kim's hostage crisis, Oshima notes the excitement he felt: "For me, it was perfect timing. Especially after working on the issues concerning Korea I thought this incident resonated perfectly with my own concerns."[54] The timing of the hostage crisis was indeed uncanny. *Death by Hanging* had opened in theaters just a few weeks before the hostage crisis broke out.

Death by Hanging takes as its basis the Komatsugawa Incident, an actual murder case committed by a resident Korean student named Ri Chin-U (Li Jin Wu) in 1958. The Komatsugawa Incident received wide press coverage because Ri himself called up the Yomiuri newspaper, offering information about the death of a Japanese high-school girl he had just killed. The police asked radio stations to broadcast the taped conversation in order to identify the perpetrator. Ri also wrote a short story based on an earlier murder he had committed and sent it to a literary competition hosted by the Yomiuri newspaper. After his arrest, Ri was sentenced to death, and was hanged in 1962. While being held in prison, Ri corresponded with another resident Korean, a journalist named Bok Junan; their letters were published in 1963. Accordingly, the case maintained a high profile, igniting public debates on surrounding political issues, including the legacy of Japan's colonialism and the systemic discrimination against Koreans. The Komatsugawa Incident drew wider attention to the inequity many resident Koreans faced (and continue to face) in Japanese society. As David Desser points out, the defense lawyers for Ri "tried to make the case that Li had been systematically denied his heritage as a Korean yet denied access to economic and social advancement because he was Korean. It was this double-bind that intellectuals were quick to point out."[55] The individual crime committed by Ri was hence perceived by many to be intimately tied to the collective crime of Japanese society against Koreans.

When analyzing Oshima's *Death by Hanging*, film scholars and critics do not fail to mention the Komatsugawa Incident as the basis of this self-reflexive work. But, usually this criminal case is interpreted as the antithesis to the film's anti-illusionist or Brechtian drama. In other words, theatricality and artifice belong only to Oshima's treatment of the subject matter. Maureen Turim, for instance, writes, "Oshima's concern with issues of justice and the state are grounded in reference to a 'real' incident, even if he addresses them in a mode that defies realism."[56] Here, Turim aligns the actual event of the Komatsugawa Incident with the effects of realism, and contrasts it to the artifice of Oshima's Brechtian treatment of this subject matter. Her emphasis is on a radical disjuncture between reality outside cinema and Oshima's cinematic appropriation of it. To be sure, *Death by Hanging* does exhibit a high degree of reflexivity. Revealing "a remarkable discrepancy in 'levels of reality'" perceived by different characters and recorded by the camera, *Death by Hanging* tests the limit of narrative filmmaking.[57] While it does not abandon the suturing effect of "narrativization," it also destabilizes and resists its unity.[58]

However, what is not sufficiently acknowledged in these preceding studies of *Death by Hanging* is precisely the film's understanding of the media event as being *itself* theatrical in nature. In fact, I would argue that the true attraction of the Komatsugawa Incident for Oshima lies in its glaringly theatrical nature, since the original crime had already contained elements of artifice and performance akin to the theatrical staging of a scripted drama in front of an audience. Here, the audience was the general public and the stage was the news media. Just like the Kim Hiro Incident, the Komatsugawa Incident hinges on the collusion between the criminal and journalists, who work together to create the arresting spectacle of the media event.

Certainly, the politicized context of these events must have interested Oshima, who had already made television documentary works focused on Korea and resident Koreans in Japan, such as *Forgotten Soldiers* (*Wasurerareta kōgun*, 1963) as well as the short experimental film *Diary of Yunbogi* (1965). Nonetheless, the heightened theatricality of *Death by Hanging* and his next feature film, *Three Resurrected Drunkards* (*Kaettekita yopparai*, 1968)—both of which focus on the plight of ethnic Koreans in Japan and experiment with a narrative structure that relies heavily on repetition—suggests Oshima's interest in the imbrication of theatrical artifice and the journalistic sensation of actuality. A performative dimension of theatrical artifice is especially apparent in *Three Resurrected Drunkards*, a film that plays with issues of mistaken identity and racial discrimination. It is not accidental that Oshima dresses one of the Korean characters exactly like Kim Hiro in this satirical drama.

We also cannot overlook the fact that one of the sets in *Death by Hanging*—a makeshift domestic space that the prison officials set up as the protagonist R's home, as they reenact the life of R—is entirely covered with newspapers (figure 2.3). It is on this set that R is forced to act out his part in the exaggerated enactment of a family drama, which the prison officials stage in order to revive R's lost memory. The ubiquitous presence of the Yomiuri newspapers covering the four walls of this

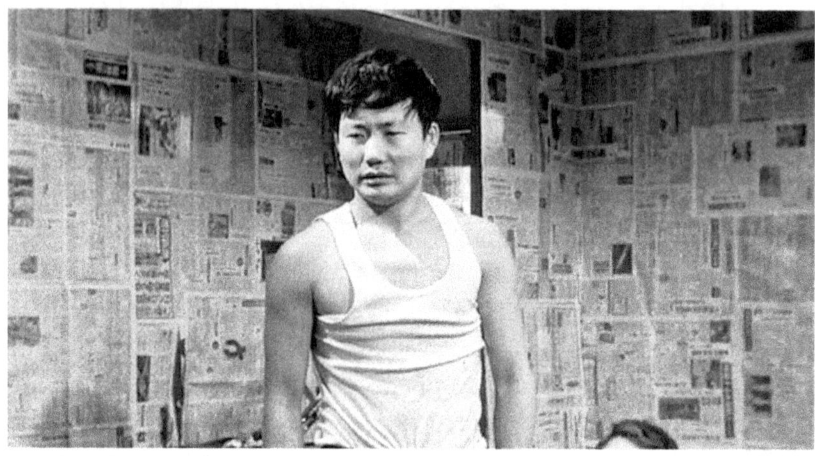

2.3. The walls are covered with newspapers. Still from *Death by Hanging* (1968), dir. Oshima Nagisa.

makeshift set visually signals the theatricality inherent in news journalism, and thus its constitutive artifice, which is at the heart of the film's deliberate appropriation of the Komatsugawa Incident.

Oshima's other works, which similarly appropriate actual criminal cases that received wide media attention, suggest his continuing obsession with theatricality and journalism. His film *Boy* (*Shōnen*, 1969) is a case in point. The film is based on an actual crime committed by a family of impostors who were making a living by "faking" car accidents. The arrest of the parents in September 1966 caused a short-lived media sensation, as the headlines of remediated newspapers in the film indicate. Like *Death by Hanging*, *Boy* focuses on the character whose criminal act was inseparable from theatrical artifice. The boy who pretended to be hit by a car so that his parents could extort compensation from the driver was "performing" his part each time he ran into a car. It is undoubtedly this artifice enmeshed with actuality that interested Oshima.

His 1967 film *Japanese Summer: Double Suicide* also draws on the case of a random shooting by an eighteen year old. In addition to the adolescent shooter, the film presents a cunning fascist-nationalist character named "Television" who carries around a TV set. Oshima again interprets an actual criminal case through the lens of theatrical artifice. Given his critique of television as an apparatus of fascism and state power, Oshima's allegorical presentation of this character as a caricature of the insatiable, self-serving journalists who willingly collaborate with alleged criminals, but inevitably betray them in the end, is significant. It suggests that television as a quintessential medium of journalism is closely aligned with state authorities, even as it offers an important venue of expression for those who are too disenfranchised to make their voice heard.[59] Oshima's films from the 1960s consistently highlight not only his obsession with journalism, but also the way in which the artifactual nature of the media event itself could become a critical source of cinematic experimentation.

FILMMAKING AS AN EVENT

The practice of experimenting with the temporal and referential proximity between cinema and journalism is not limited to the work of Oshima. The strategic incorporation of press photographs and newspapers into documentary films was already common long before the 1960s. Yet, in most cases, these appropriated images serve to enhance evidential claims, just as science and education films were incorporating charts, diagrams, and photographs to support their arguments. The critical interrogation of journalism's artifactuality undertaken by Oshima and Matsumoto among others changed the very status of journalistic materials incorporated into films. These filmmakers experimented with the temporal as well as the spatial singularity of the *event*. This singular occurrence of the event, as linked to the very act of filmmaking itself, is the last element that needs to be analyzed.

Two comparable treatments of filmmaking as an event can be found in Oshima's *Diary of a Shinjuku Thief* and Matsumoto's *Funeral Parade of Roses*, two films that best capture the eventful atmosphere of 1968 and 1969. In both films, the filmmakers and their crews appear in what seem like extradiegetic documentary sequences. These self-reflexive moments are further accentuated by the films' deliberate mixing of the diegetic world of fiction and the extradiegetic, nonfictional world of 1968–69. The most conscious blurring of the two worlds is seen in Oshima's and Matsumoto's strikingly similar deployment of *angura* theater troupes. For instance, after the opening montage of intertitles conveys a sense of global synchronicity, *Diary of a Shinjuku Thief* cuts to a sequence in which Kara Jūrō, the celebrated leader of the Situation Theater, is seen running through the streets of Shinjuku. We hear voices shouting "Thief!" and see a few men chasing after Kara. Once they catch up with him, he takes off his clothes, revealing an exquisite tattoo above

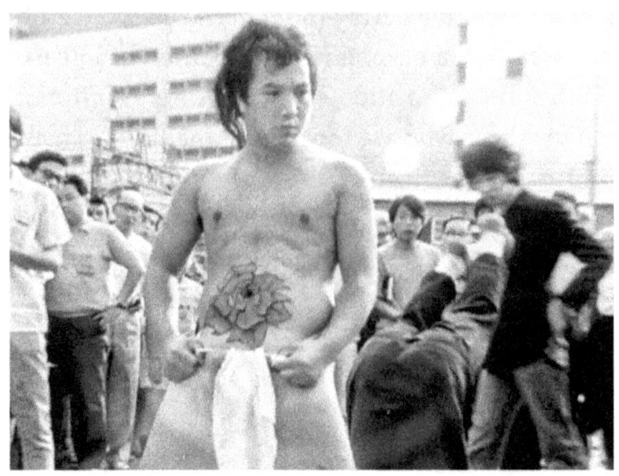

2.4. Kara Jūrō performing at Shinjuku Station (foreground) and Yokoo Tadanori watching the performance (background). Still from *Diary of a Shinjuku Thief* (1969), dir. Oshima Nagisa.

his navel. At this point it becomes clear that both Kara and his pursuers are *performing* a skit, which turns out to be a playful advertisement for their upcoming performance at a nearby shrine. Importantly, among a crowd of onlookers gathered around these performers is the character of Torio, played by the young graphic designer Yokoo Tadanori (figure 2.4). The subsequent cut to a close-up of Torio watching this street performance unfold in the eastern square just outside Shinjuku Station, effectively brings together two types of theatrical artifice: the performance of the Situation Theater actors and the performance of the actor Yokoo Tadanori. These two modes of theatrical performance are further connected when Yokoo *as the character of Torio* joins Kara in his staging of *Yui Shōsetsu*, a play about a man who attempts to steal his nation.

This doubly folded theatricality is, however, counterbalanced by a cinema verité sequence in which Yokoo *as himself* appears and receives sex counseling from a prominent sexologist, Takahashi Tetsu, together with the actress Yokoyama Rie, with whom he performs a sex scene after his staged performance as a substitute actor for the Situation Theater.[60] Toward the end, the film shifts the register of representation once again, and presents a gritty documentary sequence that captures the start of a riot on 29 June 1968. This is the document of another theatrical event in which social actors are seen "performing" their parts as protesters on the streets. The dramatic nature of this street action, epitomized by the stone that shatters the police station's window, is an unscripted event that further blurs the boundary between fiction and nonfiction, theatricality and actuality, and diegetic and nondiegetic worlds. This decisive breach of generic boundaries in order to foreground the contiguity between the screen and the world outside it is made even more palpable by the deliberate transformation of filmmaking itself into a spectacular street performance. Oshima takes pains to suggest that the act of on-location shooting is also theatrical, a spectacle in its own right.

Take, for instance, the moment when ordinary shoppers inside Kinokuniya Bookstore turn and glance back at the camera, acknowledging its presence, as the camera films Yokoo browsing through the shelves before he performs his scripted act (shoplifting of books). This is the moment when the film offers the process of filmmaking itself as a spectacle, an event that solicits the attention of the passersby and shoppers who happen to be there during the on-location shooting. A similar dynamic is at play in the opening sequence in which the members of the Situation Theater are performing their skit in front of Shinjuku Station; a crowd of onlookers gathers around Kara Jūrō and his troupe, and the camera partakes in this event. The unscripted actions of the passersby staring back at or turning away from the camera are part of the profilmic reality, of the nondiegetic world outside cinema. The film's inclusion of such moments underscores the simple fact that Oshima's filming of *Diary of a Shinjuku Thief* itself was a singular event that took place in Shinjuku in the summer of 1968.

The singularity of filmmaking as an event is hinted at the very beginning when the first intertitle appears on screen: "Shinjuku, Summer 1968, Saturday, 5:30PM." The journalistic insistence on the specificity of the day and the place reminds us that the shooting of the film on the streets in 1968 took place alongside street performances and protests. This self-conscious staging of the filmmaking itself as an event that competes for the attention of passersby and crowds in the urban space (especially around the eventful space of Shinjuku) negates the categorical differentiation of fiction and nonfiction, or of artifice and actuality. Instead, the film presents the process of its own making as an artifactual event.

A similar insistence on theatrical artifice and eventfulness characterizes *Funeral Parade of Roses*. Here, too, we see a filmmaking crew being filmed, appearing alongside cinema verité-style interviews with actors and passersby. We see the leading actor, Peter, who performs the role of a beautiful drag queen named Eddy, meandering through the streets of Shinjuku only to be filmed as one of the onlookers who watches an actual street performance of a funeral staged by the members of the avant-garde performance group Zero Dimension. Again, the distinction between fiction and nonfiction quickly dissolves as the camera *doubly documents* the actual event of Zero Dimension's street performance and Eddy's reaction as its spectator, incorporating both into the fictional diegetic space. The scripted and unscripted performances are constantly folded onto each other in this manner, giving rise to our awareness of the inseparability of artifice and actuality, fiction and nonfiction (figure 2.5).

The film's final sequence, in which Eddy stumbles out of his apartment in bloody lingerie, holding a knife with which he has just stabbed his own eyes, only amplifies the film's complex play with the theatricality of street performance and the camera's participation in it, a point which the Zero Dimension sequence had already introduced. The camera slowly circles Eddy, who is, in turn, encircled by a ring of passersby who stop and eagerly watch his dramatic performance on the street. The camera closes in on the faces of these onlookers, recording their reactions and expressions, as it films Eddy acting out the spectacular ending of this modern oedipal tragedy. Here, the very process of filmmaking—the on-location shooting of a fictional scene—attains the status of a singular event, analogous to the happening-style funeral performed by Zero Dimension (figure 2.6).

What do we make of the strong analogy between the eventfulness of filmmaking and the eventfulness of street performance? One way to interpret Oshima's and Matsumoto's deliberate staging of the process of filmmaking itself as a theatrical spectacle in its own right is to read it as a critical gesture meant to oppose the sensation of actuality generated by filmmaking to the sensation of actuality generated by journalism. The prominent presence of the crowds of onlookers that keep appearing in *Diary of a Shinjuku Thief* and *Funeral Parade of Roses* is significant in this regard, since it is precisely the presence of the onlookers that confers the status of spectacle on a performance. Returning to Rancière's definition of theatrical spectacle as bodies in action before an assembled audience and to Tarde's analysis of the sensation of actuality that requires a community of simultaneous recipients, I argue that the staging of filmmaking as a spectacle is aimed to generate its own sen-

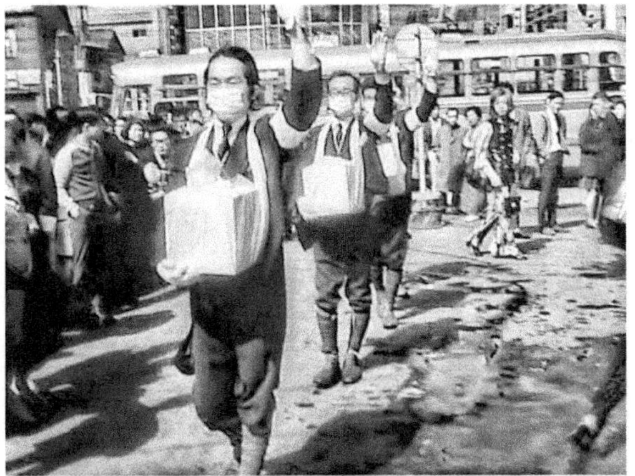

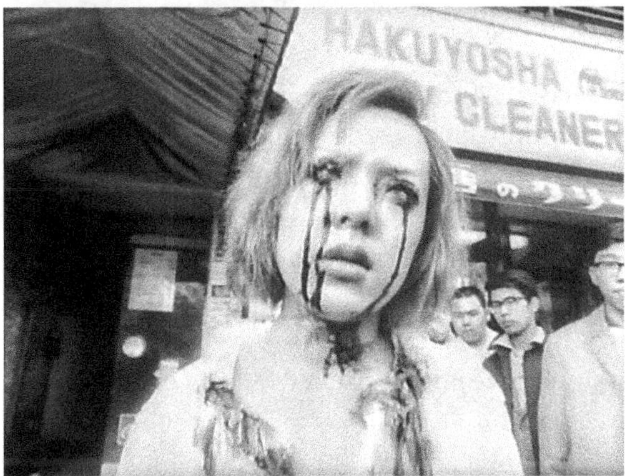

2.5. Eddy turning to watch a street performance by Zero Dimension. Still from *Funeral Parade of Roses* (1969), dir. Matsumoto Toshio.

2.6. Eddy surrounded by onlookers. Still from *Funeral Parade of Roses* (1969), dir. Matsumoto Toshio.

sation of actuality, both approximating and countering the actuality-effect of journalism. Or, to push this interpretation one step further, the journalistic sensation of actuality that these two films mimic is that of television, an exemplary medium of actuality, simultaneity, and mass receptivity.

By staging the process of filmmaking as a theatrical spectacle and by documenting this spectacular event of filmmaking itself as part of the documented reality, *Diary of a Shinjuku Thief* and *Funeral Parade of Roses* both confront and complicate the perceived actuality-effect of television, or more precisely, of television news. Oshima and Matsumoto were clearly aware of the power of television to produce media events and spectacles that generate strong sensations of actuality. If they both turned to the actuality-effect of performance to restore the eventfulness of cinema in 1968 and 1969, it is most likely because of their desire to address the power of television, a medium they saw as posing a serious challenge to avant-garde filmmaking. The late 1960s, and the years of 1968 and 1969 in particular, were the time when the artifactual power of television intensified as political activism on the streets became heavily mediated and sensationalized. Student protesters and police were staging confrontations on a daily basis alongside avant-garde performers and happenings. In the meantime, media-savvy "criminals" and activists were demanding airtime on television to advance their causes. In the midst of this increased imbrication of politics and the media, filmmakers like Oshima and Matsumoto were searching for the most effective way to address cinema's proximity to and its difference from television.

It is thus not without significance that both *Diary of a Shinjuku Thief* and *Funeral Parade of Roses* treat student protests as a form of spectacle imbued with elements of theatricality. *Diary of a Shinjuku Thief* playfully links Kara's street performance in the opening sequence to the closing documentary sequence (which works as a synecdoche of a series of protests and riots that broke out on the streets in 1968) through the motif of a broken clock.[61] In the case of *Funeral Parade of Roses*, the iconic presence of helmeted student protesters is condensed into one wounded character whom Eddy accidentally meets. The student faces the camera, delivers an impassioned speech on progressive violence as if on a stage, and quickly disappears from the narrative.

The direct remediation of television that Matsumoto used in *For the Damaged Right Eye* also returns with an interesting twist in *Funeral*

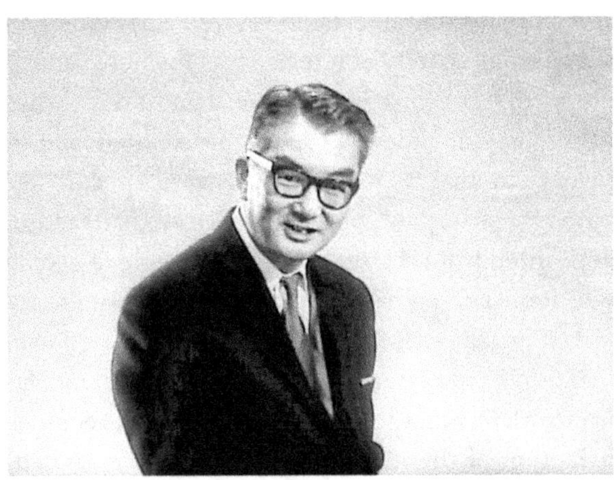

2.7. The TV commentator Yodogawa Chōji interrupts the drama. Still from *Funeral Parade of Roses* (1969), dir. Matsumoto Toshio.

Parade of Roses. In one scene the film mockingly mimics television by inserting fake commercials in the midst of narrative actions: an advertisement for eye drops follows a character taking a bottle of eye drops out of his pocket. Or, to offer another example, the film cuts from the most gripping theatrical climax, the scene in which Eddy stabs his eyes in despair after realizing that his dead lover was his own father, to a comical shot of Yodogawa Chōji. Yodogawa was a famous film critic and television commentator who presented popular films on television (in a manner comparable to Hitchcock's role in *Alfred Hitchcock Presents*). Yodogawa, framed in a medium close-up, wearing a business suit, turns his head toward the camera and says with a knowing smile, "Frightening, isn't it? The cursed destiny of man. What a mix of cruelty and laughter it is! Let's look forward to the next program. Goodbye, goodbye, goodbye" (figure 2.7). The film then abruptly cuts back to a close-up of the knife held in Eddy's hand, slowly emerging out of the bathroom. This scene both mimics and mocks the televisual economy of suspense constantly interrupted by advertisements and punctuated by commentaries. As indicated by a note on this scene in the published script of *Funeral Parade of Roses*—it reads, "An imitation of television"—Matsumoto quite consciously appropriates the segmented structure of television.[62]

Interruption and discontinuity, however, are not the only attributes of televisual time. Oshima argues that television revived early cinema's *eventfulness*. While the apparent novelty of television is liveness (which cinema cannot compete with, since the event captured on film is always already belonging to the past), it indeed repeats and revives one of the characteristics of early cinema: its propensity toward spectacular events. He thus compares the attraction of television to the attraction of early cinema, which profited from the scale and magnitude of events captured by the camera. Referencing early actuality and documentary films, such as *Momijigari* (1899), a record of the kabuki play, *Russo-Japan War: The Actual Scene of Lüshun* (1905), and *The Record of Lieutenant Shirase's Arctic Exploration* (1912), Oshima suggests that television recuperates the irresistible attraction of these early films in its effort to capture events that are spectacular and topical. Taking the example of *gaitō terebi* (open-air television set up in the public space), a form of viewing prevalent in the early years of Japanese television culture, Oshima writes, "People who gathered around the open-air television set on the street gathered there precisely because the image of the event transmitted on the screen was happening at the present moment."[63]

Oshima's observation hits the mark. It points to an uncanny loop in media history; television imitating cinema in order to supplant its production of actuality, and cinema imitating television in order to surpass it. In the early 1950s, television aimed to bring back the sensation of actuality associated with the cinema of its incipient years, but in the 1960s, cinema tried to revive this sensation by appropriating television. In 1965, Marshall McLuhan argued, "Indirectly, the new art films of our time have received an enormous amount of encouragement and impact from the television form. The television form has remained quite invisible—and will only become visible at the moment that television itself becomes the content of a new medium."[64] McLuhan's remark seems to resonate with the kinds of cinematic experiment analyzed here. As television was consciously appropriated by Japanese avant-garde cinema and remediated into the latter's content, its form became gradually visible. Here, we have come full circle: we are back to the question of cinema's relation to other media. The problematic of actuality is inseparable from the rapidly changing media environment wherein cinema's singularity as the medium of the moving image was challenged. A series of avant-garde experiments that took journalistic materials and theatrical performance as their objects of remediation and imitation was responding precisely to this changing status of cinema. Furthermore, the desire to reinvent cinema anew against television coincided with the era of revolutionary politics that seized the streets in metropolitan cities like Tokyo and Osaka.

The constellation of these related events becomes visible—or readable—if we look through the lens of the problematic of actuality: social actors, revolutionaries, and alleged criminals collaborating with journalists to produce sensational media events; filmmakers and intellectuals aligning themselves with the revolutionaries and sympathizing with criminals who command media attention; and filmmakers and performance artists competing with journalists to produce street-based events that confer sensations of actuality. Films like *Diary of a Shinjuku Thief*, *Death by Hanging*, *For the Damaged Right Eye*, and *Funeral Parade of Roses* are salient examples of the cinema of actuality that emerged out of this constellation.

three

remediating journalism

Politics and the Media Event

On 25 November 1970, the famed novelist Mishima Yukio and his private army, Tate no Kai (the Shield Society), occupied the general's office at the Ichigaya headquarters of the Self-Defense Forces in broad daylight. To a rather indifferent crowd of soldiers gathered below the balcony, Mishima delivered his passionate plea to take part in the direct action he staged and to die with him in the name of patriotism. Television crews and journalists who had been called in by Mishima himself were also present at the scene. In spite of the spectacular and meticulously planned staging of his speech, replete with the on-site television cameras and news reporters, the soldiers refused to join his cause. Mishima's speech was broadcast live, and the subsequent ritual suicides by Mishima and another member of the Shield Society, which took place inside the general's office and away from the eyes of journalists, were immediately and widely reported. The news of his anachronistic ritual suicide and failed coup were on the front pages of every newspaper the next day. For the following weeks, the incident repeatedly appeared on television programs, in the headlines of newspapers, and on the front covers of weekly magazines. The incident became one of the most well-known media events in the history of Japan.

Less than a month later, a black-and-white film entitled *Sexual Reincarnation: The Woman Who Wants to Die* (*Segura magura: Shinitai onna*, 1970) made its quiet appearance in small movie theaters.[1] The film was directed by none other than Wakamatsu Kōji, a maker of pink films renowned for his association with New Left student activists and for his daring formal experimentation in the 1960s. The film was scripted by his close collaborator, Adachi Masao, and released by Wakamatsu Production.[2] With its ample, formulaic erotic scenes, the film looked like any ordinary pink film or soft-core erotica but with one notable exception. It included several montage sequences composed of remediated press photographs and headlines from newspapers and weekly magazines reporting on Mishima's failed coup and subsequent suicide. As would have been evident to viewers at the time, and as is evident from a close reading of the film's citational strategy, the film operates as a timely parody of the incident at multiple levels (including a parody of the media that capitalized on Mishima's suicide in its immediate aftermath). The film implies, for instance, that one of the protagonists is a member of the Shield Society. This character fails to participate in Mishima's attempted coup as he spends a night with his girlfriend. This motif of failure to participate in the revolutionary event because of personal affair is one that Mishima himself used in his novel *Patriotism* (*Yūkoku*, 1961) and its 1966 filmic adaptation, which he scripted, directed, and screened at the Art Theatre Shinjuku Bunka.

Sexual Reincarnation thus makes multiple references to Mishima's sensational suicide and his work, and the manner in which it draws the spectator's attention to this spectacular media event is anything but subtle. Montages composed entirely of still images culled from newspapers and magazines flash across the widescreen. The film's remediation strategy is overt and eye-catching. The timely and conspicuous citation of journalistic images is part and parcel of the style of Wakamatsu's work produced in the 1960s and early 1970s; a number of his films from this period similarly appropriate, remediate, and directly cite then current news and media events. It is this citational practice that renders his films "actual" and confers a sense of topicality akin to television news and tabloid newspapers.

Certainly, we who watch these films years later may not immediately recognize the timeliness of their journalistic reference, as the spectators of the time would have done; the topicality of the news may be lost on us. But we can sense the strange openness of the films and their lack of narrative closure, as we gaze at these remediated photographs and magazine articles on-screen. Despite being fictional, the diegetic worlds of Wakamatsu's films are clearly contiguous with the historically "real" world outside the screen. At the same time, the purported realness of the historical world referenced by Wakamatsu's films is itself heavily mediated by journalism and the news media. The referential status of Wakamatsu's films should thus be called *artifactual*.

In this chapter I extend the analysis of artifactuality to its economic and temporal conditions, focusing on the tension between two economies of the image—cinema and journalism—that characterizes Wakamatsu's timely appropriation of journalistic materials. These materials run the gamut from high-profile media events involving well-known political figures to generic advertisements, crime photos, and pornographic images. On the one hand, his work critically intervenes in the journalistic economy of the production, circulation, distribution, and consumption of news information as spectacles; on the other hand, it participates in and is sustained by the corresponding economy of cinematic spectacles. By foregrounding the referential connection between the cinematic image and an ongoing media event, such as the Mishima Incident—which was contemporaneous to the production of his film and hence still vivid in the minds of many filmgoers—Wakamatsu's work from the 1960s and early 1970s also exposes a crucial discrepancy between these two economies of the image. While these economies overlap and intersect at institutional and aesthetic levels, they are clearly not identical. And the fundamental difference that divides the two is speed: the pace with which the image gains currency and exhausts it is much faster within the journalistic economy of the image. By contrast, the cinematic economy of the image moves slower, especially when it comes to the production, circulation, and consumption of narrative films. What happens, then, when the filmmaker deliberately mixes the two, appropriating and mimicking the temporal attributes of one through the other?

Coming out of the growing pink-film industry, where the shooting-time was extremely short in comparison to the general timeline of major studio productions, the work of Wakamatsu offers us a unique vantage point from which to analyze the temporal gap between the cinematic economy of the image and the journalistic economy of the image. As evident from the incredibly swift appropriation of the Mishima Incident in *Sexual Reincarnation*, Wakamatsu's work often plays up the temporal proximity between the widely circulated media event *and* its calculated repetition. It is the calculated timing of the cinematic repetition that commands our attention, and the critical edge that sets Wakamatsu's work apart from other soft-core filmmakers hinges on this calculated and timely remediation of journalism.

The strategy of cinematic remediation first used by Matsumoto and Oshima draws our attention to the material gap between cinema and appropriated media such as the comic book and still photography. Wakamatsu's remediation of newspapers, photographs, and magazines similarly directs our attention to the material gap between the cinematic image and the appropriated journalistic image. But this gap is also heightened and accompanied by the closeness in time of the production of the original to its remediation. By exploring the political stakes of the temporal proximity between journalism and its cinematic remediation through the exemplary Wakamatsu Production films made during the late 1960s and early 1970s—the so-called season of politics—I suggest how this investigation complicates our understanding of the New Left politics with which Wakamatsu is commonly aligned.

THE PINK FILM AND THE CITATION OF THE MEDIA EVENT

The timing of *Sexual Reincarnation* was, indeed, well calculated. Wakamatsu and Adachi began working on the script while watching the evening TV news about the Mishima Incident the very night of that shocking event.[3] As the film critic Hiraoka Masaaki observed at the time of the film's release, the speed with which Wakamatsu Production made *Sexual Reincarnation* was on par with tabloid journalism. By 29 November (four days after the incident) Adachi had finished writing the script. By 9 December the production crew finished shooting the film on location at a small inn in Minakami, a remote town located in the northern part of Japan. According to Hiraoka: "Merely two weeks after the incident, the film was complete. Its pace was comparable to that of weekly magazines."[4] As the news media continued to speculate, analyze, and circulate information about Mishima's suicide and his political goals, the film was already showing at theaters.[5] The film appears to be quite self-conscious of its temporal and referential proximity to tabloid journalism. For instance, one image that is inserted twice in the film—once at the beginning and once at the end—is a two-page spread taken from the weekly magazine *Shūkan Yomiuri*'s "emergency special issue" dedicated to Mishima's death, published on 11 December.[6] The film reproduces the press photograph of Mishima placed next to an arresting headline that reads "Madness or Sincerity? A Shocking Hour and a Half" in a tight close-up (figure 3.1). All of this suggests an exceptionally

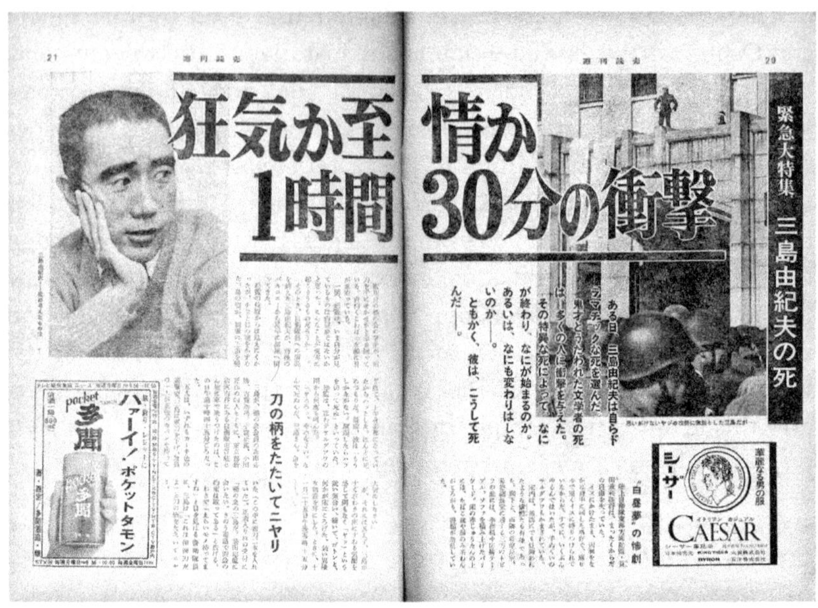

週刊読売

緊急大特集 三島由紀夫の死

狂気か至情か

1時間30分の衝撃

ある日、三島由紀夫は自らドラマチックな死を選んだ。鬼才とうたわれた文学者の死は、多くの人に衝撃を与えた。その特異な死によって、なにが終わり、なにが始まるのか。あるいは、なにも変わりはしないのか——。ともかく、彼は、こうして死んだ——。

刀の柄をたたいてニヤリ

"白昼夢"の惨劇

3.1. The original weekly magazine special on Mishima's suicide, which Wakamatsu remediates in *Sexual Reincarnation: The Woman Who Wants to Die* (1970). From *Shūkan Yomiuri* 29.55 (December 1970), 20–21.

journalistic sensibility toward timing on the part of Wakamatsu and his crew. The film is actual, up-to-date, and topical on all fronts as it holds a tight referential relation to the sensational media event that it unabashedly appropriates.

Since *Sexual Reincarnation* falls into the generic category of the pink film, and since many of Wakamatsu's films that bear the same journalistic elements are said to belong to this genre, we may surmise that this proximity to journalistic media has something to do with the generic structure of the pink film itself. As Donald Richie points out, during the height of the production of pink films, most production companies were shooting one film per week on average.[7] This seems to explain, at least partly, the strong affinity between journalism and Wakamatsu's work.

To be sure, Wakamatsu's work was not always shown at movie theaters specializing in soft-core pornography. Theatre Scorpio programmed the special screenings of Wakamatsu's films as early as 1968, one year after the screening of Adachi's experimental film *Galaxy* (*Gingakei*, 1967), which inaugurated the opening of the theater. Wakamatsu's collaboration with ATG in *Ecstasy of the Angels* (*Tenshi no kōkotsu*, 1972) also indicates his foothold in the art-cinema circuit. But this is not to say that Wakamatsu stopped being a pink filmmaker and became an art filmmaker. As Sharon Hayashi argues, the controversial showings of his earlier pink films, such as *Secrets behind the Wall* (*Kabe no naka no himegoto*, 1965) and *The Embryo Hunts in Secret* (*Taiji ga mitsuryō suru toki*, 1966) at the Berlin International Film Festival in 1965 and 1966, attest to the permeability of generic boundaries that demarcate "sex film" from "art film."[8] The special screening event, aptly titled "Wakamatsu Kōji's Soulful Demonstration," which featured six films including *Secrets behind the Wall* and *The Embryo Hunts in Secret* at Theatre Scorpio in August and September 1968, suggests that the same kind of generic permeability existed in Japan at the time. The history of the pink-film industry also indicates that the timely appropriation of topical, sensational news events (especially those involving violent crimes) was a common industry practice. Given the history of this generic practice, it is worth starting our analysis of the temporal economy of Wakamatsu's work with a consideration of the pink film as a genre, to see if it had something to do with his calculated remediation of journalistic materials.

THE ECONOMY OF THE PINK FILM

Kobayashi Satoru's *Flesh Market* (*Nikutai no ichiba*, 1962), which is said to be the first pink film, is based on an actual rape incident that took place in the Roppongi ward of Tokyo in October 1961.[9] As Eric Schaefer suggests in his study of the American "exploitation film"—a genre comparable to the pink film—this kind of referential practice was also common among exploitation films in the United States. Schaefer notes, "Because exploitation films often drew on the headlines for their story material, they emphasized timeliness in their ads."[10] Being on the low end of film production, pink films share many of the same characteristics of exploitation films: they are low budget, produced in a short span of time (often less than a week) by small independent production companies, and habitually focus on adult-only themes and "forbidden" spectacles (mainly nudity and violence). They are usually distributed and exhibited through independent venues and rarely through major film studios or their distribution channels.[11]

In fact, this last point on distribution is key to the generic definition of the pink film. Coined by Murai Minoru, a news reporter and a film critic, the term *pinku eiga* (pink film) was explicitly used to differentiate independently produced and distributed soft-core pornographic films from similarly themed films made by the major studios. As the film critic Suzuki Yoshiaki reminds us, films such as Imamura Shōhei's *Insect Woman* (*Nippon konchūki*, 1963), which was hailed for its tasty eroticism, did not qualify as "pink" because Nikkatsu, one of the major five studios of the time, produced and distributed it.[12]

Another element that is indispensable for distinguishing the pink film from other erotic or pornographic films is its postwar origin. Its putative "beginning" is traced back to Kobayashi's *Flesh Market*, the first independently produced soft-core erotica made after the establishment of Eirin (Film Ethics Regulation Control Committee), a nongovernmental organization that sets Japan's self-regulatory rating system.[13] The pink film is also a product of the era when television eclipsed cinema and led to the decline of major studios, which in turn allowed small independent companies to gain more control over the circuits of production and distribution. In this sense the pink film is not strictly equivalent to what Schaefer has called classical exploitation films (sex-hygiene films, science films, burlesque films), though these pre-pink erotic films were frequently screened in Japan long before the emergence of the pink film in the 1960s.[14]

In addition to its growing popularity among young male audiences, the pink film, with its marginalized status and its constant struggle against censorship, benefited from an aura of oppositionality in the 1960s. In order to understand the habitual association of Wakamatsu's work with the New Left, one cannot overlook the ideological positioning of the pink film as defiant and oppositional to the mainstream cinema. The historical situation of the 1960s—the general decline of the film industry, the increased militancy of the New Left student movement, and the explosion of countercultural and underground art activities—had much to do with this perception of the pink film in general and Wakamatsu's work in particular.

Interestingly, Oshima was first among the critics and filmmakers who took this politicized view of the pink film. Oshima compared the marginalized position of the pink film to the victims of social and economic discrimination in the essay "Wakamatsu Kōji: Discrimination and Carnage," published in the October 1970 issue of the film journal *Eiga Hihyō II*. Despite their stylistic and institutional differences,

Oshima and Wakamatsu worked in similar social circles, and by the time Oshima's essay was published in *Eiga Hihyō II*, their paths had begun to run in parallel. After graduating from the elite Kyoto University, Oshima began his filmmaking career at the major Shōchiku studio, and was soon applauded by the media as the leader of Japan's New Wave generation. Wakamatsu, on the other hand, started his career in the burgeoning television industry after spending a few years as a day laborer, a yakuza, and even some time in prison. Wakamatsu's directorial debut was a minor pink film, *Sweet Trap* (*Amai wana*, 1963), produced by the independent production company Tokyo Kikaku, for the meager amount of $1,800.[15] Meanwhile, Oshima left Shōchiku in protest against the repressive measures taken by the studio against the screening of his film *Night and Fog in Japan* (1960). After working in the television industry, mostly shooting documentary programs, Oshima returned to cinema and resumed making features in 1965, the same year that Wakamatsu established his namesake production company.

Throughout the 1960s, Oshima and Wakamatsu similarly dealt with polemical issues such as militant political activism, crime, sex, and the emperor system. They often shared the same actors (e.g., the Situation Theater actor Kara Jūrō) and the same crews (e.g., Adachi Masao, who worked as a scriptwriter for both Wakamatsu and Oshima), and the two directors both collaborated with ATG. Wakamatsu also produced Oshima's *In the Realm of the Senses* (*Ai no koriida*, 1976), a controversial hardcore film that reignited debates about pornography and censorship in Japan.

It is within this historical context that we should place Oshima's sympathetic portrayal of Wakamatsu as an oppositional filmmaker. In "Wakamatsu Kōji: Discrimination and carnage," Oshima introduces Wakamatsu as a fellow outcast who poses moral and political threats to the mainstream film industry and who is thus constantly "purged" from it.

> The decline of the Japanese film industry that began in 1959 necessarily led to the birth of the so-called pink film, though the industry continues to discriminate against it. The most horrifying fact is how unaware the Japanese film industry is about its own discriminatory attitude toward the pink film. I repeat: the Japanese film industry gave birth to this bastard child, the pink film. The form of discrimination expressed in this relation is the archetype of every mode of

discrimination. And Wakamatsu Kōji continues to be discriminated against as the very symbol of this form.[16]

The metaphor of discrimination against the internal "other" that Oshima uses in this essay shrewdly aligns Wakamatsu with the leftist discourse on minoritarian politics, a gesture that other critics seem to repeat and Wakamatsu himself cultivates retroactively. But the representation of leftist politics in Wakamatsu's films is more ambivalent than it first appears.

Consider the example of *Sex Jack* (*Seizoku*, 1970), a film which was selected for screening at the Cannes International Film Festival in 1971.[17] *Sex Jack* draws on the notorious airplane hijacking known as Yodogō Haijakku Jiken (Yodogō Hijacking Incident). In this incident, the members of an ultra-Left communist group, the Red Army Faction, hijacked a commercial airplane and defected to North Korea on 31 March 1970. On 15 June 1970, when student-led street protests against the imminent renewal of the Japan-U.S. Security Treaty (ANPO) were at their height, Wakamatsu began shooting the film. It opens with a long sequence of documentary footage of helmeted student protesters gathering and marching at Yoyogi Park on the day of the renewal of the ANPO. Given the film's timely release in July 1970, we can safely assume that the topicality of its reference to these two events was not lost on its initial audience. The film's reference to the Yodogō Hijacking Incident is made even more explicit by its direct appropriation of the hijackers' manifesto, including the famous passage, "We are *Tomorrow's Joe*," in which the young hijackers compared themselves to the hero of the popular contemporary manga, *Tomorrow's Joe* (*Ashita no Jō*), by Chiba Tetsuya.[18]

The fictional narrative of *Sex Jack* revolves around a group of leftist student activists (implied to be Red Army Faction members) who regard themselves as a militant vanguard for the masses, along with the young protagonist—a lone unemployed laborer—who lives on "the other side of the river." As Oshima astutely points out, the term *kawamukō* (the other side of the river), used by this young protagonist to introduce himself, functions as a subtle signifier of social discrimination: it is a term used to describe and invoke the image of the poor neighborhood where social and ethnic minorities, shunted from the eye of the general public, live. Using this topological framework of the divided city, the film juxtaposes the idealist student activists to the pragmatic proletariat who clandestinely carries out solitary terrorist attacks on police stations and the Communist Party headquarters.

After a dramatic shoot-out between the policemen and student activists (all of whom the protagonist eventually kills), the film cuts to a striking color sequence. Since the film is shot mostly on black-and-white stock, this sequence delivers a sudden visual jolt. Here the camera slowly pans upward from drops of red paint ("blood") spattered on the muddy riverbank to the horizon, taking the point of view of the protagonist who stands on the "other side" of the river. The film cuts to a close-up of the lower body of the protagonist who zips up a red jacket. Then the film cuts to the celebrated final shot: the handheld camera mimics the subjective point of view of the protagonist who walks *across* the bridge. For Oshima and other critics who enthusiastically hailed this particular shot as a metonymic gesture of social resistance, the defiant act of crossing the river is more politically subversive and provocative than the student activists' purported revolutionary action.[19] Matsuda Masao goes a step further and proposes an anarchist reading of the final sequence. He argues that the invisible target of assassination hinted in the closing shot is none other than the emperor, as indicated by the location of the bridge. According to Matsuda, the ultimate violence that the film condones is antistate terrorism: the violence aimed at the body of the symbolic sovereign.[20]

In spite of the film's explicit reference to the Yodogō Hijacking Incident, its focus is displaced from the militant form of student activism that envisions the worldwide uprising of the proletariat. Instead, the film foregrounds the solitary act of violence exhibited by the lone protagonist who refuses to join the organized revolutionary movement. While it is possible to interpret this narrative as a critique of social and economic discrimination (Oshima) or a critique of the sovereign power (Matsuda), I want to approach it from a slightly different angle in order to highlight the tension that exists between the film's generic structure and its representation of violence. This entails rethinking the gender politics inherent in the very genre of pink film in relation to the political violence, which the film's topical reference to the Yodogō Hijacking Incident evokes.

The critical examination of gender politics is notably absent from Oshima's and Matsuda's otherwise astute analysis of *Sex Jack*, a film that presents gratuitous scenes of nudity and pornographic images of ecstatic women and men. Their appraisals of the film also do not question the taken-for-granted primacy of the male hero as the agent of resistance and narrative action. As the feminist film scholar Saitō Ayako rightly points out, women's bodies in the work of Wakamatsu (as well as of Adachi) are frequently put on screen simply to provide a blank canvas on which to paint vivid pictures of social contradictions.[21] The women thus occupy the position of the passive object, an inert surface for masculine inscription. Recurrent representations of violated women in Wakamatsu's films seem to corroborate this reading. From *The Embryo Hunts in Secret* (1966), which portrays a captive woman who gets constantly whipped by a middle-aged man (named Marukido Sadao, a pun on Marquis de Sade), to *Violated Angels* (1967), in which nurses are murdered by an adolescent boy, Wakamatsu's work shares the narrative tendency in classical Hollywood cinema to sadistically punish women who assert their sexual desire and agency, a disposition that has been roundly critiqued by feminist film scholars such as Laura Mulvey.[22]

However, focusing solely on the on-screen representation of violated female bodies would risk overlooking the historical specificities of these pornographic films. For instance, as Hayashi insightfully argues, the films of Wakamatsu Production from the 1960s onward engage in a close dialogue with emergent discourses on gender and sexuality in Japan by foregrounding a particular set of problematics (e.g., infertility, impotence, sexual reproduction, and abortion) present in these discourses.[23] In addition to their conscious engagement with topical issues such as sexual reproduction and abortion, Wakamatsu's films often blur the boundary between sexual violence and political violence. In spite of its apparent endorsement of male dominance, his work often oscillates between the representations of the violated female body and those of the male body that gets "perversely eroticized through exploration of its weakness and vulnerability."[24] The images of violated male bodies are prevalent, and the male protagonist frequently takes on the vulnerable position of the bearer of sexual violence. It is precisely the spectacle of the violated male body that complicates the representation of political violence in films like *Go, Go, Second Time Virgin* and *Sex Jack*.

The solitary protagonist in *Sex Jack* is exemplary in this regard. The unemployed, working-class "outcast" who lives on the other side of the river and carries out a series of terrorist attacks against the authorities is also the one who is subjected to sexual humiliation and violence. His vulnerability is accentuated in the scene where he is coerced into having sex with the female member of the activist group. The protagonist's physical struggle against this coercion and his ultimate refusal to enter into sexual relationships with women becomes pivotal to the film's allegorical depiction of another kind of violence: the violence inherent in the purportedly democratic structure of consensual politics. One way to complicate the generic structure of Wakamatsu's films is hence to focus on the tension between political activism and sexual activities, and to ask why this tension is accompanied by unremitting topical references to actual incidents of violence, including airplane hijackings, terrorist bombings, homicides, and other sensational crimes.

THE MEDIATIZATION OF POLITICS AND THE POLICE ORDER

The 1960s saw an intensified mediatization of politics through the proliferation of television. It is worth repeating that this decade in Japan also opened, in 1960, with the first televised assassination—the assassination of Asanuma Inejirō, the head of the Socialist Party, by a young ultranationalist right-wing activist—which was followed by countless spectacles of violence relayed by television, from the images of armed riot police clashing with workers and student protesters to the images of U.S. military aggression in Vietnam, of the civil-rights movement, and of the spread of decolonization struggles in Latin America and Africa. This was also the decade that witnessed the most air hijackings, seajackings, and other direct-action tactics carried out by media-conscious militant activists. It was within this general atmosphere of media saturation that Kim Hiro staged his hostage crisis, the Yodogō hijackers stole the Japan Airline's flight 351 and defected to North Korea, and Mishima Yukio staged his failed coup d'état and performed his ritual suicide. Like Oshima and Matsumoto, Wakamatsu was quick to incorporate these sensational news items into his films, often with the help of Adachi's clever scripts.

In the course of this decade the process of consuming violence through the mediation of spectacular images and imagining politics through violence became thoroughly imbricated. In this sense the mass media and the state worked together to manage the public perception of political violence. The Japanese state and media had, of course, historically engaged in institutionalized practices of regulating and managing news consumption in order to produce a disciplined, productive population. The postwar growth of the private sector of the journalism industry seemed to liberate the mainstream news media from the grip of the state, but it continued to serve as an effective means of policing the population, often in collusion with the conservative regime of the Liberal Democratic Party government. The ostensibly democratic media that capitalize on images of violence and the consolidation of liberal governance at the height of Japan's economic growth offer a broader context for Wakamatsu's incessant appropriation of journalistic materials. Read in relation to the questions of mediated violence and governance, his appropriation of widely reported incidents such as the Yodogō air hijacking and Mishima's coup attempt in *Sex Jack* and *Sexual Reincarnation* gains new meanings. They are more than a timely citation of the sensational news, if we consider how the media shape the public expectation of political violence. At stake here is a broader mechanism of policing, which operates within and without the institutionalized apparatuses of law and order.

It is therefore not enough to simply attribute the actuality-effect of Wakamatsu's films to the generic structure of the pink film. Rather, the strategy of remediation and the temporal proximity to journalism present in Wakamatsu's work need to be also placed within this larger historical context of the intensified mediatization of political violence in the 1960s. Only then can we fully understand the particular intervention his work makes in the parallel economies of cinema and journalism.

If Wakamatsu's engagement with journalism goes beyond a mere sensationalist appropriation of topical news, and if it is historically grounded in the era of an intensified mediatization of political violence, how might we understand its significance? One way to answer this question is to step back and think about the kind of political actions made visible through Wakamatsu's citational use of journalistic materials. In order to analyze this point, I turn to the theoretical distinction between police and politics made by Rancière.[25] Following Foucault's work on the historical development of the modern police, Rancière makes a useful distinction between two ways of understanding politics; he separates what he calls the general order of "police" from the genuine acts of "politics," reserving the latter term to denote a broader range of activities that contest, disrupt, and question the very conditions of possibility that undergird the perceived social, economic, and legal orders in society, including the ostensibly democratic ones. Rancière hence uses the term *policing*—not *politics*—to refer to what commonly goes by the name of politics: the institutionalized activities of governance, regulation, and the exercise of power including the system of electoral politics: "Politics is generally seen as the set of procedures whereby the aggregation and consent of collectivities is achieved, the organization of powers, the distribution of places and roles, and the systems of legitimizing this distribution. I propose to give this system of distribution and legitimization another name. I propose to call it *the police*."[26]

Accordingly, his concept of the police significantly expands the narrow understanding of the police as an agent of law enforcement, surveillance, and legally sanctioned violence. What he calls "the police order" is a more general regulatory order of sense perception, of which the institutional apparatus of the police as the agency of law enforcement is just one element: "The police is thus first an order of bodies that defines the allocation of ways of doing, ways of being, and ways of saying, and sees that those bodies are assigned by name to a particular place and task; it is an order of the visible and the sayable that sees that a particular activity is visible and another is not, that this speech is understood as discourse and another as noise."[27]

In contrast, what Rancière calls *politics* refers to activities that upset this regulatory police ordering of the sensible and the exclusionary distribution of social roles and bodies in society.[28] Against the regulatory order of the police that predetermines what one can see, say, and do, as well as who can speak for a given political community, Rancière defines what he calls politics in the following manner: "Political activity is whatever shifts a body from the place assigned to it or changes a place's destination. It makes visible what had no business being seen, and makes heard a discourse where there was only place for noise."[29] In so doing, such political activity can expose the structure of inequality, which is constitutive of democratic society and at odds with the supposed equality among its members.

Wakamatsu's timely appropriation of media events, such as the Yodogō Incident, could be productively understood in relation to the gap that exists between the police order and political activity. Instead of focusing on political actions that appear obvious and self-evident, Wakamatsu often shifts his emphasis onto a more ambiguous element. For instance, how might we read the film's final staging of the protagonist's river crossing in *Sex Jack*? This act might be read as an attempt to dislocate and redistribute bodies from their assigned places in society rather than as a simple act of defiance against the state. The protagonist's act of crossing the river is at once a physical and symbolic gesture that exposes the perceptual order imposed by the purportedly democratic society—the order that allocates his body to "the other side of the river," the marginalized space of minorities whose presence is concealed from the public and whose voices are heard neither by elected politicians nor by activists who speak in their name.

What the film makes visible through its engagement with sexual and political violence is the uncomfortable truth that *these leftist student activists are on the side of the police* in Rancière's sense of the term. Their critique of the state and capitalism notwithstanding, the student activists in *Sex Jack* are in fact complicit with the dominant police order that forecloses the participation of those who have no political voice in representational politics, and who are excluded from the media's theatrical staging of political dissent. The protagonist's refusal to participate in the consensual model of democracy presented in the student activists' rhetoric of free sex is emblematic in this regard. While hiding inside the dilapidated apartment of the protagonist, the students pass their idle time by debating the merits of revolutionary violence, complaining about the apathy of workers, and engaging in group sex, which they call "rosy solidarity" (*barairo no rentai*). This campy caricature of solidarity depicted in the form of a run-of-the-mill, pornographic scene is suggestive; it discloses the policing power of their political vision.

The policing power of the students over the protagonist is foregrounded through this seemingly democratic rhetoric of free sex, as they invite and then pressure the protagonist to engage in the act of rosy solidarity (figure 3.2). The camera work in this sequence drives the point home. Taking a high-angle position, the camera looks on the contorted face of the protagonist who helplessly screams as he is held and stripped of his clothes. His refusal to participate in this erotic game of solidarity is interpreted diegetically as a pathetic gesture of cowardice and impotence. But if we were to understand the police order as consisting of "the set of procedures whereby the aggregation and consent of collectivities is achieved," then this scene exposes this very police order, which works through a depoliticized system of consensus in the name of liberal democracy.[30] Read in this allegorical manner, the film *Sex Jack* reveals a much deeper ambivalence toward New Left student activism than it may first appear.

This kind of ambivalence that reveals the contradictory alliance be-

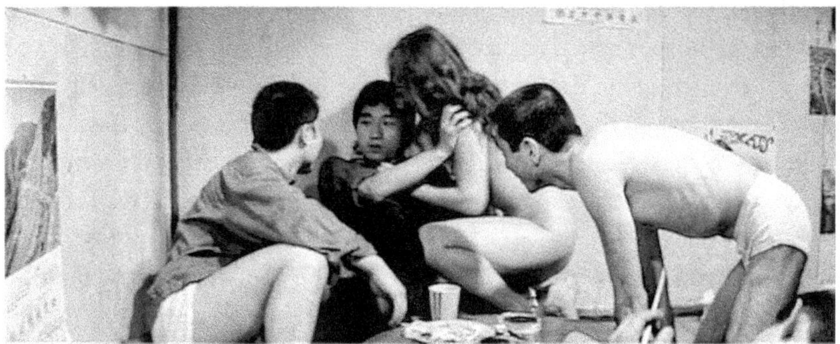

3.2. A scene of forced solidarity. Still from *Sex Jack* (1970), dir. Wakamatsu Kōji.

tween the police order and leftist politics is what makes Wakamatsu's work from the 1960s and early 1970s particularly interesting. His work is commonly interpreted as either regressively pornographic or progressively radical, and the political stance of his filmmaking from this period is predictably aligned with the New Left and with its stance of the antiestablishment.[31] As noted by the film historian Hirasawa Gō, the participation of young collaborators such as Adachi Masao in Wakamatsu Production helped ground Wakamatsu's personal hatred of police officers in a more theoretical framework of the critique of the state.[32] Wakamatsu also invited and hired former student revolutionaries and New Left activists into the production team. However, films like *Sex Jack* suggest that the question of politics in his work is much more ambivalent. If so, what does the textual ambivalence of Wakamatsu's films tell us about cinema's proximity to journalism? In order to answer this question, we need to look more carefully at the types of journalistic material appropriated by Wakamatsu.

APPROPRIATING THE SPECTACLE

The textual ambivalence of Wakamatsu's films begs the question of cinema's complicity with the existing police order that codifies our perception of political violence. Wakamatsu directly cites and remediates topical materials circulating in the journalistic economy of information, and the information appropriated by him is often quite spectacular. In so doing, his films tread a fine line between self-serving publicity and critique. By referencing then current news and media events, his work gains much needed publicity as it piggybacks on the sensational values of these events. Yet, at the same time, films like *Sex Jack* and *Sexual Reincarnation* draw attention to the policing power of journalistic media through their calculated remediation of news. It is the *delayed* repetition of the already consumed spectacles of sensational events that opens up a productive space of critique, even as it capitalizes on their value as publicity.

Exemplary in this regard are the montage sequences in *Sexual Reincarnation*, which remediate news reports and press photographs concerning Mishima's attempted coup and his suicide in close-ups. Noteworthy here is the fact the purported "political" nature of this news is aligned with the ultra-Right nationalist wing of militant activism. When read together with films like *Sex Jack*, *Season of Terror*, and *Ecstasy of Angels*, which explicitly deal with the militancy of the New Left activists, Wakamatsu's handling of journalistic materials in *Sexual Reincarnation* reveals a formal consistency; regardless of the ideological orientation, all news pertaining to the political activism of the Left *and* the Right is presented in the same manner. The direct remediation of headlines and photographs published in newspapers, magazines, and print advertisements as well as the audio sampling of radio and television news are recurrent formal techniques used in many of his films. The indiscriminate treatment of journalistic information pertaining to the political activism of this period suggests that the policing function of mediatization is not wedded to any particular ideological orientation. The process of turning activism into media spectacle erases the purported difference between the Left and the Right as it homogenizes the images of staged dissent and resistance. The attempted coup by the Right and the attempted revolutionary uprising by the Left become equivalent as information; their images become exchangeable as they circulate in the media. It is this leveling force of commodification that undergirds the constant flow of the journalistic economy of the image. However, when the same news is appropriated by cinema, it interrupts the flow of information. By creating redundancy, the cinematic repetition of the news draws attention to the policing nature of the spectacle itself.

Some of the films made by Wakamatsu in the late 1960s appropriate topical news about violence without making direct reference either to the New Left student movement or to the right-wing political activism. For instance, the film *Violated Angels*—invited to the Cannes International Film Festival along with *Sex Jack*—draws on the famous mass killing of student nurses by Richard Speck in Chicago in 1966, an incident that received much news coverage during his trial the following year.[33] Wakamatsu produced the film with his own funds in 1967, and invited Kara Jūrō, the founder of the Situation Theater, to perform the leading role. The decidedly non-pink status of the film may account for the experimental look of the work. However, its handling of journalistic materials is clearly consistent with his other films from this period.

As in *Sexual Reincarnation*, the film *Violated Angels* includes eye-catching montage sequences composed of still images extracted from newspapers and magazines, though this time the images are not directly linked to the original incident involving Speck on which the narrative is based. More precisely, the film opens with a montage sequence that mixes erotic photographs of women taken from pornographic magazines with still photographs of Kara. The film closes with another striking montage sequence, which alternates a freeze-frame shot of two policemen with raised truncheons with a series of remediated images from newspapers and weekly magazines, many of which reference then current news about the massive student protests against the Vietnam War. The formal structure of the opening and the closing sequences suggest two things: first, the sensational crime of Richard Speck is syntagmatically linked to pornography on the one hand and to political activism on the other; and second, pornography and political activism are rendered equivalent to one another insofar as they circulate as commodities in the economy of journalism.

Scholars of Japanese cinema have failed to analyze the connection between the film's timely appropriation of the crime of Richard Speck and the wider journalistic economy of news. In his discussion of *Violated Angels*, for instance, Noël Burch makes a cursory comment on these montage sequences and the journalistic sensibility of Wakamatsu: "The film was inspired by the notorious massacre of the 'Chicago nurses' and is said to have been shot within a week of that horrendous event. Actual, recent events have often provided the raw material for Wakamatsu's fantasies, as they did for Adachi Masao, his new script-writer, who was to influence the new direction of his work."[34] While Burch's observation about Wakamatsu and Adachi's appropriation of "actual, recent events" is correct, his analysis of the film misses its critical intervention into the journalistic economy of the image. Burch hastily concludes that the film creates a "mechanical association of unbridled sexual fulfillment with revolutionary politics, an association which characterizes not only much independent film-work, but also the ideology of certain ultra-Leftist groups in Japan."[35]

But, as we saw in *Sex Jack* and *Sexual Reincarnation*, it is precisely such a mechanical association between sex and revolutionary politics that Wakamatsu's work leads us to question. If sex and revolutionary politics are associated, it is because the news media have already transformed both into spectacles of equivalent value. Moreover, Burch's interpretation of the opening and closing montage sequences overly psychologizes their significance. He argues that the "two essentially extra-diegetic sequences [are] meant to ground the hero's psychosis in social reality, to designate it as emblematic of social and political repression and revolt." Burch remains skeptical of the film's purported distancing effects, noting that it simply draws a homology between "sexual alienation" and "the economic, political and ideological alienation" endemic in capitalist society.[36] However, this reading obscures the crucial difference between the police order and politics proper. Politics in Burch is reduced to a one-dimensional sphere of repression, alienation, and senseless revolt.

Burch also posits sex and politics as categorically different elements—as if one is "private" and the other is "public"—and the connection between the two is assumed to reside in the classical Marxist framework of alienation. Yet if we were to consider the mediatization of political activism that blurs the boundary between the Left and the Right, a simple analogy between sex and politics based on the concept of alienation does not hold. At stake in *Violated Angels*, as well as in other films made by Wakamatsu in the 1960s and early 1970s, is the policing *effect* of this mediatization itself, which renders political activism and sex as equivalents at the level of spectacle. Once they enter into the journalistic economy of the image, spectacles of politics and sex equally command the attention of the consumers. Understood in this manner, the relation between the pornographic photographs used in the opening montage sequence and the still images of policemen and student protests in the closing montage sequence becomes clear—this is the relation of exchangeability. By formally treating sex and politics as exchangeable spectacles, *Violated Angels* also directs our attention to the mediating role of journalism. This is done through the timely remediation of sensational images extracted from the newspapers and magazines. What becomes visible through this process is the very force of journalistic media to flatten the difference between different types of spectacles in accordance with the commodity logic of exchangeability.

Another film that directly references a violent crime is *Go, Go, Second Time Virgin*, made in 1969, two years after *Violated Angels*. Stylistically, this film closely resembles *Sexual Reincarnation* in its use of a rapid montage sequence that flashes across the screen without a clear narrative motivation. As in the case of *Sexual Reincarnation*, this sequence parades shocking images concerning the murder of the American actress Sharon Tate by the followers of Charles Manson in 1969. The news reports and press photographs about Tate's murder alternate with comic-book images that graphically depict scenes of death and violence. In his analysis of *Go, Go, Second Time Virgin*, David Desser also comments on the film's citational strategy. Like Burch, he too focuses on the narrative effect of this sequence and reduces it to character psychology: "As in *Violated Women* [*Violated Angels*], Wakamatsu shows still images drawn from commercial exploitation forms, except in this later film, he shows them at the end, forcing a kind of retrospective understanding of the hero's motivations."[37] However, explaining this sudden intrusion of nondiegetic journalistic materials through the framework of the character's motivation misses the point. The graphic violence in this montage works in the exact same way as the opening and closing montages in *Violated Angels*. They guide the spectator's attention to the journalistic production of spectacles that equates crime, sex, and politics. In so doing, these montages place the cinematic remediation of these spectacles in quotation marks, as it were.

In order to better understand the rhetorical strategy of remediation used by Wakamatsu, we also need to note the temporal proximity between the original news and its reappearance in the film. As with *Sexual Reincarnation* and Mishima's infamous spectacle, the time lag between the release date of *Go, Go, Second Time Virgin* and the date of Sharon Tate's murder is quite small. One month after the news of Tate's murder, the film was already playing in theaters. Citational practice of remediation in relation to the *speed* of the journalistic economy of information, especially news, bears further investigation here. Remediation presupposes repetition, and the cinematic repetition of journalistic information implies its belatedness. This belatedness of repetition suggests a critical gap between journalism and cinema; it is this gap or the time lag that interrupts an otherwise steady flow of news as information. The lag is short enough for the film's citational gesture to appear timely and actual, but long enough to prove that the temporality of the two economies of the image is not exactly the same. It is this temporal element of *proximity*—very close, but not simultaneous—that heightens the spectator's awareness of the marked difference between the journalistic economy of the image and the cinematic economy of the image.

Two months after the release of *Go, Go, Second Time Virgin*, Wakamatsu released yet another film, *Season of Terror*, which again opens with a spectacular montage composed of remediated press photographs and newspaper headlines. The sequence begins with an enlarged snapshot of riot police clashing with demonstrating students. The rough, grainy texture of the image and the vertical lines running across it suggest that the photograph is printed on inexpensive newsprint. The film cuts to a partial image of a newspaper headline and an accompanying photograph of a burning building. The montage proceeds to other stills, which include more images of the riot police, mass protests, arrests of demonstrators, and the military training session of a right-wing group. Meanwhile, the fragments of headlines report on the record-breaking number of student arrests, riots, and interfactional conflicts among the militant New Left students. Although the sequence itself is composed of still images, the use of fast fade-in and fade-out adds an optical rhythm, generating a subtle impression of movement.

However, as if to remind the spectator of the rhetorical function of this sequence as citation, the sequence ends with an abrupt cut to a medium shot in which a magazine with a right-wing nationalist group pictured on its cover is thrown down on the table by an invisible hand. The film then cuts to a long static shot of a housing complex and the fictional narrative of the New Left activist finally begins.[38] The artifactual effect of this sequence indicates that the images of political activism presented in the film are mediated by journalism, and the film belatedly remediates its products. The temporal factor of *belatedness* marks this process of remediation, which ultimately questions the legitimacy of the original.

Taken as a whole, Wakamatsu's films from the 1960s and early 1970s consistently play with the temporal lag between the journalistic production of information and the cinematic reproduction of it. In so doing, they draw attention to the artifactual nature of the information and the spectacularity of political activism, sex, and crime when mediated by journalism. The recurrent motifs of political activism, sex, and crime in his work are also deeply implicated in the differing economic structures of attention management in cinema and journalism. The cinematic production of spectacle is inseparable from the economic management of attention. As Jean-François Lyotard notes, the management of attention in cinema is doubly economic, as it attempts to secure a financial return by imposing the good order (in a sense of *oikonomia*), channeling the libidinal investment of the spectator into the narrative order through the staging of the mise-en-scène and the calculated processes of editing and framing.[39] Moreover, the effective orientation of the spectator's attention often works through the combination of stillness and movement, and thus the commanding power of the spectacle in cinema often takes advantage of the freeze-frame. As Mulvey and others have noted, the attention-commanding power of the cinematic spectacle is especially heightened when the image remains still and thus halts the flow of the moving image.[40] Something similar happens with the deliberate mixing of the journalistic economy of the image and the cinematic economy of the image. Wakamatsu's calculated remediation of already spectacularized images of sexual and political violence, such as Tate's murder, the anti-Vietnam war protests, and the Yodogō Hijacking Incident, halts the flow of the journalistic economy, reorients its direction, and commands critical attention from the spectator as it plays up the temporal gap between these two modes of image consumption and circulation. In so doing, it suggests that the temporal structures of cinema and journalism are not the same.

CINEMA AND THE LOGIC OF EXPIRATION

Another issue that emerges from the tension between the temporality of cinema and that of journalism is expiration. With the issue of expiration, we return to the question of journalistic actuality, which requires us to rethink the concept of actuality in relation to the temporal attributes of news. Wakamatsu's well-timed appropriation of high-profile media events and sensational crime news is marked by the belatedness of their repetition. The idea of belatedness deserves scrutiny if we are to fully understand the temporal difference between the cinematic and journalistic economies of the image. As Tosaka reminds us, "A news report stops being news if it loses its current relevance."[41] The concept of journalism, which etymologically suggests a link to the cyclical concept of the diurnal (*diurnalis* in Latin), is inseparable from the temporal attribute of being current or existing now; this attribute is what he calls "actuality."[42] As is often noted, journalistic information loses its value as time passes; the actuality of news quickly becomes obsolete. The value of information so central to journalism is time-sensitive. The temporally bound value of information in the journalistic economy has been repeatedly pointed out by scholars such as Walter Benjamin, Mary Ann Doane, and Niklas Luhmann, to name a few. To repeat Benjamin: "The value of information does not survive the moment in which it was new."[43] What defines the obsoleteness of journalistic information is, in short, its status of being out-of-date. Conversely, the temporal attribute of actuality that defines journalism is threatened by its *expirability*; the inevitability—and threat—of expiration is constitutive of journalistic actuality. Journalistic actuality is thus defined by this capacity to expire, and it operates in a particular mode of temporality punctuated by the cyclical rhythm of news production. This is why the notion of actuality is opposed to the notion of eternity.[44] The logic of expiration that structures the production of news and the expirable nature of actuality define the temporal economy of journalism.

Yet a third element also defines this temporally bound economy of journalistic information. This is *non-redundancy*. According to Luhmann, "Information cannot be repeated; as soon as it becomes an event, it becomes non-information. A news item run twice might still have its meaning, but it loses its information value."[45] In other words, repetition is detrimental to the "actual" value of the journalistic information, as it creates redundancy. Coming out of the pink-film industry, which capitalizes on a fast cycle of production and sensational news, Wakamatsu's work seems to align itself with the journalistic economy of the image. Nonetheless, his films also work against the economic logic of information; the redundancy of the sensational news quoted and repeated undermines its information value. If we take this point seriously, the time lag that Wakamatsu introduces between the cinematic and journalistic economies of the image through his citation and remediation of news gains new significance. The repetition opens up a critical interval between journalistic actuality and cinematic actuality, and this interval allows the viewer to separate information from citation. Accordingly, we may surmise that the dissemination of newsworthy information is neither the goal nor the intended effect of his remediation strategy. On the contrary, the divestment of information value seems to go hand in hand with the investment in something properly cinematic.

Here, Wakamatsu's work urges us to consider another important historical shift that took place concurrently with the mediatization of politics: the changing perception of cinema as commodity. Japan in the 1960s witnessed the dramatic decline of the major studios, which in turn helped small independent film productions to thrive and alternative modes of distribution and exhibition to flourish. The complementary developments of the pink film and art cinema (exemplified by the establishment of ATG, which specialized in the distribution, exhibition, and production of art films) indicate the changing configuration of the Japanese film industry at the time. As art cinema flourished, the status of film changed from being a temporally bound commodity stamped with a short expiration date to being an enduring work of art worthy of being archived and appreciated time and again. Wakamatsu's work straddles these two fields of filmmaking, which diverge significantly in terms of their temporal logics. The turnover time of the pink-film market critically differs from that of the art-cinema market. While the fast-and-cheap production and exhibition cycle of the pink film in the 1960s maintained the journalistic speed of the so-called program pictures, the production and exhibition cycle of art films did not follow the weekly cycle of the program picture. In this regard, the establishment of ATG, in 1961, was groundbreaking, as it clearly set the nonjournalistic pace of production, distribution, and exhibition.

In addition to fostering close interactions among avant-garde and more commercially oriented filmmakers, ATG made a particularly noteworthy contribution to the transformation of the cinematic economy of the image. It revolutionized the exhibition cycle, adopting the so-called long-run screening style. As Roland Domenig points out, "One of ATG's basic rules was to show each film for at least a month, irrespective of attendance. In the 1960s, the repertoire was usually changed weekly, and a four-week run was exceptional even for box-office hits."[46] ATG thus deviated and broke free from the previously dominant temporality of the cinematic economy of the image grounded in the weekly cycle. This dramatic shift in the exhibition cycle was significant, since it freed cinema from the structure of periodicity that the system of the program picture established and maintained during the 1950s.

It is here that our earlier examination of the journalistic logic of expiration becomes relevant. The Japanese film industry in the 1950s produced films that were branded with an expiration date. Films as commodities had to be consumed—much like news—within a particular time span and according to a periodic cycle. Cinema had a parallel temporal economy to journalism during the 1950s, when the system of the program picture was upholding the industry, insofar as the cinema, like journalism, was based around a cycle of expiration. Arguably, however, the temporal distance between cinema and journalism became much greater in the 1960s, when independent production companies and avant-garde filmmakers started to set up an alternative circuit of production, distribution, and exhibition.

In this regard it is suggestive that in 1961 Oshima published "A Challenge to Vulgar Beliefs about Cinema," an essay in which he protests the general public's perception of cinema as a commodity "that disappears in a week or two." He squarely contests a journalistic view of film as a commodity branded with an expiration date.

> Japan is now finally entering the era of big-budget, long-run filmmaking. This reflects a logical demand of the time, since we are finally realizing that a film cannot entertain without aspiring to be an artwork, a quality without which cinema cannot compete against other forms of entertainment. Accordingly, a work of film that attains this artistic quality does not lose its value after a short period of time, which is why it generates a demand for the long-run exhibition of great films.[47]

Oshima presses his point that the "vulgar" conception of cinema as a mere commodity needs to be abandoned if cinema is to survive its competition with television. Oshima's affirmation of cinema's artistic value over its journalistic value is an argument for its timeless quality over its expirability. It is precisely this shift from being an *expirable* commodity to being a *timeless* artwork that marks the cinema's liberation from its subordination to the temporal economy of journalism.

As if to echo Oshima's sentiment, Wakamatsu argues that the filmmaker is always responsible for his work and that "there is no statute of limitations or parole for a filmmaker."[48] As the legal metaphor of the statute of limitations suggests, Wakamatsu's positioning of cinema as something timeless foregrounds not its artistic merits, but the responsibility of the filmmaker for his work. Yet Oshima and Wakamatsu share the view that the temporality of cinema must be distinguished from that of journalism; it is not dictated by the logic of expiration. Wakamatsu's remediation strategy can be read in relation to this changing conception of cinema's *own* temporality, which is no longer subordinated to and modeled after journalism. Crucial here, once again, is the difference between the two types of image economies that Wakamatsu's citational use of journalism makes visible and analyzable.

In conclusion, let us return to *Sexual Reincarnation*, a film which openly parodies the Mishima Incident. This film draws on the most sensational aspects of Mishima's failed coup attempt and his suicide, by remediating numerous photographs of Mishima clad in the uniform of his private army and even his handwritten death poems. Importantly, *Sexual Reincarnation* parodies not only the media event that occurred on 25 November 1970, but also Mishima's film *Patriotism*. The reference to *Patriotism* is made explicit by the character traits of the protagonist, a right-wing nationalist and member of Mishima's private army who was described as having failed to participate in Mishima's actual coup attempt. Furthermore, not only does Wakamatsu replicate the whole setup of the young man who misses the historic opportunity to participate in a coup d'état, but he also appropriates Mishima's own appropriation, in *Patriotism*, of an actual historic event, the famous February 26 Incident. This incident, which took place in 1936, also was a failed coup, carried out by young ultranationalist officers of the Imperial Japanese Army who revolted against the government in the name of their loyalty to the emperor. Several top cabinet members were assassinated and martial law was declared, putting Japan under a state of emergency. In the end the emperor refused to support the insurrection, just as the soldiers of the Self-Defense Forces refused to respond to Mishima's call for insurrection.

Key to this layering of textual and historical references is the *untimeliness* of the action taken by those who envision revolutionary change. The trope of failure to participate in major revolutionary actions, a point made by both *Patriotism* and *Sexual Reincarnation*, is bound to the untimely nature of insurrections that failed to make history. In this regard Mishima's deliberate staging of his coup attempt as a media event appears self-conscious. He orchestrated this historic event for the camera, called the Mainichi newspaper and NHK television reporters, and thus anticipated *timely* responses from journalists.[49] The media indeed responded to the call for timely coverage and collaborated with Mishima to stage his final act, a political spectacle that clearly echoed and imitated the fictional ending of the spectacular suicide in *Patriotism*. Nonetheless, Mishima failed to realize his coup d'état. What *Sexual Reincarnation* parodies, then, is not simply the Mishima Incident of 25 November 1970, but the mediatization of politics in which journalists and revolutionaries equally participate. Even the unlikely choice of classical music Wakamatsu used in *Sexual Reincarnation* is a reference to Mishima's film *Patriotism*, which uses the score of Wagner's magnanimous opera *Tristan und Isolde*.[50] By remediating the journalistic coverage of Mishima's coup attempt and his subsequent suicide, and by appropriating Mishima's fictional work that prefigured these actions, *Sexual Reincarnation* exposes the fundamentally theatrical—and artifactual—nature of actuality staged for and through the media.

Wakamatsu's work exploits the artifactual dimension of media events and competes with the journalistic economy of information and the image without ever coinciding with it. The element of belatedness that marks his strategy of remediation, which relentlessly cites, parodies, and recycles sensational news, allows us to see the critical difference between the temporal economies of journalism and cinema. While Wakamatsu's films display the generic traits of the pink film and may appear to stand apart from more straightforwardly experimental works of filmmakers such as Matsumoto and Oshima, their work shares something fundamentally similar: a critical attitude toward the proximity between cinema and journalism. Wakamatsu's work constantly toys with this proximity, and in so doing draws our attention to the critical potential of cinema to interrupt the smooth flow of the journalistic economy. This calculated intervention into the journalistic economy of the image during the height of the intensifying mediatization of politics is what makes Wakamatsu's films so provocative, insofar as they complicate the presumed alliance between political activism and the cinema of actuality.

four

diagramming the landscape

Power and the Fūkeiron Discourse

On 7 April 1969, breaking news of the arrest of a nineteen-year-old teenager named Nagayama Norio was all over the front pages of Japanese newspapers. Nagayama's arrest and his subsequent fame as a self-made novelist during his incarceration turned his case into one of the most memorable juvenile crime cases in postwar Japan. The media dubbed Nagayama a "pistol serial killer" in reference to the four homicides he committed in October and November 1968. His arrest and the ensuing blanket coverage of his background—poverty-stricken childhood, job-hopping, stowaway attempts, and petty thefts—highlighted the fact that he had relocated from a rural village to a metropolis in search of menial jobs right after graduating from junior high school. In narrating Nagayama's life, the media frequently invoked the clichéd trope of urban alienation to explain his fall into criminality. The 8 April editorial of the national newspaper *Asahi shinbun*, for instance, faulted the solitude of living in the city, all the while stressing the ordinariness of the criminal ("a typical youth who can be found anywhere").[1]

The timing of Nagayama's arrest explains the media's insistent reference to the idea of an ordinary youth turning violent, which metonymically links this stand-alone crime to the continuing stream of news on escalating violence among student activists. Violence was always newsworthy, but particularly so in the late 1960s, when the student movement turned visibly militant. Physical confrontations between armed riot police and student demonstrators were frequent, and the images of riot police and helmeted students gathering en masse flooded the news media. Indeed, these images had functioned, and continue to function, as the most recognizable icon of the "season of politics." The height of this intensely mediatized era of political activism was 1968 and 1969, the years that witnessed widespread combative and spectacular forms of student protests led by the Zenkyōtō (All-Campus Joint Struggle Committee) generation.[2] Universities across Japan were barricaded and occupied one after the other. Students armed with wooden staves (*gebabō* or "Gewalt Staves") and colorful helmets marking their sectarian affiliations openly embraced violence—or *Gewalt*, as they called it—as a legitimate means of opposing state power.

In Japan—as in Europe and the United States—the widely circulated images of armed protesters and barricaded campuses came to represent the years immediately preceding and following 1968. There was a sense of global synchronicity among student activists. Echoing the jubilant mood of May '68 in France, the students called occupied streets of Tokyo *Kanda Quartier latin*, and the anti-Vietnam War protest movement organized by the Beheiren group was calling for pan-Asian solidarity.[3] Several events that took place during 1968–69 became particularly central to the historiography of the Japanese student protest movement. In October 1968—the same month when Nagayama killed two security guards and one taxi driver—a massive anti-Vietnam War protest broke out in the nearby Shinjuku Station. Thousands of protesters and onlookers gathered around Shinjuku station and clashed with riot police. The government reacted by invoking the Riot Law, and hundreds of arrests were made overnight.

Another pivotal incident that received wide media coverage was the so-called fall of the Yasuda Auditorium in January 1969. Taking place at the prestigious University of Tokyo, this event came to emblematize the blatant suppression of the student movement by the state as well as the intensified media consumption of such an act of suppression as spectacle. When the government finally ordered the Tokyo Metropolitan Police to break through the barricaded auditorium, which had been occupied by the students since the summer of 1968, the two-day battle that ensued was broadcast live on television, with a record-breaking viewer rating.[4]

In the fall of 1969 and in the aftermath of the violent student-police confrontations earlier that year, a small group of filmmakers, including Adachi Masao and Matsuda Masao, started to document urban landscapes where Nagayama had lived and worked. While referencing the highly mediatized case of Nagayama's crime, the resulting experimental documentary film, *A.K.A. Serial Killer* (*Ryakushō renzoku shasatsuma*, 1969), carefully avoids showing recognizable images of violence. Immediately following the completion of *A.K.A. Serial Killer* a series of articles devoted to the question of "landscape" emerged, giving rise to a critical discourse known as *fūkeiron* (landscape theory). While it was primarily the production of *A.K.A. Serial Killer* that spurred the discourse of *fūkeiron*, another film played an equally significant role: Oshima's experimental narrative film *The Man Who Left His Will on Film* (*Tokyo sensō sengo hiwa: Eiga de isho o nokoshite shinda otoko no monogatari*, 1970), which contains a film-within-a-film similarly focused on urban landscapes. When considered together, these two films—*A.K.A. Serial Killer* and *The Man Who Left His Will on Film*—allow us to see how filming a banal landscape became a critical strategy to counteract and question the codified media representations of violence and activism, and, furthermore, to explore a new way of conceptualizing state power.

In the last chapter I noted how Wakamatsu, with the help of Adachi as his scriptwriter, drew attention to the journalistic economy of information and news. I now return to the tension between the cinema of actuality and journalism, but with a different perspective, no longer emphasizing the direct remediation of sensational news and topical journalistic images, but rather the deliberate effacement of the spectacularity associated with these materials. The guiding thread here is the problematic of landscape, an image that is utterly ordinary, eventless, and devoid of any visible conflict. In the discourse of *fūkeiron*, the landscape occupies an antithetical relation to the dramatic, spectacular images of violence and militant struggle that dominated the mass media as well as the political imagination of student activists.[5] The landscape becomes a privileged locus of analysis and critique of media representations of violence for critics as well as filmmakers.

The turn toward the landscape by filmmakers such as Adachi and Oshima in, respectively, *A.K.A. Serial Killer* and *The Man Who Left His Will on Film* indicates a twofold attempt to differentiate cinema's engagement with political violence from its journalistic counterpart and to complicate the standard conception of film as a political weapon. The concurrent theorization of landscape by the fūkeiron critics, including Adachi himself, also marks a crucial shift in the conception of state power. The critique of the state generated by the discourse of fūkeiron directs attention toward the nonspectacular and nonrepressive mechanisms of control and governance built into the everyday environment. Instead of focusing on the repressive forces of the state that make themselves visible in the spectacular form of antagonism between protestors and police, the discourse of fūkeiron focuses our attention on the ways the governmental power of the state operates through the built environment itself. Which is to say, the relation between the landscape and the state articulated by the fūkeiron critics hinges on the broader operation of *governmentality*.[6] The cinematic landscapes examined by the fūkeiron discourse and captured in the two films mentioned above thus function as a diagram of governmental power.[7]

LANDSCAPE FILMS

The main theorist of the fūkeiron discourse is Matsuda Masao, a former professional Marxist revolutionary, a chief editor of the activist film journal *Eiga Hihyō II*, and one of the creators of *A.K.A. Serial Killer*.[8] Matsuda appeared in Oshima's *Death by Hanging* along with Adachi, another key participant of the fūkeiron discourse and the principal director of *A.K.A. Serial Killer*. Two years after the making of *A.K.A. Serial Killer*, Adachi returned to a more overtly militant mode of filmmaking with the agitprop newsreel *The Red Army/PFLP: Declaration of World War* (*Sekigun-PFLP: Sekai sensō sengen*, 1971).

Because little has been written on Adachi's work, it is worth providing a brief overview of his filmmaking career. While a student at Nihon University, he started to make experimental films and joined the legendary Nichidai Eiken (Nihon University Film Study Group), a radical student organization closely associated with the university's branch of the Japan Revolutionary Communist League (BUND) and founded by experimental filmmakers such as Hirano Katsumi, Jōnouchi Motoharu, and Kanbara Hiroshi, who worked closely with avant-garde artists and musicians such as the members of Neo-Dada Organizers and Group Ongaku. Together with Jōnouchi, Kanbara, and a few others, Adachi founded the experimental film collective VAN Film Research Center (VAN Eiga Kagaku Kenkyūjo) in 1960. VAN became a popular hang-out for radical activists and artists who worked in various areas of cinema, photography, music, theater, and graphic design.[9] For instance, Adachi appears in Jōnouchi's *Hi Red Center Shelter Plan* (*Hai reddo sentaa sheru-taa puran*, 1964), an experimental documentary film that records the happening staged by Hi Red Center, an avant-garde collective formed by Akawasegawa Genpei, Nakanishi Natsuyuki, and Takamatsu Jirō.[10] Before joining Wakamatsu Production, Adachi also directed several renowned experimental films made with the Nihon University Film Study Group, including *Bowl* (*Wan*, 1961) and *Closed Vagina* (*Sain*, 1963). For *Closed Vagina*, Adachi collaborated with the avant-garde composer Ichiyanagi Toshi, and the film was later screened at Art Theatre Shinjuku Bunka.[11] This late-night screening of *Closed Vagina*, in 1965, influenced the manager Kuzui Kinshirō to commission Adachi to make an experimental film, *Galaxy* (*Gingakei*, 1967), which inaugurated the opening of the underground Theatre Scorpio, in August 1967. The film was publicized as "the first work of underground cinema" in Japan.[12] From the mid-1960s to the early 1970s, Adachi worked for Wakamatsu mostly as a scriptwriter. During this time, he directed several feature-length films, including *Contraceptive Revolution* (*Hinin kakumei*, 1966), *Sex Zone* (*Sei chitai*, 1968), and *School Girl Guerrilla* (*Jogakusei gerira*, 1969). In the late 1960s, Adachi also worked as a scriptwriter for Oshima.[13] Adachi's involvement in the making of *A.K.A. Serial Killer* and the discourse of fūkeiron thus followed years of close collaboration with a wide range of avant-garde artists, activists, and filmmakers.

A.K.A. Serial Killer was a collaborative work of filmmakers and critics who worked closely with Oshima and Wakamatsu.[14] Noteworthy here is the participation of Sasaki Mamoru in the making of *A.K.A. Serial Killer*. Sasaki was a co-scriptwriter for *The Man Who Left His Will on Film*. Made a few months after *A.K.A. Serial Killer*, *The Man Who Left His Will on Film* is a fiction film dedicated to the "War of Tokyo." In Oshima's view, the New Left student movement that intensified during 1968–69 and culminated in the occupation of Tokyo University and the antiwar demonstrations in Shinjuku was a failed revolution. This revolutionary struggle, "at its peak, was dubbed the War of Tokyo by the Red Army Faction," and it ended "in a mood of defeat."[15] In direct reference to the ongoing student movement, which continued after the unsuccessful insurrection by the Red Army Faction in the fall of 1969, Oshima incorporates in *The Man Who Left His Will on Film* timely documentary footage of a mass demonstration filmed during Okinawa Day on 28 April 1970. This footage is thematically and visually juxtaposed to the film-within-a-film, which presents a remarkable formal similarity to *A.K.A. Serial Killer*. The visual predominance of static long shots of cityscapes often devoid of human presence characterizes *A.K.A. Serial Killer* and the film-within-a-film of *The Man Who Left His Will on Film*.

Both films are equally obsessed with the eventless space of everyday life subsequent to a systemic crackdown on the student movement. They are "landscape films" (*fūkei eiga*), as the fūkeiron critics called them.[16]

But why landscape? What is the significance of shooting utterly ordinary, unremarkable scenery that lacks both drama and human action? One way to answer such questions is to examine the formal elements of the landscape films. The distinctive aesthetic of the landscape films, which seems to appropriate and imitate the pre-documentary genre of actuality films, stands in opposition both to the dominant aesthetics of the mass media as well as the forms of militant documentary filmmaking prevalent in the late 1960s.

FILM AS A POLITICAL WEAPON

The late 1960s is often singled out as the most vibrant era of militant documentary filmmaking, which traversed national borders in association with various waves of revolutionary movements. One may cite as its most celebrated example the Argentine filmmakers Fernando Solanas's and Octavio Getino's manifesto, *La hora de los hornos* (*The Hour of the Furnaces*, 1968), a cornerstone of the Third Cinema movement. Here we have the sound of machine guns firing in perfect synch with a rapid montage of still images of fashion models, Batman, cowboys, and bleeding Vietnamese children—a famous sequence emblematizing the activist notion of film as a political weapon, a militant ideal engraved deeply in the history of leftist filmmaking. The sound of machine guns and the image of bullet holes also mark the final shot of the Cuban filmmaker Santiago Álvarez's *Now* (1965), a work of remediation that creates a dramatic montage of audiovisual materials appropriated from American media sources.[17] Solanas and Getino spell out the alliance between cinema and militancy: "The camera is the inexhaustible *expropriator of image-weapons*; the projector, *a gun that can shoot 24 frames per second*."[18]

Crucially, this militant vision of film activism analogized to armed resistance was not limited to Latin America, but was widely shared among leftist documentary filmmakers in other parts of the world. In the United States, for instance, the New Left documentary collective Newsreel, with its machine-gun logo, is most closely associated with the militant vision of film as a weapon.[19] In Europe, Jean-Luc Godard and Jean-Pierre Gorin formed a militant film collective, the Dziga Vertov Group, in the immediate aftermath of the insurrection of May '68.[20] In Japan, a new form of collective documentary filmmaking exemplified by the work of Ogawa Shinsuke and Tsuchimoto Noriaki responded to the increasing demands by student activists and workers to document and support their protest movements. Like Newsreel, Ogawa and Tsuchimoto turned their cameras toward students, workers, and farmers behind barricades, and joined their struggles not as distant observers but as intimate participants. The most emblematic examples of such direct participation in political activism are perhaps Ogawa's *Report from Haneda* (*Gennin hōkoku: Haneda tōsō no kiroku*, 1967) as well as his Sanrizuka series, and Tsuchimoto's *Prehistory of the Partisan Party* (*Paruchizan zenshi*, 1969).[21]

Yet at the height of such political upheaval and the spread of activist filmmaking in Japan and abroad, Adachi and his associates decided to turn their camera to mundane landscapes devoid of dramatic action. Although *A.K.A. Serial Killer* presents itself as nonfiction, its approach to its subject matter is antithetical to the Griersonian ideal of classical documentary filmmaking, famously defined as "the creative treatment of actuality."[22] Nothing exciting happens or appears in *A.K.A. Serial Killer*. In its insistence on a lack of drama, the film's strategy appears to resonate with some of the contemporaneous political avant-garde works of European filmmakers, especially with the work of Chantal Akerman. Akerman's *News from Home* (1976), for instance, similarly focuses on the eventless landscapes of New York City, eschewing dramatic action in favor of the mundane sight of the urban environment. Nonetheless, *A.K.A. Serial Killer* significantly differs from *News from Home* because of its temporal and referential proximity to a contemporary media event: Nagayama's crime. While taking on one of the most "actual" news events of the time, *A.K.A. Serial Killer* adamantly refuses to reproduce the sensationalist and sentimental tone of the mass media. Furthermore, because of its peculiar obsession with quotidian landscapes, *A.K.A. Serial Killer* stands apart from the majority of militant, leftist documentaries of the time, which emphatically turn the camera toward the individual faces of social actors engaged in critical situations.

Among the classical images presented by the leftist documentary films of the 1960s are those of police brutality, picketing workers, and marching students. These images convey a sense of urgency, eventfulness, and excitement. Despite the susceptibility of images to commodification by the media, many filmmakers felt it necessary to produce and circulate these images at the time. As Michael Renov notes in his discussion of Newsreel, "There was a perceived need for immediate coverage of events from a leftist perspective."[23] Japanese filmmakers shared this awareness of the need to document political struggles. In a 1967 interview, Ogawa speaks of the sense of urgency he felt about getting involved in the filming of student activism: "I had a gut-level fear that I was becoming apathetic toward politics while making P.R. films [public-relations films]. . . . And when I saw the struggle of student protesters at Meiji University, I felt a strong urge to do something about the reality presented there from my own [professional] position."[24] This interview took place immediately after Ogawa finished making *Forest of Pressure* (*Assatsu no mori*, 1967), a widely acclaimed documentary film about student activism at the Takasaki City University of Economics.

Japanese film critics welcomed Ogawa's work with enthusiasm. Along with the work of Tsuchimoto, who directed *Prehistory of the Partisan Party* with Ogawa Productions, Ogawa's documentary films significantly changed the way in which leftist filmmakers expressed their commitment to activism. As Abé Mark Nornes observes, "Ogawa and Tsuchimoto's films documented the thrill of independence, of crossing barricade lines and taking sides. This bold move attracted the burgeoning student movement, making the filmmakers cultural heroes of the left."[25] At the time of its release, Matsuda hailed Ogawa's *Forest of Pressure* for taking an activist stance. Commenting on the sequence from *Forest of Pressure* wherein student protesters violently clash with police in front of the courthouse, Matsuda writes: "A riot policeman reaches his hand forward with the intention of taking off the white cloths masking the students' faces. Even a piece of white cloth, here, can become a weapon. And when the documentarian gives up his camera and tries to guard the masked fighters—the student troopers—with his own body, this documentary proves itself to be a masterpiece."[26] Matsuda celebrates the determination of the filmmaker to stand by student activists as he relinquishes his camera in order to offer his own body as a shield to block the advancing riot police. Although Matsuda became critical of Ogawa's subsequent films, he was quite supportive of *Forest of Pressure*. Another critic who expressed similar admiration for Ogawa was Oshima. In an essay published in the film journal *Eiga Hihyō II* in 1970, Oshima gave the highest praise for Ogawa, calling him a filmmaker who deserves his "utmost respect."[27] Oshima was deeply impressed by Ogawa's ability to document not only the dramatic sights of armed struggle, but also the introspective moments of group discussion held by students and farmers.

Although it was made only two years after *Forest of Pressure*, Adachi's *A.K.A. Serial Killer* radically departs from this celebrated tradition of militant documentary filmmaking. There are no iconic, urgent images of historic events or heroic figures in *A.K.A. Serial Killer*. A simple intertitle that flatly states Nagayama's crimes ("Last fall four murders were committed in four cities using the same pistol / This spring a nineteen-year-old boy was arrested / He was called a pistol serial killer") and the occasional voiceover by Adachi (who offers chronological information about Nagayama's frequent moves from one city to another) are the only narrative contextualization the film offers. Neither Nagayama nor his victims' families appear on-screen. No interview is conducted, and no press photograph is included. Instead, the film offers us a series of discontinuous shots: houses, alleyways, train tracks, apple orchards, empty school yards, bus terminals, bridges, city streets with pedestrians, cyclists on the road, deserted metro stations, stairways leading to Nagayama's apartment, an empty jazz club, and so on. While several shots of the Self-Defense Forces and uniformed riot police strolling among pedestrians briefly appear on-screen, these images are no more privileged than the shots of anonymous boys delivering milk cartons or bundles of newspapers. Unlike Solanas's and Getino's *The Hour of the Furnaces* (1968), it does not offer an analysis of cultural imperialism or a clear indictment of the systemic violence of capitalism. In contrast to Newsreel's *Columbia Revolt* (1968) or Ogawa's *Report from Haneda* (1967), the film also steers away from focusing on iconic sights that bespeak political struggle. The lack of diegetic sounds and the use of free jazz in the soundtrack also heighten the sense of detachment. The film-within-a-film in *The Man Who Left His Will on Film* similarly generates this effect of detachment or "exteriority," an effect which derives from the film's appropriation of what Burch calls the Primitive Mode of Representation.[28]

The first thing to note is that landscape shots in *A.K.A. Serial Killer* and *The Man Who Left His Will on Film* appear self-contained, discrete, and discontinuous. While *A.K.A. Serial Killer* makes frequent use of camera movement—often starting with a static shot followed by a lateral pan—the overall effect of the two landscape films remains remarkably similar: the exteriority of the spectator in relation to the image. This effect is more strongly demonstrated in the film-within-a-film in *The*

Man Who Left His Will on Film, which is composed of six static long takes, each shot lasting more than sixty seconds.[29] The relations between the shots are not clear, since there is no apparent narrative logic to the order of the shots. We are presented with a tranquil view of rooftops, a narrow shopping street and pedestrians, a guardrail occasionally obscured by passing cars, a mailbox standing beside an underpass, a small tobacco shop seen across railway fences, and television antennas and telephone lines against the empty sky. A sense of banality permeates these urban landscapes (figures 4.1, 4.2, 4.3, 4.4, 4.5, and 4.6).[30]

Similarly, *A.K.A. Serial Killer* consists of a series of quotidian scenes: alleyways, houses, docks, rice fields, train stations, railway tracks, pedestrians, newspaper delivery boys, school girls commuting by bicycle, and housewives shopping (figures 4.7 and 4.8). The film does not offer identifiable characters or a focus on individuals. The lack of diegetic sounds also enhances a sense of distance between the spectator and the images that pass across the screen. In addition to the use of the long shot, *A.K.A. Serial Killer* makes use of lateral pans and horizontal tracking shots that move along the walls, streets, and moving vehicles. The camera does not penetrate into the space, but *looks on* the space it captures. The obtrusive lateral blurs of shadows, fences, and cars passing across the frontal plane, which momentarily but repeatedly block the full view of objects, thwart the spectatorial desire to see. The result is a frustrating experience for the spectator, who is forced to take a position external to the unsutured screen space.

Taken together, these shots present many of the characteristics of early cinema, namely, "the autarchy of tableau," "horizontal and frontal camera placement," the "maintenance of shots," "centrifugality," and "narrative non-closure."[31] Here, the spectator's position in relation to the screen space remains external. The transition from what Burch calls the Primitive Mode of Representation of early cinema to the Institutional Mode of Representation of classical narrative cinema occurs when the spectator, who was positioned outside the screen space as a distant onlooker, becomes *emplaced* within it. This "psycho-physiological orientation of the spectator" is done through the use of continuity editing and the subordination of cinematic techniques to the narrative function. The historical emergence of narrative cinema is marked by "the cinema's *centering* of the spectator," which makes her the privileged point of reference around which the entire diegetic world is organized.[32] However, the formal composition and presentation of

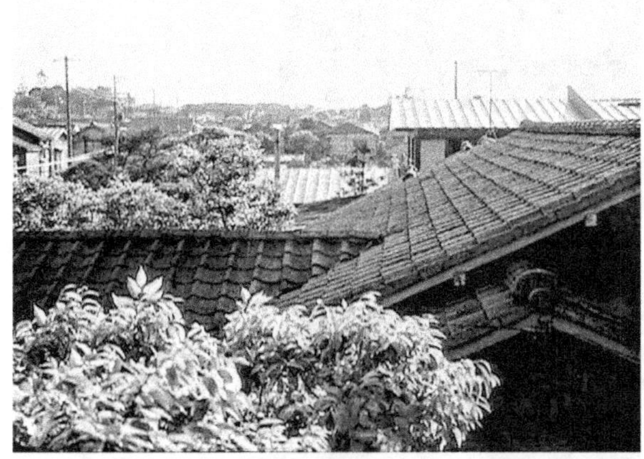

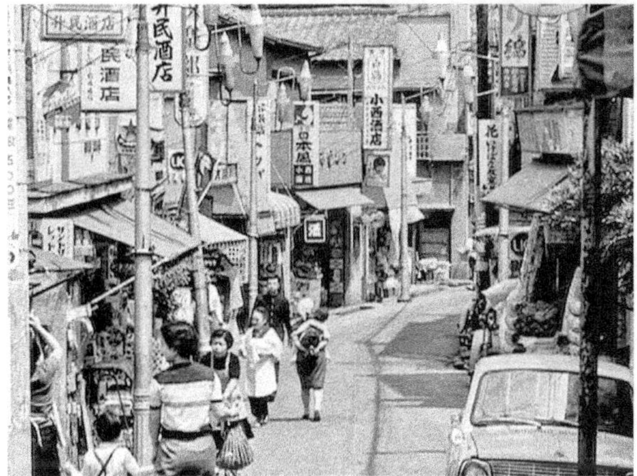

4.1. A landscape shot of rooftops. Still from *The Man Who Left His Will on Film* (1970), dir. Oshima Nagisa.

4.2. A landscape shot of a narrow shopping street. Still from *The Man Who Left His Will on Film* (1970), dir. Oshima Nagisa.

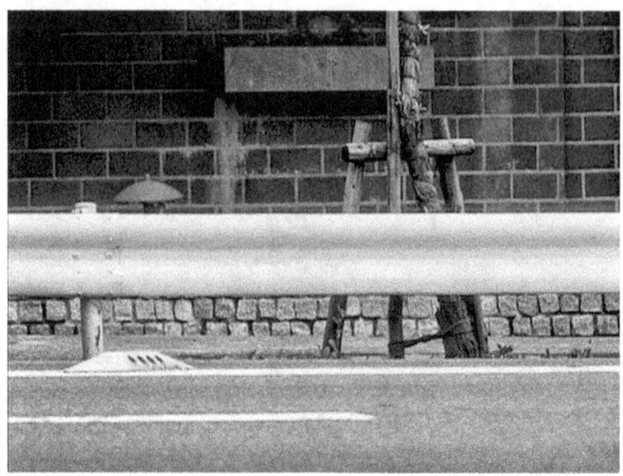

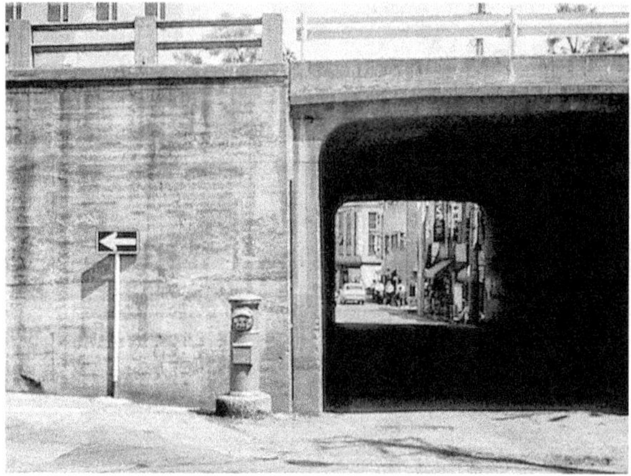

4.3. A landscape shot of a guardrail. Still from *The Man Who Left His Will on Film* (1970), dir. Oshima Nagisa.

4.4. A landscape shot of an underpass and a mailbox. Still from *The Man Who Left His Will on Film* (1970), dir. Oshima Nagisa.

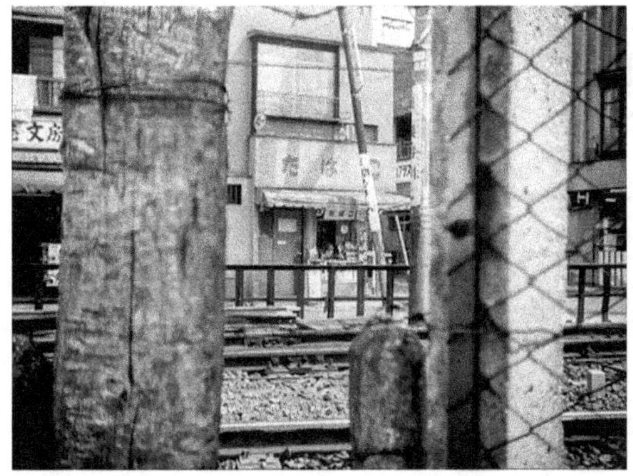

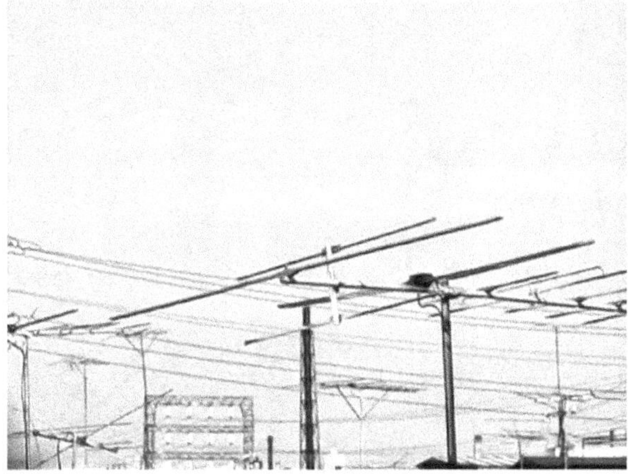

4.5. A landscape shot of a tobacco shop. Still from *The Man Who Left His Will on Film* (1970), dir. Oshima Nagisa.

4.6. A landscape shot of television antennas. Still from *The Man Who Left His Will on Film* (1970), dir. Oshima Nagisa.

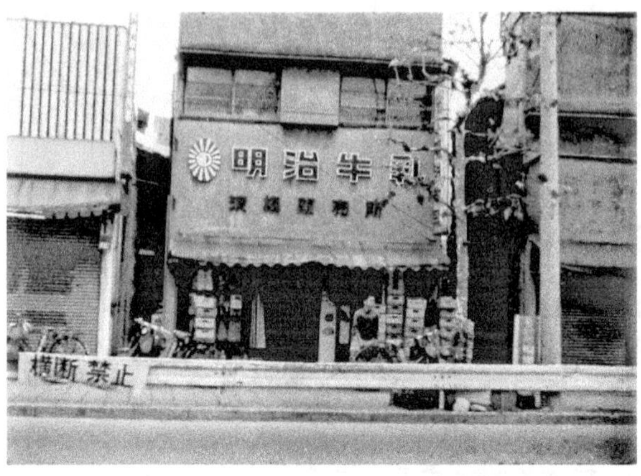

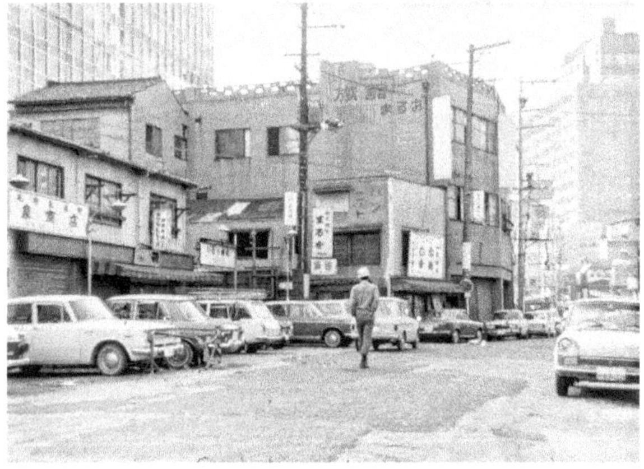

4.7. A landscape shot with a guardrail. Still from *A.K.A. Serial Killer* (1969), dir. Adachi Masao. Courtesy of Adachi Masao.

4.8. A landscape shot of an alleyway. Still from *A.K.A. Serial Killer* (1969), dir. Adachi Masao. Courtesy of Adachi Masao.

urban landscapes in *A.K.A. Serial Killer* and the film-within-a-film of *The Man Who Left His Will on Film* do not allow this crucial emplacement of the spectator into the screen space.

These landscape films also lack a clear sense of narrative closure and, most important, of dramatic development. The lack of narrative continuity in *A.K.A. Serial Killer* and the film-within-a-film of *The Man Who Left His Will on Film* sets these films apart from most documentary films, if we are to understand the term *documentary* as signifying a genre of filmmaking structured by what Philip Rosen calls "the centralization of meaning through internal sequenciation."[33] Rosen's phrase refers to the way in which shots are organized in documentary films such that they delimit and regulate meanings communicated by the filmic text. The unity of signification supported by internal sequenciation is, therefore, not limited to mainstream narrative cinema but is also observed in documentary film. In contrast, as Tom Gunning notes, early cinema lacked this "dramatic articulation of a story."[34] What connects documentary film to narrative cinema is the process of such dramatic articulation. When John Grierson defined documentary film as the "creative treatment of actuality," what he had in mind was precisely this process of dramatization. For this reason he rejected early actuality films. "They do not dramatize, they do not even dramatize an episode: they describe, and even expose, but in any aesthetic sense, only rarely reveal. Herein is their formal limit, and it is unlikely that they will make any considerable contribution to the fuller art of documentary."[35] Grierson invokes the same ideology of narrativity that characterizes mainstream narrative cinema. It is an ideology of unity and coherence; both documentary film and narrative cinema emphasize narrative coherence and control over the production of meaning. The actuality film, in contrast, puts an emphasis on display, and the Griersonian style of documentary developed through the rejection of this particular genre.[36]

A.K.A. Serial Killer and the film-within-a-film of *The Man Who Left His Will on Film*, however, seem to embrace the stylistic tendency of actuality films. Take, for instance, the second landscape shot in the film-within-a-film of *The Man Who Left His Will on Film*. The camera is positioned on the right side of a narrow shopping street. Pedestrians walk in and out of the frame while a small pickup truck passes slowly by. The use of the long shot and the camera's fixed position on the side of a city street evokes a number of actuality films, such as *New York: Broadway at Union Square* (1896) by the Lumière Brothers or *Lower Broadway*

(1903) by American Mutoscope and Biograph Company. Here, we have a similarly quotidian cityscape in which pedestrians freely walk in and out of the frame as trolleys pass by. Slow traveling shots around ports and cities filmed from a moving vehicle in *A.K.A. Serial Killer* also find striking resonance in early actuality films such as *Skyscrapers of New York City from North River* (1903) by G. A. Smith. The use of nondiegetic music throughout *A.K.A. Serial Killer* further contributes to this formal resonance with silent actualities.

A.K.A. Serial Killer's and *The Man Who Left His Will on Film*'s appropriation of the form of actuality films enables these films to do two things: to loosen the meanings imposed on the image, and to position the spectator externally in relation to the image. The appropriation of the actuality genre here points to a decisive move away from the dominant aesthetics of documentary filmmaking, including the politically committed kind. Further, the landscape films' affinity with early actuality films functions as an implicit rejection of the militant documentary filmmaking that privileges dramatic actions over static landscapes, and clarity of meaning over ambiguity. Rejection of militant documentary filmmaking is indeed built into the main narrative of *The Man Who Left His Will on Film*; the film-within-a-film, which presents landscape shots, is opposed to the jerky handheld sequences of street protests filmed by student activists.

Of course, while *A.K.A. Serial Killer* and the film-within-a-film of *The Man Who Left His Will on Film* share the aesthetics of early cinema, there are notable differences between the two films. Most important, *The Man Who Left His Will on Film* is structured as a narrative film that contains the non-narrative landscape film within it. This landscape-film sequence, which exhibits the formal characteristics of early actuality films, is preceded and followed by the main narrative of the film, which is clearly organized in the style of classical narrative cinema. *The Man Who Left His Will on Film* frequently uses close-ups, the shot–reverse shot sequence, and the mobile camera that follows the actions of its main characters. The camera penetrates into the illusory diegetic space, constantly orienting the spectator in relation to the narrative. Moreover, the plot of *The Man Who Left His Will on Film* is driven by the actions of its two protagonists: Motoki and Yasuko, lovers who belong to the same activist group of student filmmakers. This character trait allows *The Man Who Left His Will on Film* to directly incorporate the militant ideal of film as a political weapon.

The Man Who Left His Will on Film sets up an opposition between a documentary sequence that embodies this ideal and the landscape film (or the film-within-a-film). The latter is presented as a "testament film" of an unidentified cameraman, who appears to be an imaginary double of Motoki. At one point, voice-overs of student activists loudly denounce this testament film (or this is how Motoki imagines it). They argue that the cameraman who shot the testament film is morally and politically bankrupt, as he wasted film by shooting mundane settings that could be filmed "anywhere, anytime." These students see no need to film landscape, because *it is not considered political* (unlike the scenes of student protests they film). This assessment of landscape as an apolitical image by student filmmakers is crucial, since the logic of *The Man Who Left His Will on Film* proves to be the opposite; it urges us to politicize landscape. The politicization of landscape, however, is made possible on the negation of the militant mode of documentary filmmaking that privileges the exceptional, dramatic acts of human actors. In place of such documentary filmmaking, Oshima offers the landscape film as a possible alternative means of engaging with politics.

As Maureen Turim suggests in her analysis of *The Man Who Left His Will on Film*, it is the character of Motoki who first questions the political validity of the idea of film or the camera as a political weapon.[37] He confronts Yasuko, who tries to remind Motoki of their collective effort to document student protests on Okinawa Day: "Making film into a weapon? Do not make me laugh!" Motoki's rejection of militant documentary filmmaking in favor of the landscape film, however, is complicated by the fact that his attempt to reshoot the same landscapes that appear in the film-within-a-film gets foiled by Yasuko's repeated intervention. In the end Motoki's failure to reshoot the same landscapes enables us to see what was absent in the original landscape film.[38]

Consider, for instance, the first landscape shot Motoki decides to reproduce: the tableau shot of a mailbox placed beside an underpass. To his frustration, after Motoki sets up the camera, Yasuko suddenly enters the scene and stands in front of the mailbox, preventing him from reproducing an identical landscape to the original that appears in the film-within-a-film. A postman then arrives and tries to remove Yasuko from the spot. She refuses. Suddenly, a policeman rushes into the frame from the off-screen space on the left and runs to assist the postman. He wrestles with and pins Yasuko down. As the policeman arrives, Motoki slowly backs out of the frame. The whole scene is filmed in a static long shot, replicating the exact composition and scale of the original tableau shot in the film-within-a-film. The film then cuts to a low-angle medium close-up of Motoki's face looking through the viewfinder. The following long shot shows the policeman holding down Yasuko, as the postman hurriedly drives away with his van. If the spectator sees more in this reshot sequence than in the original landscape film, this seeing is clearly enabled by Yasuko's presence; it is she who introduces the violence absent in the original landscape. The act of reshooting the landscape film, in other words, reintroduces the human presence that brings about the drama of individuated violence.

While I agree with Turim that much of the violence enacted in this sequence is sexual, as it targets Yasuko, whose body solicits aggressive reactions from male characters, I believe that the full theoretical and historical significance of this sequence cannot be understood without taking into consideration the concurrent discourse of fūkeiron. Certainly, the psychoanalytic framework of the unconscious offers one way of interpreting the structure of repetition present in this sequence.[39] However, the psychoanalytic reading of the film, in terms of dream logic and the return of the repressed, does not explain *why the image of landscape matters* in this film. The centrality of landscape as a motif is signaled by the original title of the film: *Tokyo Landscape War* (*Tokyo fūkei sensō*). The sequence where Motoki and Yasuko carry a map of Tokyo in order to identify the exact location of each landscape shot is also called "Tokyo Landscape War."[40] According to Sasaki—the co-scriptwriter of *The Man Who Left His Will on Film*—the map that appears in this sequence is named "Tokyo Landscape War Operation Diagram" ("Tokyo fūkei sensō sakusen youzu").[41] The connection between the militant student movement and the theme of landscape is made even more explicit in this sequence, where Motoki and Yasuko run around the city of Tokyo with the operation diagram of the Tokyo Landscape War, dressed in activist gear replete with helmet, *gebabō* stick, and cotton gloves. All of this suggests that landscape is the central problematic of the film. The political efficacy of documentary filmmaking and the visualization of violence—two thematic concerns of *The Man Who Left His Will on Film*—are inseparable from the film's presentation of landscape shots. And it is the problematic of landscape that links *The Man Who Left His Will on Film* to *A.K.A. Serial Killer*. How are we supposed to read these two films' concern with the problematic of landscape? In order to answer this question, we must return to the historical context that surrounds the making of these two films: Nagayama's arrest and militant student activism.

HOMOGENEOUS LANDSCAPES

Unlike student activists depicted in *The Man Who Left His Will on Film*, Nagayama Norio was born into a poor working-class family and never attended university. He was neither a student nor an activist. As he recounts later in his novelistic works, poverty forced him and his family to move around, preventing him from attending school regularly. In 1968, he stole a pistol from the U.S. navy base in Yokosuka and killed two security guards and two taxi drivers. He was arrested and sentenced to death. While he was imprisoned, he learned to read, turned to political philosophy, and began to write. In 1971, he published his first autobiographical novel, *Muchi no namida* (Tears of ignorance), which became an instant bestseller, gaining enthusiastic support from Left-leaning youth. Nagayama became an icon of radical leftism and the agitating voice of the so-called lumpenproletariat. His statements—such as "The bourgeoisie does not have the right to pass judgment on the proletariat"—gained sympathy from intellectuals. When he wrote passages like "At midnight on a certain day of a certain era / a fool who knew neither East nor West / declared war in solitude / against the Japanese capitalist State," Nagayama retrospectively positioned himself as the solitary rebel.[42] Consequently, numerous writers, filmmakers, and intellectuals turned to Nagayama in order to speak *for* and *about* him, as if he were the symbolic meeting point of the political, economic, and cultural strata of postwar Japan.

The independent filmmaker Shindō Kaneto, for instance, turned the life of Nagayama into a sentimental narrative film, *Hadaka no jūkyūsai* (*Live Today, Die Tomorrow!*) in 1970. Unlike *A.K.A. Serial Killer*, *Live Today, Die Tomorrow!* focuses on Nagayama's social and familial relationships. It tells a heart-rending story of his plight by articulating a chain of dramatic events propelled by the main characters' actions. In contrast, *A.K.A. Serial Killer* refuses the narrative impulse toward dramatic storytelling. In recalling the production of *A.K.A. Serial Killer*, Adachi notes that they resisted the temptation to *narrate* Nagayama's life. Landscape, according to Adachi, emerged as an alternative way of organizing the film while they followed the migratory footsteps of Nagayama from one location to another.

> The impression that every city is the same as the one before did not disappear. While I held my breath, stood still, and wondered about the origins of this stifling feeling in these cities, the landscapes in front of my eyes appeared as beautiful as postcards. Yet precisely because their beauty was like that of picture postcards, I realized that this was the source of our suffocation. Perhaps everyone knows about this suffocation, yet it continues to spread everyday as people walk through the city in order to simply survive. I felt that perhaps these suffocating landscapes had been Nagayama's enemy. Then, we thought we could turn these landscapes that keep stealing from us into a method of interrogating landscapes, ourselves, and the images of Nagayama.[43]

Adachi's visual analogy between the clichéd images of picture postcards and homogeneous scenery is translated into the formal style of *A.K.A. Serial Killer*, in which the majority of shots appear as composed as the static view of picture postcards. Adachi's reference to postcards also sheds light on the visual uniformity and banality of the images that appear in this landscape film. Noteworthy here is Adachi's deliberate positioning of the landscape that changes so little from one city to another as "Nagayama's enemy."

By referencing Walter Benjamin who argues that Eugène Atget photographed the empty landscapes of nineteenth-century Paris as if they were deserted crime scenes, Matsuda similarly discusses the making of *A.K.A. Serial Killer* in the 1970 essay titled "Fūkei to shite no toshi" (City as landscape). Matsuda reverses Benjamin's formula by noting, "We filmed crime scenes just like landscape [photographs]."[44] The deserted landscape shots, in other words, become the evidence of violence that has already taken place. The *absence* of visible violence is key to Matsuda's interpretation of *A.K.A. Serial Killer*. Like Adachi, he draws our attention to the uniformity of the landscapes in various cities and Nagayama's migratory footsteps through them.[45] The following passage from the essay "My Archipelago, My Landscape" echoes Adachi's observation: "When we tried to see another Japanese archipelago with visionary eyes by following the footsteps of a member of the masses who grew up in the lower-class strata of society and who had to form his own class position through constant vagrancy as his only state of being, surprisingly or not surprisingly, we ended up discovering a common element that cannot be called anything but *landscape*, which existed like the end point of a line's segment."[46] As Matsuda writes in another essay, what he calls the "common element" that repeatedly confronted the crew of *A.K.A. Serial Killer* is the uniformity of landscapes.[47] For Matsuda and Adachi, Nagayama's crime is aimed at the uniformity built into the everyday environment. They hence interpret Nagayama's violence as a form of revolt against the homogenizing forces of urban development and the restructuring of cities during Japan's high-speed economic growth. The hint of romanticization notwithstanding, what is important to note here is the connection Matsuda and Adachi draw between the homogenization of landscapes and an accelerated process of urbanization led by the government in the 1960s. Though not explicitly discussed by Matsuda and Adachi, this connection between the rise of uniform landscapes and the state-led urban-planning projects during the 1960s allows us to approach state power, not in terms of its repressive forces (as exemplified by the iconic image of the riot police), but in terms of its productive forces, which mold and shape the everyday environment in order to maintain order and security.

In "Closed Chamber, Landscape, and the Power of Domination" (1969), Matsuda explains how he and others involved in the making of *A.K.A. Serial Killer* turned to landscape as a central motif.

> The reason why we, including Adachi Masao, in making a strange work—which can only be called a "landscape actuality" or an "actual-scenery film" [*jikkei eiga*], rather than a documentary film—followed the footsteps of the "serial killer" Nagayama Norio by passing through the eastern half of Japan—Abashiri, Sapporo, Hakodate, Tsugaru Plane, Tokyo, Nagoya, Kyoto, Osaka, Kōbe, and even through Hong Kong—and filmed only the local landscapes, which Nagayama would have seen with his own eyes, is because we became conscious of the landscape as the antagonistic "power" itself.[48]

Matsuda's suggestion that *A.K.A. Serial Killer* should be aligned with the actuality film rather than with documentary corroborates my point about the formal affinity between landscape films and early actuality films. But what is more intriguing here is his statement that landscape is an embodiment of the "antagonistic power" (*tekitai shitekuru "kenryoku"*), which he specifically associates with the state.

Matsuda's statement invites us to reflect on the political use of landscape by the state. The concept of landscape evokes two different registers of perceiving and organizing space: an actual physical space seen from a particular point of view (e.g., garden); and a visual representation (e.g., in painting, photography, and cinema) of this space. Accordingly, Matsuda, Adachi, and others who use the term *fūkei* (landscape) refer to both the profilmic space as well as the cinematic image of this space.

Since the 1980s, the connection between the representational practice of imaging the landscape and the material practice of transforming physical space have been theorized widely by cultural geographers and art historians through the frameworks of modern subjectivity, visuality, colonialism, capitalism, and urban development. W. J. T. Mitchell, for instance, has argued that landscape is "a medium of cultural expression."[49] According to Mitchell,

> Landscape may be represented by painting, drawing, or engraving; by photography, film, and theatrical scenery; by writing, speech, and presumably even music and other "sound images." Before all these secondary representations, however, landscape is itself a physical and multisensory medium (earth, stone, vegetation, water, sky, sound and silence, light and darkness, etc.) in which cultural meanings and values are encoded, whether they are *put* there by the physical transformation of a place in landscape gardening and architecture, or *found* in a place formed, as we say, "by nature."[50]

Mitchell extends the notion of landscape beyond representational practices to include the semiotic functions of physical space itself. Similarly, Denis Cosgrove defines landscape as *a way of seeing*. Landscape as a culturally and historically conditioned way of seeing the external world is tied to a "practical appropriation of space." The practical appropriation of space encompasses diverse modes of reconfiguring physical space, from the discipline of urban planning to the colonial expropriation of land and natural resources. For Cosgrove, the dominant representational practices of landscape—be they painting or photography—are hence inseparable from the economic and social expansions of the urban property owners that emerged in fifteenth- and early-sixteenth-century Europe.[51]

Critics have also argued that the concept of landscape needs to be understood in relation to ideology and as a historically specific technique of vision that developed alongside linear perspective. Landscape painting and photography, these critics argue, are imbricated in the formation of the modern sovereign subject. It has been argued that the apparatus of the camera itself, with its built-in linear perspective, enforces an ideological construction of disembodied vision. This is a view held by the proponents of apparatus theory, including Jean-Louis Baudry.[52] In the West this historical mobilization of landscape and linear perspective for political or ideological purposes developed over centuries. Turning to the case of Japan, however, we find that not only cinema but also the entire practice of European-style landscape painting and photography (along with philosophy) was imported in the late nineteenth century. Hence, for critics like Karatani Kōjin, the semiotic "discovery of landscape," which entailed a seismic perspectival inversion of the world, took place only in the nineteenth century, the era of Japan's intensive industrial and cultural modernization.[53] Whether it is analyzed in the Euro-American context or the Japanese context, landscape is often seen as implicated in the emergence of the modern epistemic subject who, as Martin Heidegger has argued, sees the world as if it were a "picture."[54]

Yet, unlike Karatani or Heidegger, the critics of fūkeiron are not in fact concerned with the emergence of an epistemic subject. But they are concerned with the political connections among the state, capitalism, and landscape. The landscape as articulated by the fūkeiron critics is an embodiment of the governing power of the state. Matsuda's analysis of a black-and-white photograph shot by the documentary photographer Kurihara Tatsuo is suggestive in this regard. Shot from a low-angle camera position, the photograph shows a large manhole in the foreground on the right and a file of student demonstrators in the background, near the edge of the upper left frame. This snapshot of Tokyo University's campus is one of many photographs Kurihara took during his year-long project of documenting student protests, in 1968–69. In his discussion of the landscape and student activism, Matsuda singles out this particular photograph among more dramatic photographs, arguing, "There is nothing special about this commonplace photograph. No helmet and no *gebabō* are seen here—it only conveys a tactile sensation of the remaining heat of the summer through the cracked surface of the asphalt ground that separates the manhole and the demonstrators."[55] As the camera focuses on the empty urban space and averts its gaze from the human figures, the photograph appears to register a fleeting moment of tranquility.

But this impression is deceptive, as Matsuda goes on to argue. This photograph is in fact more political than other photographs that document student-police confrontations, because it indicates that the policing power of the state *is not reducible* to the figures of the police whom student activists confront on the street. Instead, it is embodied by urban landscapes that envelop them. The state wields its policing—or more precisely, governing—power over the students through the built environment even when there is no visible conflict. Matsuda points out an insignia on the manhole cover, which reads "Imperial University Sewage" (*Teidai gesui*). This insignia is not only a symbolic remnant of the wartime police state and Japanese imperialism, but also a concrete reminder of the ubiquity of state power: "In the University of Tokyo the presence of the Imperial University permeates from the lid of a manhole to the handle of a toilet. The popular chant 'Dismantle the Imperial University' is hence not just a symbolic slogan. Kurihara Tatsuo's snapshot offers us a glimpse of the reason why countless, anonymous fighters are revolting against this gigantic power."[56] Matsuda finds it both ironic and suggestive that the presence of the state is inscribed in the environment of the student protesters, whether or not they are aware of it. "The fighters would soon depart the scene," continues Matsuda, "and this ominous landscape is left with the sign 'Imperial University Sewage.'"[57] What remains firmly in place after the departure of the student protestors and riot police is the ubiquitous presence of the state, which continues to affect and regulate the daily conduct of students through the processes of normalization, disciplinary control, and surveillance. The insignia on the manhole cover is a subtle reminder of this governmental power, which operates through an assemblage of regulatory and disciplinary procedures, practices, and techniques. For Matsuda, this photograph, which serendipitously "documents" the presence of the state embedded in the urban environment, foreshadows the more conscious approach to landscape undertaken by *A.K.A. Serial Killer* and *The Man Who Left His Will on Film*.

Nakahira Takuma shares Matsuda's perspective on the ubiquity of governmental power manifesting itself through the urban landscape. In "Insurgency against Landscape" (1970), Nakahira argues that the landscape is an embodiment of regulatory orders built directly into our everyday environment.[58] Nakahira interprets the widespread practice of erecting barricades across streets and on campus as an attempt to physically alter and transform this environment. Instead of focusing on the physical resistance of the students against the state authorities, Nakahira emphasizes the subtle and noncoercive management of the urban environment and population. The practices of barricading the campus and demonstrating on the street are more than acts of civil disobedience; they are also subversive tactics of landscaping that literally transform the look of urban space—which in turn functions similarly to what Foucault would call "counter-conduct" (or "revolts of conduct").

Counter-conduct is a mode of resistance that has as its "objective and adversary a power that assumes the task of conducting men in their life and daily existence."[59] By formulating landscape as a political concept, Matsuda and Nakahira gesture toward something like counter-conduct. Their argument is that a fundamental connection exists between the New Left student movement and Nagayama's crime. The student activists and Nagayama are equally driven by their shared desire to "tear up uniform 'landscapes.'"[60] By emphasizing uniformity and control, Matsuda and Nakahira articulate the ubiquity of governmental power that manifests itself through spatial practices such as urban planning, sewage construction, and traffic regulation. They saw it necessary to disengage from the narrow understanding of state power as only manifesting itself in the most repressive acts of policing, arresting, or confronting the student protesters. In so doing, these fūkeiron critics turned their focus away from the spectacle of violence to the underlying conditions of such violence. The concept of landscape enabled them to shift perspective such that activities like obstruction of traffic, construction of barricades with school desks, or theft of a pistol from a U.S. Navy base could no longer be interpreted merely as expressions of political dissent or criminal acts. Instead, these activities offered a way to radically reimagine state power at a time when images of police violence and militant protests were saturating the mass media and limiting the political imagination of the public.

The potential of fūkeiron as a critical discourse lies in the connection it draws between the regulatory management of the urban environment and the governmental power of the state. The cinematic engagement with landscape plays a central role in visualizing this connection. By focusing on eventless landscapes, *A.K.A. Serial Killer* and the film-within-a-film of *The Man Who Left His Will on Film* reorient our attention, directing it away from spectacular sights of physical conflict and dramatic action toward nonspectacular elements of the urban environment. The concerted effort of critics and filmmakers to turn their attention away from exceptional scenes of conflict and violence to utterly ordinary scenes of daily activity and the increasing uniformity of urban space was a timely response to the spectacles of violence, conflict, and revolt that saturated newspapers and television programs. But the political significance of this reorientation is not easy to see if we do not situate the emergence of fūkeiron and landscape films within the media historical context of the late 1960s.

DIAGRAMMING THE LANDSCAPE

At the time of Nagayama's arrest, one of the major newspapers published a diagram of the itinerary of Nagayama, who frequently moved from one city to another.[61] According to Sasaki, an initial inspiration for making *A.K.A. Serial Killer* came from looking at this diagram, which mapped Nagayama's movement through the Japanese archipelago. The cartographic practice of mapping also occupies an important place in Matsuda's theorization of the landscape. For instance, Matsuda begins his essay "My Archipelago, My Landscape" with a reflection on cartography.

> It is well known that the atlas made in Japan and the atlases made abroad—let's say in London—have different compositions. That is, Japan is placed at the center in the former, and England in the latter. As a result, the Pacific Ocean spreads vastly, with North and South America placed on the right side and Africa on the left in the former atlas, while South America and Africa face one another closely across the Atlantic Ocean in the latter atlas. Of course the Pacific Ocean gets divided in half, and if you look for Japan, it barely retains its trace, like a stretched scar at the top corner on the right. As I write this, it may appear commonsensical and hence not move you at all, but, by way of experiment, I suggest actually buying two maps and placing them on two different walls for comparison. When placed between two maps, we would actually feel the transformation of our own *worldview*. In my case, when a printing gets shifted slightly, things whose existence I took for granted are transformed into a source of tremendous shock that even causes a sensation of nausea.[62]

Matsuda argues that the cartographic practices of different nation-states reflect different "worldviews." The innocuous surface of a page from an atlas might be read as the symbolic mapping of different geopolitical imaginations at work.

An especially noteworthy passage, which connects Matsuda's thoughts on cartography to the making of *A.K.A. Serial Killer*, appears immediately afterward. In noting how Africa and South America show up like severed "Siamese twins" in the atlas made in London, Matsuda shifts his focus from the comparison between Japan and England to the formation of the "Third World": "The innocuous existence of the map made in London triggered me to think of the meaning of the 'Third World' as *another world*. I felt that the entire history of the ones who made the map and the ones who were inscribed into the map crystallized there."[63] He observes the peripheral positioning of both Africa and South America on the maps made in two former imperial nation-states—Japan and England—and reads Third World politics into it. In so doing, Matsuda links his shock at seeing Japan marginalized on the map made by British cartographers to a critique of the equally marginalizing attitude of Japanese cartographers toward Africa and South America (which are placed at the far edges of the map). The practice of cartography allows him to move away from the dualistic comparative schema of Japan versus the West and to reflect on an interrelation between the cartographic imagination of the world and the politicoeconomic constitution of the Third World.

Matsuda's evocation of the Third World in this essay is not surprising given his avowed interest in the works of writers such as Frantz Fanon, Che Guevara, and Jules Régis Debray.[64] More important than his reference to the Third World is his understanding of cartography as a method of policing vision, which imposes culturally and historically conditioned ways of seeing the world (worldviews). These *ways of seeing*—like landscape—are directly linked to colonial and imperial relations of power. Although an in-depth analysis of Matsuda's conceptualization of the Third World is outside the scope of this chapter, it is worth mentioning that Matsuda introduces the notion of the Third World in order to connect Nagayama's plight to the disenfranchised, precarious populace that forms a symbolic Third World within Japan. Matsuda notes, "I could not help but wonder whether it is possible for us to discover *another Japan*—another Japan which is expressible as a concrete material map."[65] Following this remark, Matsuda describes his desire to rewrite the official map of Japan as his personal premise for becoming involved in the making of *A.K.A. Serial Killer*. The filming of homogeneous landscapes, which constitute an alternative "map" of the Japanese archipelago, is therefore explained as a countercartographic endeavor that aims to undo habitual ways of seeing the world.

Given the common understanding of cinema as a photorealistic medium, the use of the nonmimetic, diagrammatic practice of cartography as a model for filmmaking raises new questions. For the cinematic images of urban landscapes that appear in *A.K.A. Serial Killer* and *The Man Who Left His Will on Film* are more like mimetic documents than maps. So how do we read the filmed landscapes cartographically?

In his incisive reading of Foucault, Deleuze uses the metaphor of diagram in order to explain the specific arrangement (*agencement*) of power, which can be applied to various instances and locations (as in the case of disciplinary power, which operates through multiple institutions from prison to school, from hospital to military training camp). This mobilization of *diagram* to describe the invisible arrangement of power operative in a given social field is useful for our analysis of the landscape, as it allows us to differentiate the document from the diagram. While *diagram* originally refers to the architectural blueprint of the panoptic prison drawn by Jeremy Bentham in 1791, Deleuze uses it to describe Foucault's understanding of power as a relation of forces. Bentham's architectural drawing of the panoptic prison, in contrast, is a document, a visual aid by which to understand the disciplinary mechanism of power. The notion of diagram here refers to the general operation of power rather than to a particular type of architectural drawing.[66] Furthermore, there is not just one but multiple diagrams; every society at any given moment operates through a set of diagrams, some of them more dominant than others.

Similarly, the filmed landscapes in *A.K.A. Serial Killer* and *The Man Who Left His Will on Film* can be approached as *documents* from which the spectator can extract the dominant *diagram* of power at work in Japanese society at the end of the 1960s. Since the diagrammatic function of power may not be known to the spectator, the spectator must actively conduct a critical reading—we may call this activity diagramming—of the relations of power that are neither immediately legible nor visible on-screen. Important to note here is the intermediary process of filming the landscapes through which they become readable as documents and the diagram of power. While the formal techniques of actuality films (such as tableau shots) prevent the spectator from being immersed in the screen space and thus can help the spectator to pay close attention to the landscape shots, in order to complete the critical *reading* of these landscape shots in relation to the actual workings of power, the spectator needs the assistance of fūkeiron. This is why the contextualization of *A.K.A. Serial Killer* and *The Man Who Left His Will on Film* in relation to the discourse of fūkeiron is indispensable. The existing analyses of *The Man Who Left His Will on Film* by scholars such as Burch, Desser, Turim, and Edward Branigan fail precisely on this point. *The Man Who Left His Will on Film* is often said to be the most perplexing or "difficult" film made by Oshima, but it is only perplexing if one misses the film's interrogation of landscape.[67]

Understood through the lens of fūkeiron, *The Man Who Left His Will on Film* and *A.K.A. Serial Killer* present a way to look beyond the documentary qualities of images of urban landscapes and to extract a particular diagram of power from them—that of governmental power, which operates through subtle, noncoercive, and economic forms of policing and managing the urban population. The connection between landscape and the state is something that Matsuda repeatedly highlights in his writings. He calls landscape "a text of state power," arguing that "our landscape theory [*fūkeiron*] should be restructured as a theory of state [*kokkaron*]."[68] But Matsuda's writings fail to specify what kind of state power the landscape makes visible or readable. In order to supplement Matsuda's theorization of state power, we must return to the cinematic representation of urban landscapes in *A.K.A. Serial Killer* and *The Man Who Left His Will on Film.*

In *A.K.A. Serial Killer* and *The Man Who Left His Will on Film*, this power manifests itself first and foremost as the governmental control over pathways of commerce and information. The relations of power in question here are profoundly *economic*. To better understand this point, consider how the six "tableau" shots that comprise the film-within-a-film of *The Man Who Left His Will on Film* highlight networks of circulation. In these shots we see telephone lines, mailboxes, railways, streets and bridges, all of which support the smooth circulation of men, goods, and information. These tableau shots direct us to the general policing of space by the state. As Paul Virilio comments, "The State's political power . . . is only secondarily 'power organized by one class to oppress another.' More materially, *it is the polis, the police, in other words highway surveillance*."[69] The network of circulation here should be understood in terms of material infrastructures (e.g., highways, rivers, canals, bridges) as well as being "the set of regulations, constraints, and limits, or the facilities and encouragements" that work on the conducts of individual subjects.[70] The utterly ordinary images of urban landscapes in *A.K.A. Serial Killer* and *The Man Who Left His Will on Film* point to the incessant operation of connection and division—the networks of circulation such as highways, railroads, and antennas—which are fundamental to the circulation and distribution of goods, information, and labor. The landscape shots in these films suggest how the policing of urban space guarantees the efficient circulation and distribution of things. What is at stake here is precisely the kind of state power that Foucault calls governmentality, which works through an assemblage of techniques and institutional procedures that aim to police, guide, and manage a population according to the principle of economic rationality.[71]

A DIAGRAM OF GOVERNMENTALITY

Foucault famously locates the origin of the economic logic of governmentality, which aims "to shape, guide or affect the conduct of some person or persons," in the political concept of the police that gained currency in the seventeenth century.[72] The history of governmentality as narrated by Foucault suggests that the development and transformation of the police as a political concept *and* as a state apparatus were central to the modern conception of governance. Foucault traces the genealogy of the modern conception of governance to the German theory of *Polizei*, suggesting that its main concern was the economic art of governing a population. The term *police* as used in the political theories of seventeenth- and eighteenth-century Europe hence was broader in meaning than is our current use of it. Rather than referring to a particular institution that maintains order and enforces law, *police* understood in this context refers to a set of techniques used to govern the population: "When people spoke about police at this moment, they spoke about the specific techniques by which a government in the framework of the state was able to govern people as individuals [who were] significantly useful for the world."[73]

Grounded in the political discourse of the state, the earlier and broader conception of *police* as an assemblage of governmental techniques had as its aim the general welfare of the population. The target of policing at that time encompassed a wide range of objects, from public hygiene to security against poverty and the construction of transportation systems, including roads, bridges, and highways to ensure the smooth circulation of goods and people. The policing activities of the state over its population and the economic management of its territory, especially its infrastructure, were deeply intertwined. The modern police force, however, was developed in order to secure "the circulation of men and goods in relation to each other," which is why, Foucault continues, vagrancy became a principal object of vigilant police control: "It is the whole problem, precisely, of these vagrants, of people moving around. Let's say, in short, that police is essentially urban and market based."[74] This economic conception of the police was indispensable for the development of the modern state, including that of Japan, which modeled its police system on that of France in the 1870s.[75] Operating alongside the techniques of disciplinary power that target individuals, the modern apparatus of the police targets a population as its primary object, optimizing its productivity, health, and happiness.[76] This economic understanding of the police lies at the heart of Foucault's analysis of governmentality. In short, the policing of the population goes hand in hand with the economic conception of government, which in turn generates multiple mechanisms of security, surveillance, and social control.

The understanding of the governmental power of the state as having its basis in mundane activities such as traffic regulation resonates strongly with the discourse of fūkeiron and the cinematic experiments of *A.K.A. Serial Killer* and *The Man Who Left His Will on Film*. In these films, images of homogeneous landscapes that document the space of commerce, transaction, and transportation (railway stations, highways, docks, canals, and markets) direct us toward the diagram of governmentality, the relations of power guided by economic rationality.[77] The concept of government in question here is hence not reducible to sovereignty or to the state itself. Instead, it points to a set of techniques and procedures jointly developed and exercised by the state and by the private sector.[78]

The connection between the policing function of the state and the economic rationality of the market was apparent in late 1960s Japan. The ruling Liberal Democratic Party (LDP) worked closely with the construction industry to push forward systematic urban development. And the emergent security industry worked alongside the police force to keep the urban population under surveillance. The birth of the Japanese security guard business in 1962 was, in fact, a direct result of the intense migration of the uprooted rural population into the Tokyo metropolitan area. Two massive construction projects led by the state—the Tokyo Olympics in 1964 and Expo 70 in 1970—further accelerated the growth of the security-guard industry in Japan.[79] In the meantime, the state actively mobilized the security police (or the public-order police) in order to monitor and track down student activists. The introduction of the closed-circuit television (CCTV) for crowd control purposes during the Tokyo Olympics also marks an increasing confluence of the burgeoning security and electronics industries. The monotonous urban landscapes documented in *A.K.A. Serial Killer* and the film-within-a-film of *The Man Who Left His Will on Film* must be placed within this particular historical context. In spite of the apparent absence of visible conflict or violence, these films document the tightening of governmental power that operates through the networked systems of circulation, communication, and control.

The timely intervention of these landscape films becomes even more apparent when we consider specific techniques of policing and security measures developed during the height of the student movement. For instance, the state enforced new traffic regulations to prevent protesters from assembling in public spaces. The city of Tokyo also rebuilt its sidewalks to prevent demonstrators from tearing up paving stones to use as makeshift weapons during the protest. Compared to the mobilization of riot police, paving the streets with asphalt may not appear "political," yet the seemingly benign operation of governmental power must be discerned through such mundane, preventive security measures. Traffic control and urban planning clearly operate as part of the regulatory apparatuses of security.[80]

With this consideration in mind, let us return to the pivotal sequence in *The Man Who Left His Will on Film* involving the reshooting of the landscape film. In this sequence, violence appears as an *effect* of counter-conducts. For instance, Yasuko is violently attacked when she attempts to disrupt traffic, obstruct access to the public telephone, or prevent the postman from collecting mail. Her act of altering the landscape is directly linked to the disruption of the public order, which in turn gives rise to spectacles of violence. According to Nakahira, altering the landscape through an act of civil disobedience was exactly what student activists aimed to accomplish as they stopped the train, jammed the traffic, and halted the network of communication. However, for fūkeiron critics like Nakahira, building barricades, tearing pavement, and stopping traffic were more than acts of civil disobedience; they were acts of creative counter-conduct designed to resist the techniques of government.

Reading the fūkeiron discourse through the Foucauldian paradigm of governmentality helps us appreciate its critical insight and the timeliness of its attendant filmmaking, which emerged at the height of militant student activism and against the backdrop of Japan's high-growth economy. In Japan's dramatic economic growth of the 1960s, cities once devastated by the war were built anew, and the growing economy sustained by the construction industry further accelerated homogeneous urban planning. Accordingly, the physical landscapes of the Japanese archipelago underwent significant transformations. These changes are glaringly visible, but their political connotations often remain obscure. Critical insights offered by fūkeiron and *A.K.A. Serial Killer* and *The Man Who Left His Will on Film* make these connotations explicit and analyzable.

Attempts by the fūkeiron critics and filmmakers of *A.K.A. Serial Killer* and *The Man Who Left His Will on Film* to rethink state power through urban landscape were not isolated acts. Instead, these efforts resonate with similar attempts undertaken by avant-garde artists and activists at the time—for instance, the avant-garde performance activity of Hi Red Center in 1964. Hi Red Center's performance took place in the context of massive municipal transformations precipitated by the Tokyo Olympics, to be held that year. In anticipation of receiving foreign travelers, the state sought to beautify and restructure the city by catching stray dogs, prohibiting public urination, and constructing numerous hotels and highways. Hi Red Center playfully critiqued this beautification project in a street performance, *Cleaning Event (Campaign to Promote Cleanliness and Order in the Metropolitan Area)*. During the show, the Hi Red Center members Akasegawa, Nakanishi, and Takamatsu wore masks and white laboratory coats, and set up a sign that read "Be Clean!" According to Reiko Tomii, "Their demeanor was so serious that a patrolling policeman thanked them for their diligent work, perhaps thinking they were part of the Olympics-related beautification program. Yet, by occasionally halting automobile traffic, their project verged on unlawfulness."[81]

Given the close collaboration between Nakahira and Akasegawa in the serialized reports they published in the film journal *Eiga Hihyō II*, and given the friendship between Akasegawa and Adachi, it is perhaps not surprising to find this resonance between Hi Red Center's concern with the alteration of Tokyo and the filming of urban landscapes in *A.K.A. Serial Killer*. The Hi Red Center performance was also a type of counter-conduct in that it aimed to draw attention to the connection between the urban environment and governmental power. The dramatic transformation of cities and the homogenization of cityscapes were taking place as the LDP government was cracking down on protesters. In 1968, the year when Nagayama committed his crime, the government issued "General Outline for Urban Policy," a landmark policy for the urban planning of the Tokyo metropolitan area.[82] It was drafted by Tanaka Kakuei, a conservative politician affiliated with the LDP. Tanaka climbed to the highest political echelon through his involvement in the construction business. In 1972, the year he became prime minister, he published an influential book, *Plan for Remodeling the Japanese Archipelago* (*Nihon rettō kaizō ron*), which promoted the further homogenization of provincial cities modeled after Tokyo.

The cinematic experiments undertaken by the filmmakers of *A.K.A. Serial Killer* and *The Man Who Left His Will on Film* and the theorization of the landscape by fūkeiron critics emerged out of this historical context. Their critique of the landscape was deeply rooted in their concern over the invisible traces of state power inscribed in the everyday environment, the kind of power that was obscured by the incessant media coverage of the militant student movement and violent juvenile crimes. By deliberately turning the camera away from mediatized images of violence toward the images of eventless landscapes, *A.K.A. Serial Killer* and *The Man Who Left His Will on Film* explored the diagram of governmental power. By articulating the problematic of landscape in relation to the state and the economy, the discourse of fūkeiron tried to make sense of this diagram. In so doing, these films and fūkeiron introduced a new way of conceptualizing state power, dislodging it from the codified images of police officers and politicians.[83] *A.K.A. Serial Killer* and *The Man Who Left His Will on Film* were "actual" insofar as they grappled with the widely reported news of Nagayama's crime and the militant student activism of 1968–69, but their strategy of opposing the nonspectacular images of landscapes to the spectacular images of violence separates their experiments from the journalistic coverage of the same events. The problematic of landscape thus presented a new possibility for the cinema of actuality to engage in politics.

five

hijacking television

News and Militant Cinema

On the evening of 28 May 1971, Wakamatsu Kōji and Adachi Masao landed in Beirut with a 16 mm camera, a cassette tape recorder, and two walkie-talkies. Just before they flew to Beirut they attended the Cannes Film Festival, which had screened two films by Wakamatsu Production, *Violated Angels* (1967) and *Sex Jack* (1970), along with Oshima's *The Man Who Left His Will on Film* (1970) and *Ceremony* (1971). Wakamatsu and Adachi went to Beirut with the hopes of making a newsreel about the Palestinian liberation movement. They sought assistance from the Popular Front for the Liberation of Palestine (PFLP), a Marxist-Leninist organization known in the late 1960s and early 1970s for its spectacular hijackings and its internationalist policy. With the aid of a young Japanese Red Army activist, Shigenobu Fusako, who had been in Beirut for two months and knew some of the Palestinian artists and journalists in the area, Wakamatsu and Adachi were able to contact Ghassan Kanafani, the renowned novelist and the chief editor of the PFLP's weekly magazine, *Al Hadaf*. The PFLP granted them permission to visit refugee camps in Saida and Shatila in Lebanon, as well as their guerrilla bases in the Golan Heights in Syria and in the mountainous region of Jerash, near the border of Jordan and Israel. Wakamatsu and Adachi interviewed key PFLP members, including Kanafani and Leila Khaled, the first woman hijacker to become a media celebrity. On 27 June, Wakamatsu returned to Japan, while Adachi remained behind to finish interviewing Palestinian revolutionaries and filming camp life in

Lebanon. One month later, Adachi returned to Japan with five hours of documentary footage. The outcome of their journey was the propaganda newsreel *The Red Army/PFLP: Declaration of World War* (*Sekigun-PFLP: Sekai sensō sengen*, 1971).

At first sight, Wakamatsu and Adachi's treatment of politics in *The Red Army/PFLP* not only departs from, but in some ways contradicts and even undercuts the critical perspective put forward in their earlier works, such as *Sex Jack* (1970) and *A.K.A. Serial Killer* (1969). *The Red Army/PFLP* aligns itself with militant revolutionaries who deliberately stage spectacular media events; it takes a much more explicit ideological stance than their previous films. As is evident from its avowed status as a news film, *The Red Army/PFLP* is also an attempt to create an alternative circuit of information that circumvents the existing system of journalism. It aims to *produce* news rather than simply appropriate it. This attempt to use cinema as the basis for the construction of an alternative circuit of information departs from the preceding practice of the cinema of actuality, which strategically cited and remediated news materials from the mainstream media.

Importantly, however, *The Red Army/PFLP* does not give up these strategies, but uses them rhetorically in order to foreground a certain paradox of mediation: the political efficacy of *direct* action that needs to be transmitted through and *mediated* by the news media. As such, *The Red Army/PFLP* signals a logical conclusion to the cinema of actuality, exposing both the limitations and potentials of its image politics. I will thus extend the issues I have already covered: the relation between the condensed temporality of news and the quotidian temporality of the landscape, the spectacle of state violence and the discrete presence of governmental power, and the purported directness of political action and the presumed indirectness of mediatization.

At the time *The Red Army/PFLP* was made, the Japanese New Left student movement was increasingly facing factional conflicts and starting to take a more internationalist and militant approach to direct action, in solidarity with Third World liberation movements. Frequent references to the Black Panther Party, the Viet Cong, and the Tupamaros are made by the Japanese Red Army as well as by the PFLP activists in the film. The film's rhetoric of armed resistance against imperialist oppression and for the empowerment of people in the Third World reflects and is consistent with discourses on decolonization and the liberation movements that were popular in Japan at the time. In the words of Adachi, the film was made with a clear intention to contribute to "the construction of a worldwide revolutionary front."[1]

In the context of the cinema of actuality, however, more important than the ideological alliance with worldwide liberation movements is the film's self-proclaimed status as a *news film*. Wakamatsu and Adachi's decision to make a revolutionary propaganda newsreel at this particular moment deserves attention for two reasons. On the one hand, the making of *The Red Army/PFLP* came after Wakamatsu and Adachi had already made use of journalistic materials in a number of pink films, which mocked and critiqued the spectacular mediatization of politics. The film's embrace of armed struggle and its interview format also signal a departure from Adachi's previous investment in landscape, which was evident in *A.K.A. Serial Killer*, a film that rejected conventions of documentary filmmaking. The inclusion of readily recognizable images of armed resistance (e.g., airplane hijackings, barricades, trenches, rifles) and individual social actors in *The Red Army/PFLP* thus appears to sharply contrast with *A.K.A. Serial Killer*. Nonetheless, the theorization of landscape as a locus and a diagram of governmental power not only is present but also plays a key role in this film. Equally, *The Red Army/PFLP* inherits Adachi and Wakamatsu's view of journalistic media, especially television, as an accomplice to the existing police order. The recurrent appearance of television (its images as well as the image of the television monitor itself) in the film attests to this view.

Through a comparison with a contemporaneous project undertaken by Jean-Luc Godard and Anne-Marie Miéville, *Ici et ailleurs* (*Here and Elsewhere*, 1974), I explore the way in which *The Red Army/PFLP* remediates television. *Here and Elsewhere* is based on an unfinished film project of the Dziga Vertov Group, *Until Victory* (*Jusqu'à la victoire*). With the assistance of the Palestinian Liberation Organization (PLO), Godard and Jean-Pierre Gorin went to Jordan in order to document the Palestinian liberation movement in 1970. They eventually abandoned the project. In remaking *Until Victory* into *Here and Elsewhere*, Godard and Miéville added new footage, which depicted the ordinary life of a French working-class family (often gathered in front of a television set). Comparing *The Red Army/PFLP* to *Here and Elsewhere* will allow us to examine the political tension between cinema and television.[2]

HIJACKING AS INCORPOREAL TRANSFORMATION

On the surface, *The Red Army/PFLP* appears to be a straightforward propaganda film for the anti-imperialist and anticapitalist struggle. However, the self-evident notion of "propaganda"—a mass-mediated form of publicity designed to disseminate a certain kind of information—turns out to be much more nuanced than it first appears. The central questions raised by *The Red Army/PFLP* hinge on the process of mediation integral to an act of propaganda: how to achieve optimal publicity and media attention through direct actions, and how to construct an alternative circuit of information while usurping the mainstream news media. I approach the question of propaganda from a perspective that regards cinema as an apparatus of mediation *and* remediation.

One of the first messages delivered by *The Red Army/PFLP* is that direct, physical acts of armed struggle are the best form of propaganda. The news film as a *mediated* form of propaganda thus aims to supplement and assist the alleged *directness* of armed resistance. Accordingly, the film opens with a sequence that contains remediated news footage that focuses on the arguably most spectacular form of direct action—the hijacking of an airplane. But this opening montage complicates *The Red Army/PFLP*'s own positioning as a propaganda film that complements direct action. For a political hijacking is fundamentally designed to be a media event, whose efficacy lies in its ability to serve as "propaganda of the deed," as a means of publicity and not just an instrument of political negotiation. Furthermore, in order for it to be successful as propaganda, a hijacking needs wide journalistic coverage. What, then, would be the role of a propaganda *news film* that positions itself as an alternative medium of news production? More to the point, what do we make of the fact that the film foregrounds the mediated nature of a political action such as hijacking through its use of recycled news footage? Clearly, there is a complex series of mediations at play here.

With the song "The Internationale" blasting on the soundtrack, the film *The Red Army/PFLP* opens with a rapid montage of news reports on two internationally known hijackings: the Yodogō Incident, carried out by the Japanese Red Army faction in March 1970, and the Dawson's Field hijackings by the PFLP in September of the same year. The very first shot of *The Red Army/PFLP*, for instance, is a title shot of a black-and-white Daimai news film containing a headline that reads "A Hijacking of Japan Airlines." A shot of an airplane taking off from the runway

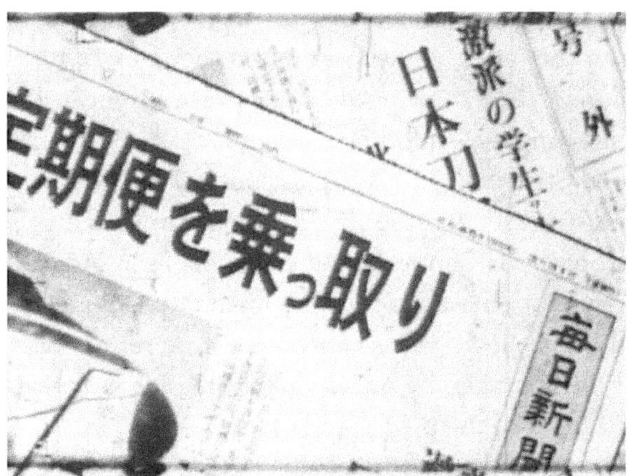

5.1. A close-up of the *Mainichi Newspaper* report on the Yodogō Incident. Still from *The Red Army/PFLP* (Wakamatsu Production, 1971).

ensues. On the soundtrack, we hear a male voice-over that calmly announces, "This is a news film for the construction of the World Red Army."

The following shot is a quick zoom on the front page of the Mainichi newspaper's report on the Yodogō Incident (figure 5.1). The film cuts back to another piece of remediated footage, one that shows a group of helmeted policemen running. A brief shot of released hostages disembarking from the airplane follows. At this point, the film's title finally appears on-screen. The voice-over applauds the spectacular success of the Yodogō Incident (the hijackers defected to North Korea after releasing the hostages in Seoul). The film then cuts to color news footage on the multiple hijackings carried out by the PFLP. A handheld camera pans along a slogan painted on the side of an airplane: "Down with Imperialism, Zionism and Israel." A long shot of three airplanes stationed on the runway at Dawson's Field in Jordan follows the pan. One of the airplanes suddenly explodes in the distance, and the voice-over notes how the PFLP's multiple hijackings garnered worldwide attention. The three empty airplanes, after the hostages were released, were indeed blown up to create a media spectacle. The opening sequence of *The Red Army/PFLP* thus draws a parallel between these two contemporaneous hijacking incidents undertaken by two Marxist-Leninist organizations in order to highlight the global scope of the anti-imperialist and anticapitalist revolutionary struggle. What is more important than the ideological alliance between the Japanese Red Army and the PFLP is, however, the film's inclusion of the following slogan (inserted right in the middle of the footage showing the exploding airplanes): "The Best Form of Propaganda Is Armed Struggle." In his discussion of *The Red Army/PFLP*, Abé Mark Nornes suggests that the affirmation of armed struggle as the best form of propaganda contradicts a claim made by Adachi, who supported the view that cinema is the best form of propaganda.[3] This seeming contradiction, however, is more than a mere inconsistency in the political position taken by Adachi; what the slogan reveals is, arguably, the very paradox of the propaganda of the deed.

For instance, what exactly is the rhetorical effect of editing the aforementioned slogan and the news footage of the exploding airplanes? The combination of the two suggests that hijacking is simultaneously a form of propaganda and an armed struggle; it serves as a media event and a direct action. But in order to be a form of propaganda, hijacking must be established first as an act of communication, a premise that complicates our understanding of the alleged directness of this action.[4] Once hijacked, an airplane deviates from its original function, a medium for transporting passengers, and becomes another kind of medium, one meant for communicating messages. It is precisely the *becoming-media* of the hijacked airplane that characterizes the paradoxical status of hijacking as a mediatized form of direct action. While hijacking an airplane might be a direct action, its communicative capacity as propaganda derives from its reliance on its journalistic coverage; the physical action alone is not enough to constitute hijacking itself as communication. The peculiarity of hijacking as the propaganda of the deed thus lies in its duality: (1) it is a means of political negotiations (e.g., it serves as leverage for the hostage and prisoner exchange); and (2) it is a medium for communicating political messages (e.g., the condemnation of the occupation of the land).

Hijacking is therefore said to belong to a special class of "mass-mediated" political violence. Its status as violence critically differs from other forms of political violence, as it is inseparable from its communicative function. Hijackings—and hostage-takings to some degree—are hence understood to be "politically motivated deeds perpetrated by groups or individuals for the sake of communicating messages to a larger audience."[5] In order for the hijacking to properly function as propaganda, however, it must capture the attention of the news media.

The communicative potential of the take-over and the becoming-media of the airplane thus depend on the participation of the news camera and reporters who help disseminate the message. Political hijacking is a direct action that rejects legally sanctioned procedures of political negotiation in favor of an alternative mode of communication. It reconfigures the institutionalized mode of political communication as it solicits collaborations by journalists. The deed is successfully transformed into propaganda when it undergoes this dual process of rerouting and mediatization. What the opening sequence of *The Red Army/PFLP* suggests is the inverted logic of *mediated direct action* as an alternative mode of political communication.

To better elucidate the idea of hijacking as an alternative mode of political communication, we may turn to Gilles Deleuze's and Félix Guattari's analysis of hijacking as a form of "incorporeal transformation," a concept that designates an instantaneous change in the incorporeal state of affairs or situations surrounding the corporeal entity. The primary examples of incorporeal transformation are the religious rite of the Eucharist and the political act of hijacking. When the bread and wine are consecrated during the rite of the Eucharist, they undergo an incorporeal transformation: they become "the body and blood of Christ." Similarly, when the hijacking of an airplane occurs, the bodies of the airplane and its passengers undergo an incorporeal transformation: "In an airplane hijacking the threat of a hijacker brandishing a revolver is obviously an action; so is the execution of the hostages, if it occurs. But the transformation of passengers into captives, and of the plane-body into a prison-body, is an instantaneous incorporeal transformation, a 'mass media act' in the sense in which the English speak of 'speech acts.'"[6] The hijacked airplane deviates from its intended path and undergoes a process of *rerouting* twice.

To put it differently, when the takeover of an airplane is declared, this speech act brings about an event of incorporeal transformation. Just as the utterance of a priest announcing the bread and wine to be the body and blood of Christ is necessary for the successful rite of Communion, the announcement of the takeover is central to the incorporeal transformation involved in hijacking. What is immaterially expressed in this statement joins the material force that concretely affects the body. Just as a sentence enunciated by a judge ("You are guilty") would transform the accused into a convict, a statement declaring the takeover of an airplane would transform passengers into hostages. The plane-body turns into the prison-body when the takeover is announced or made into a statement. The utterance of the takeover thus generates and partakes in the event of incorporeal transformation, which joins two heterogeneous orders of things and language.

That said, however, hijacking as a type of incorporeal transformation occupies a rather special place among performative speech acts. It is a *mass media act* carried out by a collective agent rather than by an individual who makes an utterance; hijacking is essentially a media event. Therefore, the physical takeover of an airplane alone does not constitute hijacking as a media event. The latter belongs to a different order of event, in which the agent of enunciation is no longer an individual—like a priest or a judge—but the apparatus of the news media that acts as the collective agent of this speech act.

The original French expression Deleuze and Guattari use for "a hijacking of an airplane" is *un détournement d'avion*.[7] The phrase aptly underscores the fact that hijacking is an event marked by the act of rerouting, a change of direction. The use of remediation as a formal strategy in the opening sequence of *The Red Army/PFLP* gains new significance when considered from the perspective of directionality: remediation is a type of semiotic rerouting. Deleuze's and Guattari's choice of the term *détournement* also resonates with the media strategy advocated by Situationist International artists and theorists. A certain similarity between Wakamatsu and Adachi's strategy of remediation and the Situationist International's artistic method of détournement might be noted. While Wakamatsu and Adachi's remediation of news is less systematic than the Situationists' appropriations of cultural texts—from advertisements to literary classics—their strategies resonate on two points: a reliance on citation and the affirmation of propaganda. As Guy Debord and Gil Wolman put it, the method of détournement is conceived as a strategy of political communication: "The literary and artistic heritage of humanity should be used for partisan propaganda purposes."[8] This affirmation of propaganda as the ultimate goal of artistic expression is a position adopted by *The Red Army/PFLP* as well. In both cases, the practice of détournement, or "hijacking," which reroutes the intended meaning of the original text, is intimately tied to the idea of propaganda, the communicative act of disseminating information and promoting a particular political message.

With this in mind, let us return to the opening montage in *The Red Army/PFLP*. Here, the formal strategy of remediating news footage mimics the semiotic act of hijacking or rerouting, mirroring the physical act of hijacking airplanes by the Red Army and the PFLP: this sequence as a whole serves as a double act of détournement. Instead of presenting the hijacking incidents as political crises or terrorism (as the original news reports did), the voice-over in this sequence presents them as revolutionary direct actions. The film thus mimics, at the semiotic level, the very process of hijacking.

As the film transforms remediated news footage into a form of propaganda, it engages in the performative speech act that brings about the incorporeal transformation of the footage. The whole sequence mimetically repeats the semiotic effects of hijacking as propaganda that deviates from the intended destination or message. The spectacular images of exploding airplanes at Dawson's Field, for instance, come to signify resistance rather than terrorism. *The Red Army/PFLP* as a propaganda film hence mirrors the hijacking as a mass-media act. The actual takeover of airplanes and the film's remediation of the news coverage of that event are parallel acts of détournement. As instances of incorporeal transformation, the physical appearance of the airplane and the surface of the image remain the same. But their expressions and significations have changed. Then, the practice of détournement is inseparable from the instrumental idea of a medium. Anything—from the body of a hijacked plane to the body of a pirated image—can be made into a medium of communication for the sake of propaganda: the medium is a means to an end.[9]

THE AMBIVALENCE OF TELEVISION

On close inspection, however, *The Red Army/PFLP* appears to contradict an instrumental conception of the medium. The film demonstrates a certain hesitancy toward such a vehicular understanding of a medium as a neutral means of transmitting a message. On the one hand, the opening sequence of *The Red Army/PFLP* clearly makes instrumental use of media. There is not much ambiguity in this sequence: the images of hijackings, the song "The Internationale," and the voice-over that declares, "This is a news film for the construction of the World Red Army." These elements are tightly organized in order to ensure the film's self-positioning as a revolutionary newsreel. The opaque materiality surrounding the medium—images and sounds—is minimized in order to guarantee the clarity of the message. On the other hand, after the opening sequence, *The Red Army/PFLP* develops an increasingly ambivalent relationship to the image. The film starts to lose clarity as it progresses. The first series of ambivalent images appears in the sequence in which a television monitor shows a myriad of information-based images (Japanese advertisements, news on the Sanrizuka farmers' armed resistance against the expropriation of their land by the state, weather reports, and so on). The second series of ambivalent images simply presents the monotonous landscapes of refugee camps and the daily activities of the PFLP guerrilla fighters. Both series of images complicate a seemingly straightforward definition of propaganda as a vehicular mode of communication.

The advertising sequence contradicts the logical premise of the opening sequence, that is, the constitutive role—and hence necessity—of the mainstream media for the publicity of armed struggle. The advertising sequence follows the second slogan, "Armed Struggle Is Reality," which appears as an intertitle. What precedes this television sequence, however, is a voice-over by Ghassan Kanafani, who defines propaganda as the means of delivering information; he notes that information is a means of communicating truth and the supreme form of truth is armed struggle. The film's first slogan—"The Best Form of Propaganda Is Armed Struggle"—reflects this definition of propaganda by Kanafani, who continues by saying: "We all know that the current propaganda system of American imperialists is the largest one in history. They control and dominate the world's television networks and newspapers, say whatever they want to say through these media, provide people with false education, and make films."[10] This critique of U.S. hegemony over the news media is followed by mostly silent documentary footage of the Shatila refugee camp, showing rows of houses, laundry on the rooftops, children on the streets, graffiti and countless bullet holes on the wall. Immediately after this documentary sequence, the second slogan appears.

After the intertitle "Armed Struggle Is Reality," the film cuts to a medium close-up of a color television monitor. A series of advertisements flash on the screen, as the voice-over asks a series of questions concerning the perception of reality: "Is reality fighting with the enemy? Who is really fighting the enemy? Are we able to fight the enemy for real?" The film then cuts to a close-up of the Red Army's banner, which is followed by another shot of the television screen. We see more advertisements for different commodities as well as a news program reporting on the Sanrizuka farmers' armed struggle—a series of protests against the proposed construction of the Narita Airport on expropriated farmers' land, which became a gathering point for New Left student activists as well as farmers from the area. The film cuts back and forth between the documentary images of the Red Army gathering and the remediated images of television news and advertisements. With its inclusion of the television monitor itself, this sequence also underscores the very fact of remediation.

Crucial to the rhetorical effect of this sequence is indeed the presence of the television monitor. With the blue glare and tracking lines typical of the filmed television screen functioning as a visual mark of remediation, this sequence draws attention to the material presence of television. Through the use of the voice-over, the film links the idea of the "enemy" to the apparatus of television. This rhetorical positioning of television as the enemy of the colonized and the oppressed echoes Kanafani's critique of the misinformation disseminated by the imperialist system of news production. However, this positioning of television as an apparatus of misinformation turns out to be not so straightforward.

Unlike the opening sequence, the remediated images in this section are not quite "readable" or transparent. For instance, one is pressed to interpret the connections between the different images: are we supposed to read advertisements and the Sanrizuka protests as equivalent in terms of their shared status as information commodities? Are they images of misinformation and hence part of capitalist propaganda? This reading is possible, yet not definite. The images of farmers behind the barricade are, after all, analogous to those of the militant revolutionaries; both are images of direct action captured by the news camera. In turn, the images of hijackings were also commodities, spectacles produced for and by television, which form an integral component of the global capitalism denounced by the voice-overs of the PFLP and Red Army militants. The metonymical association between the remediated news reports and advertisements presented in this sequence suggests their exchangeability as information commodities. They are exchangeable as information insofar as they appear on television. While the same technique of remediation is used in the opening montage, this sequence operates differently as it foregrounds the material presence of the television monitor.

In his analysis of Debord's films, which are similarly composed of remediated images from television, cinema, and print media, Giorgio

Agamben notes how Debord's use of repetition departs from a dominant understanding of artistic expression that negates the material presence of the medium: "The current concept of expression is dominated by the Hegelian model, in which all expression is realized by a *medium*—an image, a word, or a color—which in the end must disappear in the fully realized expression. The expressive act is fulfilled when the means, the medium, is no longer perceived as such."[11] In contrast, by virtue of their repetition, the remediated images in Debord's films draw attention to the stubborn presence of the medium. It does so by creating an interval between the original and its repetition, which makes visible what was invisible in the original. Thus, in Debord's films, "the image gives itself to be seen instead of disappearing in what it makes visible."[12] The same observation applies to the remediated television sequence in *The Red Army/PFLP*; the images do not disappear into the expressed contents of the advertisements and news. Instead, they draw attention to the mediating presence of television as a medium. As a result, the televisual image enters "a zone of undecidability."[13]

This is where the undecidability of television as a medium starts to destabilize the textual coherence of *The Red Army/PFLP* as a propaganda newsreel. On the one hand, the film aligns television with the capitalist mode of production and image consumption; on the other hand, it positions television as the principal conduit of publicity needed for a successful execution of propaganda of the deed. If propaganda of the deed, such as the hijacking of an airplane, exemplifies the axiom—the best form of propaganda is armed struggle—and if the political efficacy of this propaganda hinges on its journalistic coverage by the mainstream news media, including major television networks, it is not possible to simply reject television as an apparatus of misinformation. For the mediation and dissemination of direct action, such as hijacking, enacted by television are yoked to armed struggle insofar as television facilitates an incorporeal transformation of the hijacking into an act of communication. Television as the quintessential medium of mass publicity thus becomes a paradoxical object of negation and affirmation.

THE CONJUNCTIVE "AND"

Godard's and Miéville's *Here and Elsewhere*, a film that similarly raises the question of mediation and its relation to armed struggle, echoes the ambivalent position occupied by television in *The Red Army/PFLP*. A comparative analysis of the two films will help elucidate this position. *Here and Elsewhere* is based on the unfinished film project *Until Victory*, which started as a collective work of the Dziga Vertov Group under the commission of the PLO. In order to make *Until Victory*, Godard and Gorin interviewed Palestinian militants, observed gatherings, and documented the life at refugee camps. Four years later, this unfinished documentary film dedicated to Palestinian revolutionaries was transformed into a contemplative essay film that self-reflexively interrogates the manipulation of images and sounds: the cropping of images, the artificial staging of actors, the effacement of individual Palestinian voices due to a dogmatic belief in the collective voice of the people, and so on. The reflexive tone of *Here and Elsewhere* contrasts with the agitprop tone of *The Red Army/PFLP*, though both are equally concerned with the same problem of mediation: cinema's relation to revolution, the image's relation to action, and the relation between here and elsewhere.

If *The Red Army/PFLP* accentuates the geopolitical proximity between Japan and Palestine on the ground of the international alliance among Marxist revolutionaries, *Here and Elsewhere* stresses the geopolitical distance between France and Palestine, emblematically separated by the television set. While *The Red Army/PFLP* draws a parallel between the news coverage of Japanese militants and that of Palestinian revolutionaries, *Here and Elsewhere* juxtaposes images of a working-class French family watching television in their living room with images of Palestinian fighters engaging in military drills. Nonetheless, both films are concerned with and invested in the question of relationality, which is graphically expressed by the slash (/) in the title *The Red Army/PFLP* and by the conjunction *et* (and) in *Here and Elsewhere*. In other words, the central problematic for both films is relationality, which surfaces as a series of reflections on mediation and remediation. And this concern with relationality manifests itself as an interrogation of the media.

Not surprisingly, both films showcase multiple media forms on the screen, though *Here and Elsewhere* presents a more diverse range of media than does *The Red Army/PFLP*. The images in *Here and Elsewhere* include shots of multiple television monitors and slides, reproductions of still photographs and newspapers, the face of a digital calculator, the volume control of an amplifier, and the blue letters of an early computer screen. In spite of this variety, however, the film keeps coming back to television. It is the television that allows the film to interrogate its own politics of mediation and remediation. In a particularly salient sequence, Godard and Miéville comment on the 1972 Munich Olympic Games and the attendant hostage crisis, wherein several Palestinian militants kidnapped and subsequently murdered eleven Israeli athletes. During this incident, a group of Palestinian militants—named Black September after the Black September attack of 1970, in which thousands of Palestinians were killed by the Jordanian army (which in turn was a retaliation against the Dawson's Field Hijacking)—demanded the release of one hundred Palestinian prisoners from Israeli prisons in exchange for the release of Israeli hostages.

In this sequence a French family—mother, father, and two children—are watching television in their living room. The male voice-over says, "September '72. Olympic Games. A Palestinian commando seizes a dozen hostages from the Israeli team and threatens to execute them if a hundred of his Palestinian fellows, prisoners in Israel, aren't released." Overlapping the voice-over are a cacophony of cheers and live coverage of the Olympic Games. We see a close-up of one Palestinian commando being interviewed, then a medium shot of three Palestinian girls dressed in uniform. This footage was shot for *Until Victory* before the massacre of September 1970, during which many of the militants Godard and Gorin interviewed were killed.[14] The female voice-over comes in: "I don't know. I'm sure there was something else to be done. Think it over. The conditions under which it happened." The film cuts to a fixed medium shot of a television monitor—empty, blue, and static. The voice-over continues: "In Munich that day the force of imperialism was television, and billions of spectators wanted a program. So, it could have been possible to take advantage of the whole world listening and say, 'Show this image from time to time.'" At this point, a long static shot of a refugee camp appears on the screen. Though silent, this image speaks loudly of the reality of displacement. The film cuts back to the empty television monitor, and the voice-over notes that if the television networks broadcasting the Olympic tournament had refused to show this image, the hostage-takers could have threatened the captives with violence ("We'll kill the hostages and we'll be killed afterwards"). With this evocation of death, the film cuts to a still photograph of the face of a dead Palestinian man. "And for them as for us, we find it stupid to die for an image, and we are a little scared," says the voice-over, as the film cuts back to the static shot of the empty, blue television monitor, and then to a black-and-white still photograph of Holocaust survivors staring at the camera from behind the barbed-wire fence: another camp, another displacement, another death.

This sequence is structured by a series of repetitions and echoes: the image of a Palestinian refugee camp and the image of a Nazi concentration camp; the image of television viewers and the image of the television screen; the deaths of Israelis and the deaths of Palestinians; Munich of 1972 and Amman of 1970. In its insistence on the connection between images, this sequence is emblematic of the whole film. It visualizes the conjunctive logic of "and," which subtends the film's reflexive interrogation of the mediating function of various media. The sequence is also suggestive of the importance of the linkage between image and political action. As the voice-over insists, there might have been a different way of conducting armed struggle: instead of asking for the release of hostages, the Palestinian militants could have asked for the image of the refugee camp to be broadcast on television to the billions of viewers avidly watching the Olympic Games. This, she implies, would have been as important an act as that of demanding the hostage-prisoner exchange. Read this way, the sequence explicitly foregrounds the relationship between an image and action, and implicitly the relationship between an image and death. To die for the image seems "stupid," she says, and yet this option is proposed as a possible alternative form of action ("There was something else to be done").

Commenting precisely on this sequence from *Here and Elsewhere*, Adachi recalls how assured he felt, since this commentary on dying for the image suggested to him the necessity of making politically committed films such as *The Red Army/PFLP*.[15] But what does it mean to die for an image? How does it relate to the efficacy of making films? At the least, the proposed "option" of dying for the image here is not a simple affirmation of militant cinema. Rather, it points to a triangular relation among three media of communication: armed struggle, cinema, and television. In fact, the proposition of risking one's life to show the image of the refugee camp on television turns out to be much more ambiguous.

First, the voice-over comment points to the presence of fear underneath the veneer of stupidity ("We are a little scared"). This evocation of fear in relation to the image is suggestive. One implication is that none of us wish to risk our life for just a few seconds of television time, yet the film's insertion of the press photograph of the dead Palestinian militant suggests that some have already died for that very reason. The same photograph appears earlier in *Here and Elsewhere*, with the caption "Amman, 1970." This photograph is thus a metonymic reminder of Black September, a civil war in which the King of Jordan declared martial law and his army crushed Palestinian guerrillas. This attack was a direct retaliation against the successful hijackings (Dawson's Field Hijackings) that had been carried out by the PFLP. This spectacular hijacking incident was not only an instrument of political negotiation, but also an effective means of propaganda, with the explosion of three airplanes at Dawson's Field, just outside the city of Amman in Jordan, being staged for the media, and for television in particular. In light of this historical context, we may read the photographic image of the dead Palestinian militant as an icon of death dedicated to propaganda. The proposition to die for an image can then be taken literally, as a reference to the history of hijackings carried out by Palestinian revolutionaries who demanded that their acts be broadcast and publicized to the entire world.

However, this initial reading, based on the affirmation of televised propaganda, is challenged by the film's insertion of the landscape of a refugee camp. While *Here and Elsewhere* does not show actual news footage of the Munich hostage-taking, the voice-over suggests that such a spectacle of violence was staged for and preferred by television. The rhetorical juxtaposition of these two types of images—the landscape and the hostage crisis—makes them antithetical to each other from the perspective of the televisual economy of the image. Television demands spectacular images that command the attention of the viewer. And what television prefers in particular—and what the news media prefers in general—is the image of crisis: an image that ruptures the fabric of the everyday, an image that can be translated into "breaking news." Understood in this manner, the film's insistence on the image of the refugee camp becomes crucial to the film's critique of television, a medium that capitalizes on visible and readable political violence, such as hostage-taking and hijacking.

TO DIE FOR AN IMAGE

Let us look closely at the image of the refugee camp, which appears when the voice-over says, "Show this image from time to time." On the screen is a long shot of dusty white tents and crumbling barracks standing on the parched land, decorated only by rows of colorful laundry. In the distance residents are walking across the camp. It is a serene image in which nothing spectacular or dramatic is taking place. The image lacks action. To demand that this image be broadcast on television instead of the live coverage of the Olympic Games would be tantamount to forcing television to deviate from its economy of spectacle. The voice-over in *Here and Elsewhere* suggests that the hostage-takers demand that network television replace the action-packed images of sports with this image of inaction. Arguably, what this sequence proposes is an alternative economy of exchange contrary to capital. It proposes to exchange an image filled with dramatic action for an image devoid of dramatic action, to exchange a spectacle for a nonspectacle. Insofar as the attention of television viewers is already a commodity to be sold to advertisers, forcing this exchange would amount to hijacking or enacting a détournement of television, which the film directly equates with the imperial system of capital ("In Munich on that day the force of imperialism was television"). To divert the attention of billions of television viewers from the spectacles of the Olympic Games to the image of the refugee camp would be to hijack the airwaves and reroute the economy of spectacle. If this exchange of images fails, the film suggests, the Palestinian hostage-takers and Israeli hostages will all be killed. They will be killed for an image and be killed by the imperial force of capitalism (embodied by television), which rejects this exchange for the sake of spectacle. The repeated images of the empty blue television monitor thus rhetorically stand in for the invisible presence of the third party—capitalists—who refuses images that do not fit into the televisual order of information and crisis.

But this reading of the sequence as a call for hijacking the airwaves is challenged and countered by another possible interpretation. As the film cuts from the photograph of the Palestinian militant to the photograph of Jewish prisoners in the Nazi concentration camp, the voice-over says, "We are a little scared." The evocation of fear in relation to the image of Jewish prisoners standing behind the barbed-wire fence complicates the previous affirmation of death for propaganda purposes. This poignant photograph suggests that people have not only voluntarily died for images, but also that some have been killed for images against their will. The Nazi Party's obsession with its own image, for instance, demanded that the Jewish prisoners be annihilated for it.[16] History thus tells us that the voluntary act of *dying* for the image cannot be separated from the involuntary act of *being killed* for the image.

The use of montage by Godard and Miéville in this sequence (and indeed throughout the film) not only highlights the articulation between two images, but also points to the mediating presence of the third party that makes this articulation possible. In presenting a series of still images that includes photographs of violence and political conflict as well as advertisements, the film raises a question—"How does one discover one's own image?"—and answers by juxtaposing images and displaying them side-by-side on nine screens, and by editing them one after another. The film thus spatially and temporally makes visible the relation between images. Yet the correlation between the self and the other is mediated by the camera, which functions as "the gaze of a third person who is not yet there, but is already represented by a photographic lens." One's self-image, suggests the film, depends on the image of the other mediated by the apparatus of the camera. We see a still photograph of a man pointing a camera at something off-screen. The film camera then pans down to reveal the rest of the photograph: the man is taking a picture of a dead person lying on the ground. On the soundtrack, the voice-over notes, "As a matter of fact, it is likely that one constructs one's own image with the other's." The process of self-representation is a process of *appropriation*, an act of making one's own what belongs to the other, which in turn is linked to finding a proper image of the self (as the voice-over claims, it is about the question of "rediscovering one's own image": *retrouver sa propre image*).

When analyzed through the question of the proper self-image, the relation between the photograph of the dead Palestinian commando and the photograph of Jewish prisoners at the Nazi concentration camp becomes more complicated. Beyond the causal relation of displacement and beyond the ontological relation to death, this montage of two disparate images draws attention to the presence of the principal mediator: the camera. With this acknowledgment of the invisible agent behind the camera who makes and takes images, *Here and Elsewhere* redirects its critique of television toward its own medium as well. Whether mediated by television or by cinema, images are never simple; this is the point *Here and Elsewhere* repeatedly asserts. "There is no simple image," says the voice-over in a sequence that presents four television monitors showing four different programs; in another sequence, the voice-over says, "Too easy and too simple to simply divide the world in two."

This point is further complicated by the film's interrogation of sound, which functions as an additional framing device that delimits the meanings of the image. Just as the camera can crop the still photograph, showing only the cameraman but not the corpse, sound can delimit the image by overpowering its signification. As the film self-critically suggests, the 1970 version of *Until Victory* suppressed and replaced the individual voices of Palestinians with Godard's voice, which interpreted the images according to his Maoist vision of the people's war. This critique is visually presented through close-ups of a volume meter and of a hand manipulating the volume control of an amplifier. The voice-over suggests that power operates not only through domination but also through appropriation, through taking over what belongs to the other and making it one's own. Here, the question of appropriation is directly linked to the question of representation, as it interrogates representation in its double sense: the aesthetic sense of re-presentation and its political sense of speaking for the other. The film thereby complicates the relations between images, between sounds, and between images and sounds as relations of appropriation, property, and proper boundaries.

TELEVISION AND LANDSCAPE

If *Here and Elsewhere* and *The Red Army/PFLP* insist on showing the television monitor, as they remediate and appropriate televisual images, it is because television is the other that enables cinema to discover its own image. The tension between the two media manifests itself through complex relations of appropriation and domination in both films, but often this tension is displaced onto a gap between two types of images: those of violence or armed struggle and those of landscapes or refugee camps. What is the significance of these two types of images? A short answer to this question points to differing economies of attention. While cinema and television both demand and manage the attention of viewers, their systems of attention management differ. Television fragments time more rigorously than cinema, constantly translates representation into information, and prevents viewers from engaging in contemplation even more forcibly than cinema.

As John Fiske, Jane Feuer, and others have argued, television structures the economy of attention through the dialectic of flow and segmentation. The endless flow of television—one can turn it on and watch something at any point of the day—generates a sense of continuity, yet this continuity is predicated on the succession of disconnected and discrete segments.[17] Television exploits the shock value that accompanies the unexpected, the instantaneous, and the discontinuous, all the while rigorously structuring and programming what appears on the monitor. For every second of the airtime is an investment and must be programmed with an understanding of attention as the prime commodity for advertisements. While this classic understanding of television in terms of its economy of attention management may have limitations, it offers a framework by which to analyze the ambivalent positioning of television as cinema's "other" in *Here and Elsewhere* and *The Red Army/PFLP*. While *Here and Elsewhere* clearly offers a more extensive reflection on television, both films present television as a medium directly linked to the spectacular economy of attention and capitalism.[18]

In both films a television monitor appears as a profilmic object. This fact in itself does not tell us much unless we understand the central role television played in disseminating images of political violence in the early 1970s. But considering that both films are deeply concerned with the Palestinian armed struggle *and* with cinema's relation to armed struggle, the gesture of filming the television monitor must be read critically. *Here and Elsewhere* includes the television set as a major element of its mise-en-scène. Similarly, in the abovementioned sequence, *The Red Army/PFLP* films the television monitor as it presents an array of advertisements and news reports on the Sanrizuka farmers' struggle. The inclusion of the monitor punctuates this sequence, drawing our attention not so much to the content of each segment—whether it is an advertisement or a news report—but rather to the material presence of the screen itself. Television is thus presented as a profilmic object. This framing of television as an object enables *Here and Elsewhere* and *The Red Army/PFLP* to visually differentiate their textual practice from that of television programs.

The distance between cinema and television, moreover, is rhetorically presented by the use of strikingly similar visual elements in *Here and Elsewhere* and *The Red Army/PFLP*. Both emphasize images of refugee camps, which they set against televisual images of advertisements and news. We may recall that the alternative image proposed to be aired during the Munich Olympics in *Here and Elsewhere* is the long shot of the refugee camp. Remarkably similar images of refugee camps appear in the documentary sequences of *The Red Army/PFLP* (figures 5.2 and 5.3). There is something peculiar about the way in which these land-

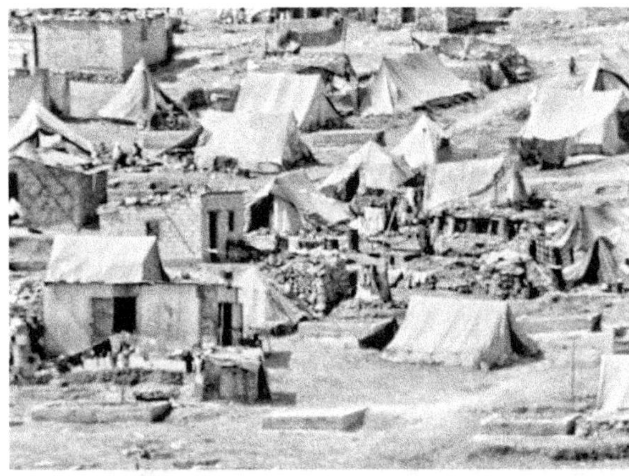

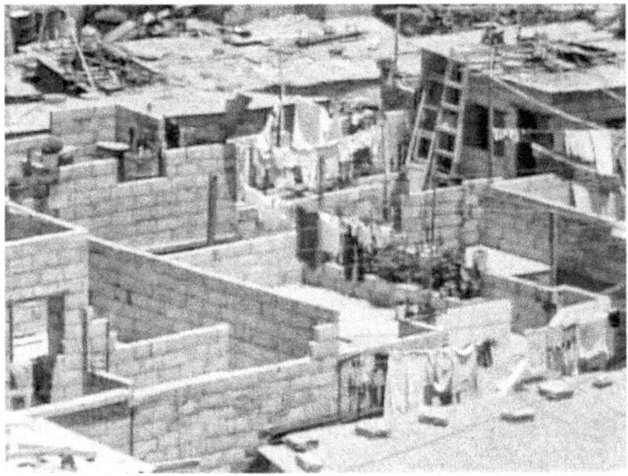

5.2. A Palestinian refugee camp. Still from *Here and Elsewhere* (1974), dir. Jean-Luc Godard and Anne-Marie Miéville.

5.3. Shatila refugee camp. Still from *The Red Army/PFLP* (Wakamatsu Production, 1971).

scape shots are used in the two films. The refugee-camp landscapes are similar precisely in their unremarkable quality and their lack of spectacularity. They are also similar in their scale, duration, and high camera angle. The camera lingers on the scenery, composed of tattered barracks and rows of tents, in which nothing dramatic is happening. Lacking the immediate sign of action, let alone violence, these landscapes do not fit the televisual order of "breaking news" or crisis, with which the Israeli-Palestinian conflict became increasingly associated in the 1960s and 1970s. These landscapes are antithetical to dramatic images of hijacking, hostage-taking, and bombing, which television eagerly transforms into spectacles. Thus, these landscapes can be read as forming a rhetorical counterpoint to the commodified flow of televisual images.

The nondramatic quality of landscape as a cinematic image was important for Adachi. The concept of landscape theorized by Adachi, Matsuda, Nakahira, and others who participated in the fūkeiron discourse goes beyond a readily visible sight or scene. Instead, the filmed landscape functions as a diagram of governmental power, and landscape films, such as *A.K.A. Serial Killer* and *The Man Who Left His Will on Film*, actively endeavor to diagrammatically map—and make visible—the invisible yet ubiquitous relations of power. Landscapes as they appear in these films are more than documentary images. Certainly, they could function as mimetic or photorealistic documents of particular places at particular moments. However, their political significance lies in their ability to indirectly point to—or index—what remains invisible. In the case of *A.K.A. Serial Killer* and *The Man Who Left His Will on Film*, it was the governmental power of the Japanese state. This is why the images of landscapes must be understood in the dual sense of indexing or pointing; the cinematic image of landscape is both a document of a singular place and a diagram of governmentality.

A diagrammatic understanding of landscape is relevant to our analysis of *The Red Army/PFLP* as well as of *Here and Elsewhere*. The images of landscapes are equally tied to the question of state power, and they play a pivotal role in these two films' critique of television's implication in its operation. In the history of the Israeli-Palestinian conflict, the political significance of land is indisputable. As Eyal Weizman argues, since the 1967 War, the physical transformation and the political interpretation of the landscape in the occupied Palestinian territories of the West Bank and Gaza have been directly implicated in the military control and the civilian system of governance that the Israeli state developed, not only through the violent means of acquiring land by warfare, but also through the much more subtle yet equally effective means of strategic settlements, forced land requisition, urban planning, and calculated constructions of roads, highways, bridges, and tunnels. Throughout the 1970s, "architecture and planning were thus used as the continuation of war by other means. Just like the tank, the gun, and the bulldozer, building matter and infrastructure were used to achieve tactical and strategic aims."[19] In the 1970s the transformation as well as the maintenance of the landscape formed the focal point of the military and civilian organization of space. From barbed-wire security fences to trenches to bullet holes in the walls of houses inside camps, the landscape images that appear in *The Red Army/PFLP* and *Here and Elsewhere* also bear witness to the history of reciprocal violence waged over and in the name of sovereignty, territory, and security.[20]

Understood in this context, it makes perfect sense that the image of a refugee camp occupies the central place in *Here and Elsewhere* and *The Red Army/PFLP*. The visible image of the refugee camp points to the invisible diagram of power relations that give rise to various techniques of governing a population without directly engaging in war. Furthermore, the centrality of the landscape as a key motif in these films needs to be examined in relation to a particular kind of temporality that characterizes camp life.

Consider, for instance, the documentary footage of the Jerash camp from *The Red Army/PFLP*. The camera repeatedly pans from close-ups of objects (such as a bullet hole in the wall) to expansive landscape shots containing the camp, such as the long-shot of rows of barracks standing against the blue-grey sky and hills, or the shot of houses, with tattered windows and bullet holes, lining both sides of a dusty narrow street. Adachi's camerawork alternates between pans and fixed long takes, just as it did in *A.K.A. Serial Killer*. At one point, the film shows an overview of the camp from what appears to be the rooftop of a building—the serene but mundane landscape of a Palestinian encampment in Jordan, which was established as a temporary "emergency camp" in 1968. As the image-track shows the mundane landscape inside the camp, the soundtrack presents the voice-over of Leila Khaled, who narrates how she gave up her career as a schoolteacher along with her "petty-bourgeois life" in order to join the PFLP's armed struggle, whose ultimate aim, she notes, is proletarian revolution.

This sequence is interesting not for its overt affirmation of Marxist-

Leninist ideology, but for the way it complicates our interpretation of the first slogan presented in the film ("The Best Form of Propaganda Is Armed Struggle"). The banality of the landscapes at the Jerash camp in this sequence also contrasts starkly with the spectacular quality of the news footage in the opening sequence, which presents the violent explosions of hijacked airplanes. This contrast points to alternate understandings of the temporality of "armed struggle." On the one hand, armed struggle means engaging in combat or militant action. On the other hand, armed struggle includes the patient state of waiting and not directly engaging in militant action. It is to this second temporal modality of armed struggle that the landscape images are linked. This focus on the quotidian temporality of waiting and on the nonspectacular sight of the refugee camp complicates the film's seemingly straightforward embrace of violence. Armed struggle, in other words, is neither equivalent to violence, nor reducible to militant direct action.

In this regard it is worth noting that the slogan "Armed Struggle Is to Be On Standby" appears in the scene that observes the day-to-day lives of Palestinian commandos. This slogan complicates the semantic association drawn between the images of airplane hijackings and the first slogan. While the first slogan implies that hijacking and other forms of direct militant action, which capture the attention of the mass media, are the best way to propagandize the cause of political struggle, the second slogan suggests that the best form of propaganda is the image of waiting and being ready; the latter does not require the spectacle of violence as a medium of communication. The film's persistent focus on routine activities—such as cooking, drinking, sleeping, talking, and reading, all engaged in by the residents of various refugee camps as well as by the PFLP guerrilla fighters—indicates that communicating this quotidian landscape and the temporality of camp life *is* the best form of propaganda.

Crucial here is the monotonous rhythm of daily life, which contrasts with the condensed time of mediatized violence and political crisis that characterizes the news coverage of the Israeli-Palestinian conflict. The tedium conveyed by the images of banal landscapes and refugee camps allows the film to differentiate its status as a *newsreel* from the conventional journalistic practice of newsmaking, especially by television. The sense of urgency, rupture, and interruption marks the televisual economy of news, and among information deemed newsworthy, a political crisis such as the hijacking of an airplane often generates the greatest sense of urgency. The televisual temporality of crisis—be it a hijacking, hostage-taking, assassination, or coup d'état—compresses time and intensifies its experience with a desire for dramatic resolution.[21] The monotonous time of waiting and living embodied by the emblematic landscape of the refugee camp, which the documentary sequences of *The Red Army/PFLP* make felt, is diametrically opposed to the condensed temporality of crisis. Given Adachi's critical stance toward television (which he aligns with state power), it is reasonable to read this opposition allegorically. The monotonous temporality of waiting and living in a temporary refugee camp is aligned with the medium of cinema, whereas the condensed temporality of crisis and violence is aligned with the medium of television. This reading explains why all the violent images of armed conflict in the film are *not* shot by Adachi or Wakamatsu, but remediated from television.

According to Adachi, what he wanted to film most in Palestine was the repetitiveness and tediousness of everyday life. His desire to document the most mundane aspects of daily life was, however, a source of tension during the filming of *The Red Army/PFLP*. Shigenobu Fusako, who was working as a translator for Adachi and Wakamatsu at the time, recalls how frustrated Adachi became at one of the guerrilla bases in southern Lebanon: "Cinema meant action for most of these commandos. Fixated on the perception of cinema based on Hollywood, they didn't accept ideas such as 'surrealism' and 'fūkeiron.' Adachi would then get angry and put his camera down, shouting, 'No! I want to film your life, its everydayness, and the attitude of being on standby for revolution!'"[22]

Adachi confirms how he struggled to communicate his vision of an *alternative* newsreel, one which privileged the nondramatic and the ordinary over the dramatic and the extraordinary.

> When we arrived, there were other filmmakers from Europe, such as those related to the French socialist solidarity movement and the Italian socialist group associated with the newspaper *Il Manifesto*. They were also there to make documentary propaganda films, but their approaches were identical to the methods of making ordinary P.R. films. This shocked me. For example, they would light up the entire classroom at a school inside the refugee camp as they documented the lesson. They would even embellish things. The PFLP officers would chime in and invite us to film it, saying, "This is a really

> good condition which doesn't come so often—you should film this!" But since we refused to shoot it, saying, "There is no use filming things that are already understood," we ended up arguing. Then they asked us, "What do you want to film then?" I replied by saying, "We want to document situations like the one where women are washing clothes in the kitchen, right next to a Kalashnikov." They would then treat us as if we were crazy by saying, "That's so ordinary, why do you want to film that!"[23]

Adachi's insistence on shooting the everyday scenery wherein nothing extraordinary was happening clearly echoes his stance toward the landscape as expressed two years earlier in *A.K.A. Serial Killer* and the discourse of the fūkeiron. Ironically, the finished version of *The Red Army/PFLP* includes a dramatic "reenactment" of a battle scene performed by the PFLP soldiers, a sign of compromise between the filmmakers and their collaborators. While this inclusion of the reenactment scene undermines Adachi's stance toward the landscape developed in *A.K.A. Serial Killer*, his skepticism toward the spectacle of violence that feeds the mainstream news media clearly is carried into the making of *The Red Army/PFLP*.

FROM LANDSCAPE TO NEWS REPORT

The decisive break between *A.K.A. Serial Killer* and *The Red Army/PFLP*, however, is not merely the latter's use of reenactment. A more profound difference is to be found in *The Red Army/PFLP*'s emphasis on cinema's capacity to intervene directly in the journalistic economy of the news. The starting point of *A.K.A. Serial Killer* is the media's sensational coverage of Nagayama's crime, which the film appropriates in order to interrogate the connection between the landscape and the state. The news of Nagayama's arrest still serves as the basis of the film, even though its focus is on the ubiquity of the governmental power that operates through urban planning, traffic control, and infrastructure building. The starting point of *The Red Army/PFLP*, in contrast, is the production of an alternative kind of news that serves the goal of revolutionary struggle. Instead of referencing already produced news, *The Red Army/PFLP* aims to construct an alternative circuit of information. In short, *The Red Army/PFLP* appropriates the very practice of journalism itself as the operative ground of militant cinema.

Adachi himself articulates the strategic shift from *A.K.A. Serial Killer* to *The Red Army/PFLP*. Together with Matsuda, Adachi describes the shift away from landscape (*fūkei*) to news report (*hōdō*) as a necessary step to continue an activist mode of filmmaking and film criticism in the 1970s. A number of essays published by Adachi in the film journal *Eiga Hihyō II* between 1970 and 1973 foreground the notion of the news report. Similarly, Matsuda notes in the afterword to his 1973 book, *Impossible Media (Fukanōsei no media)*, that he and Adachi conceived of the strategic transition from landscape to news report as a means to further politicize cinema.[24] The goal of *Eiga Hihyō II*, for which Matsuda and Adachi both served as editors, was also to reinvent film criticism as activism. They envisioned the activist filmmaker as both a journalist *and* a revolutionary. "We had no model to rely on," writes Matsuda, "but we were struggling to position ourselves as *journalists* living in the transformative age, and the activities of the Dziga Vertov Group were the only indirect help we found in this process."[25]

While this way of envisioning film criticism was not new—the preceding incarnation of the journal *Eiga Hihyō I* (1957–59) similarly upheld the transformative power of film theory and criticism—its emphasis on defining cinema as a form of activism or movement (*undō*) attained added significance in light of the revolutionary filmmaking in Latin America, the Middle East, and Europe. It is not a coincidence that *Eiga Hihyō II* published a number of seminal texts on revolutionary filmmaking, including Solanas's and Getino's "Towards a Third Cinema" in 1973. According to Adachi, Solanas's and Getino's proposition for Third Cinema resonated strongly with his own vision of militant cinema and the film-screening movement.[26]

It is also important to note that the publication of *Eiga Hihyō II* started after the making of *A.K.A. Serial Killer* and the emergence of the fūkeiron discourse, which reached a certain theoretical impasse as various critics began to indiscriminately appropriate the notion of "landscape" as a convenient metaphor for different purposes. Adachi's and Matsuda's decision to move away from landscape as a key term was therefore strategic. Interestingly, the first issue of *Eiga Hihyō II*, published in 1970, features a photomontage composed of the diagram of an eye and a photographic portrait of Adachi, with the caption "Landscape as an institution bequeathed from the past" (figure 5.4). The caption anticipates, perhaps inadvertently, Adachi's eventual abandonment of landscape as a key word in his own writing in the early 1970s. This

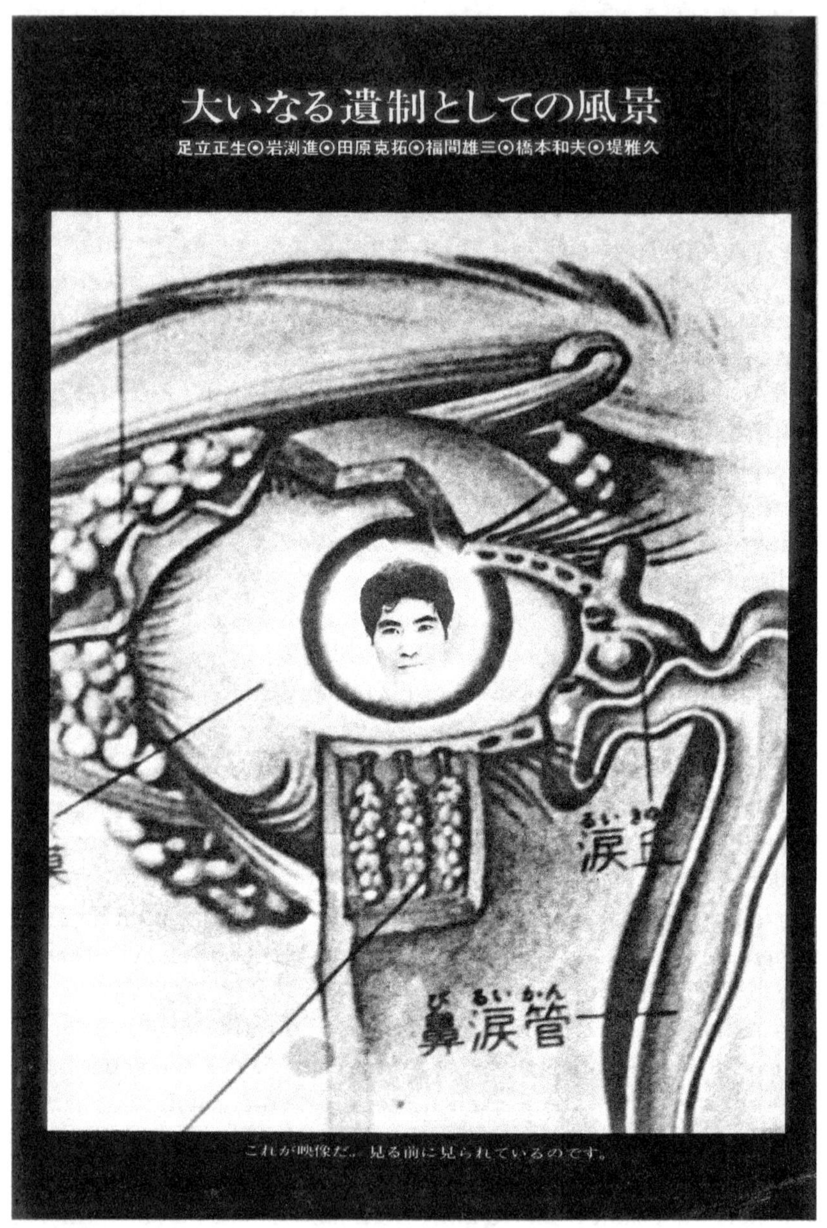

5.4. A photomontage, including a photograph of Adachi, published in the inaugural issue of *Eiga Hihyō II* (October 1970).

issue of *Eiga Hihyō II* also includes an essay by Hara Masato, which questions Oshima's treatment of landscape in *The Man Who Left His Will on Film* in light of the discourse on fūkeiron, and Tsumura Takashi's seminal essay on Godard and *Vent d'est* (1970), in which Tsumura advocates the need to reinvent cinema as a revolutionary mode of journalism that keeps an eye on the Third World. As is evident from the contrast between these two essays—one focuses on the landscape, the other on the news film—the intermediary role of *Eiga Hihyō II* as an organ of activist filmmaking and criticism was crucial in facilitating the transition from *A.K.A. Serial Killer* to *The Red Army/PFLP*. The journal served as a nodal point of theory and practice, and offered a productive venue for discussions and debates among the filmmakers associated with the cinema of actuality.

The reclaiming of the newsreel as a militant mode of filmmaking clearly came out of this discursive milieu, and the work of the Dziga Vertov Group offered much inspiration to Adachi, even as he criticized Godard's use of the black screen as a sign of philosophical introspection.[27] The recurrent use of intertitles in *The Red Army/PFLP* is also indebted to the preceding work of Godard, who in turn is indebted to the work of Vertov.[28] Given their engagement with journalism, it is not surprising that Adachi and Wakamatsu turned to the project of making a militant newsreel. However, their attention to Palestine and to the rhetoric of Third World liberation movements was clearly a timely response to the discursive milieu of Japanese film criticism at the time. Here, it is worth noting that *Kikan Firumu* [Film quarterly]—another influential film journal edited by none other than Matsumoto Toshio—published two specials, one on the work of Glauber Rocha (presented as an auteur from the Third World) and the other on *Vent d'est*, in November 1970, just a few weeks after the publication of the inaugural issue of *Eiga Hihyō II*. The front cover of *Kikan Firumu*, designed by Awazu Kiyoshi, features a playful photomontage of the title character from Rocha's *Antonio das Mortes* (1969), a film which had just opened at Art Theatre Shinjuku Bunka in late October (figure 5.5). In March 1971, only two months before Adachi and Wakamatsu flew to Beirut, *Eiga Hihyō II* published translated scripts by Vertov, and *Kikan Firumu* published another special on Rocha along with a large special on Vertov. The special includes seven translated essays by Vertov and the translation of his production proposal for *The Man with a Movie Camera* (1929), as well as a translation of Marcel Martin's interview with Godard on the formation

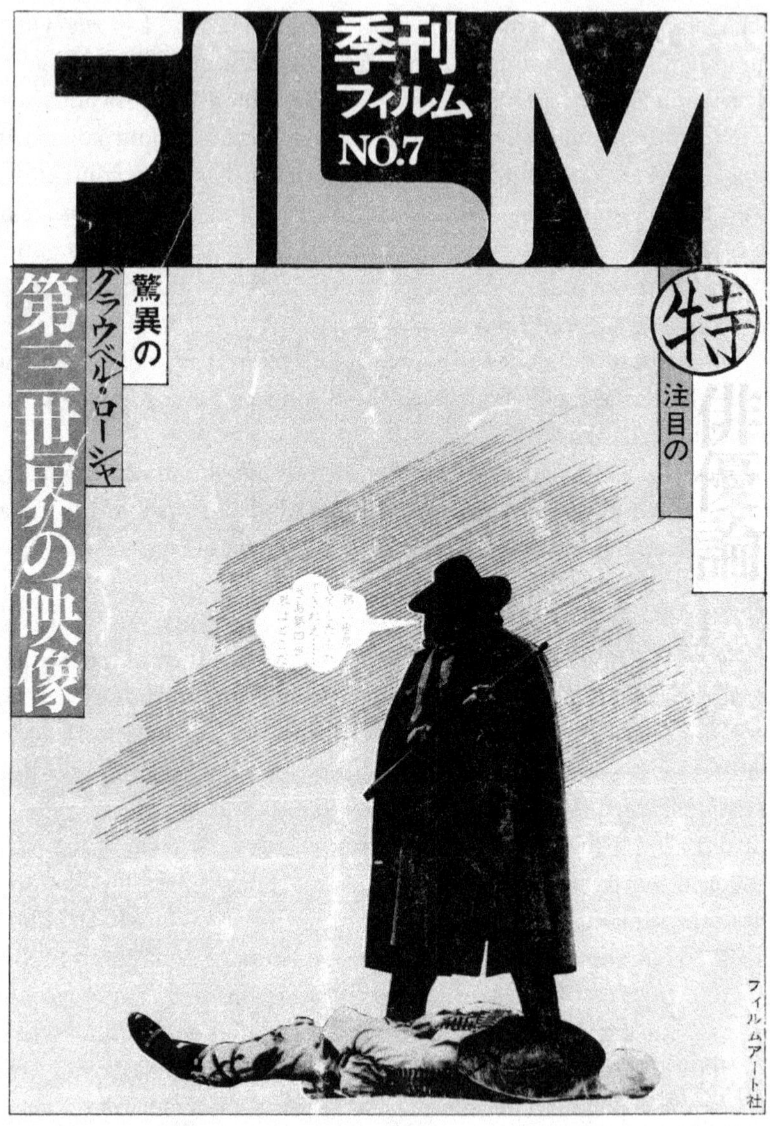

5.5. Front cover of *Kikan Firumu* (November 1970), featuring a photomontage of Antonio das Mortes with a word bubble: "I can't get stuck in the Third World. . . . Where is the Fourth World?"

of the Dziga Vertov Group, originally published in the December 1970 issue of *Cinéma*.

It is likely that the attention directed toward political filmmakers such as Godard, Rocha, and Vertov in 1970–71 laid the groundwork for Adachi and Wakamatsu's decision to make *The Red Army/PFLP*, though other factors, such as their personal connection with Shigenobu, a founding member of the Japanese Red Army in the Middle East, no doubt had a more immediate impact. A concern with actuality—especially with its journalistic attributes of topicality, newsworthiness, and timeliness—was central to the radical cinematic experiments undertaken by Oshima, Matsumoto, Wakamatsu, and Adachi. Arguably, the cinema of actuality reached its logical conclusion with the making of *The Red Army/PFLP*, which embraced journalism as an exemplary mode of militant, revolutionary filmmaking. The militant conception of newsreel as a means of directly participating in revolution, moreover, extends to the film's performative use of intertitles and to the screening movement, which functions as an integral component of the film's efficacy as propaganda.

SLOGANS AND THE SCREENING MOVEMENT

A final element in *The Red Army/PFLP*, which complicates the idea of mediation and direct action, is the series of intertitles that display militant slogans such as "The Best Form of Propaganda Is Armed Struggle," "Armed Struggle Is to Be On Standby," "Revolution = World War," and so on. Insofar as these slogans aim to mobilize the audience to support the film's political cause, they operate as what Deleuze and Guattari call "order-words" (*mot d'ordre*). Order-words function as performative speech acts, and hence help bring about incorporeal transformations. For instance, the Marxist political slogan "Workers of the world, unite!" was not merely a motto that expressed an already existing ideology. Rather, it affected the state of affairs and created a new condition of possibility for politics, as it "constituted an incorporeal transformation that extracted from the masses a proletarian class as an assemblage of enunciation *before* the conditions were present for the proletariat to exist as a body."[29]

Much as the act of hijacking transforms an airplane into a medium of communication, the order-word as a speech act incorporeally transforms the established order of things. As a means of incorporeal transformation, the order-word relies on a certain redundancy between the act and the statement; whether it be an invention of the proletariat class through a slogan or a transformation of airplane passengers into captives by a (mediatized) statement, language is directly implicated in the changes happening to bodies and things.[30] This is where words induce actions, and we might say that the slogans in *The Red Army/PFLP* aim to solicit actions from the spectator. The slogans that appear in the film are designed to agitate, mobilize, and solicit the incorporeal transformation of spectators into activists. The closing sequence is exemplary in this regard.

On the image-track appears a long tracking shot filmed from the rooftop of a driving car, which shows nothing but a hilly desert landscape intersected by a single, narrow, winding road that stretches into the distance. On the soundtrack is a polyphony of voices (Shigenobu, Kanafani, Khaled, and so on). This long take of the landscape ends with a montage of intertitles, each composed of simple white letters on a black background: "Revolution Is World War," "Revolution," "Revolution = World War," "For Armed Struggle!," "Take Weapons!," "Guns," "Bullets," "Weapons," "Gunpoint," and "Trigger."[31] The monotonous desert-landscape images dominate the sequence. The absence or the lack of the direct representation of people in this long take of the desert landscape is compensated by the presence of slogans that call for a global insurrection. These slogans operate as order-words insofar as they aim to extract the revolutionary masses out of the masses of spectators. The film's positioning of armed struggle as propaganda and its self-positioning as a propaganda newsreel finally come together in the performative use of order-words. Here, the mediated message on-screen joins the immediacy of action off-screen, as it were.

The emphasis on the off-screen activities was crystallized in the very form by which this film circulated: a caravan tour organized and executed by Adachi, who drove a red minivan to accompany the film as it traveled throughout Japan.[32] It is of no small importance that Adachi and Wakamatsu took the formation of the revolutionary masses out of spectators so seriously as to create new circuits of circulation and exhibition for the film itself. Clearly, this film would not produce revolutionaries as effectively if it relied on existing circuits of distribution and exhibition. Adachi's writings at the time corroborate this interest in new filmic modes of distribution, which he calls *jōei undo*—a term which may be translated as "screening activism" or, perhaps more appropriately, "screening movement." Adachi envisioned this screening movement as a form of direct action, in which three parties (the film, filmmakers, and spectators) meet on equal ground. Especially for Adachi, who advocated the idea of "Cinema = Movement" before he started to make *The Red Army/PFLP*, this screening movement was theoretically and practically an important step forward. For instance, Adachi's "Towards a Restructuring of Our Battlelines" (1972) indicates that the mobilization of spectators through the organization of screenings was central to his understanding of activist cinema.[33]

One of the catalysts that allowed Adachi to develop this activist conception of cinema was the Suzuki Seijun Affair of 1968 (often compared to the Langlois Affair in 1968 in France). Just as the firing of Henri Langlois from his position as the director of the Cinématheque Française became a focal point of protests, the firing of the director Suzuki Seijun by the head of the Nikkatsu Studio became an occasion for Left-leaning Japanese filmmakers, critics, and fans of Suzuki Seijun's films to organize a coalition of protesters.[34] Adachi, along with Oshima and other outspoken filmmakers, was a leading figure of this protest movement. Central to the movement was the idea of the active audience who demand to see films that they want to see, rather than simply consume what the film industry puts out. Adachi's "What Is Not to Be Done" (1971) reflects on the Suzuki Seijun Affair. Published in *Eiga Hihyō II*, and written just a month before Adachi flew to Beirut to make *The Red Army/PFLP*, this essay indicates a nascent vision of revolutionary cinema in which the mobilization of the audience plays a key role.[35]

This screening movement is the third form of relation cinema can have with armed struggle. *The Red Army/PFLP*, which positions itself as an auxiliary of armed struggle, helps us understand the paradoxical logic of mediation involved in the film's emphasis on direct action. First, there is the film's remediation of televisual spectacles, including the images of hijackings. Since the hijacking appears as an exemplary form of armed-struggle-turned-propaganda, it complicates our understanding of the relation between the immediacy of political violence and the mediatedness of propaganda as a form of communication. This transformation of immediacy into mediation—hijacking into propaganda—is a type of incorporeal transformation. Second, cinema's relation to armed struggle is further complicated when it tries to critique television, the principal medium that assists the incorporeal transformation of hijacking into propaganda. In comparing *The Red Army/PFLP* to *Here and Else*-

where in terms of their treatment and appropriation of television, we can see that cinema's ambivalence toward television manifests itself most critically in its use of landscape as a cinematic counterpoint to televisual spectacle such as hijacking. The monotonous time associated with the landscape of refugee camps is diametrically opposed to the televisual order of the crisis, which condenses time in order to generate a sense of urgency. Third, cinema that aimed to compete with television had to generate an alternative circuit of production, distribution, and exhibition. In the case of *The Red Army/PFLP*, the move toward alternative means of disseminating information and images gave rise to the complementary screening movement. This activist vision of the film screening saw it as a form of direct action whereby cinema extracted the revolutionary masses out of the masses of spectators, engaging in what I have referred to as the incorporeal transformation of spectators.

Ultimately, however, the conflation of activism with filmmaking risks codifying what counts as proper political action. In spite of its underlying ambivalence, the film *The Red Army/PFLP* threatens to take up the act of policing in its own right, as it highlights militant armed struggle as the political ideal. On the one hand, *The Red Army/PFLP* is the logical conclusion to the cinema of actuality insofar as it aspires to establish an alternative system of journalism, albeit as an auxiliary of revolutionary movements. On the other hand, the film embodies the limitations of a leftist political imaginary that perhaps fails to address its own complicity with the existing police order that determines what counts as proper political action. Nonetheless, the film's ongoing negotiation with television, its critical use of remediation as a cinematic strategy, and its insistence on the landscape as a diagram of power clearly deserve attention. For these elements are precisely what confers a critical edge to the cinema of actuality that redefined the political potential of Japanese avant-garde filmmaking in the 1960s and early 1970s.

conclusion

At the end of December 1974, Theatre Scorpio and Art Theatre Shinjuku Bunka closed. The closure of these two iconic sites of avant-garde film and underground art culture coincided with the waning of the cinema of actuality. By the mid-1970s, the once ubiquitous sights of student protests, performances, and happenings that transformed urban streets into temporary theaters of spectacle had also disappeared. At the same time, many of the filmmakers discussed in this book had turned away from a critical engagement with actuality and media events; avant-garde filmmaking's proximity to journalism and its contiguity to street politics were fading fast. It is certainly possible to attribute the decline of cinematic engagement with actuality and media events to the withering of the New Left student movement and the corporate financing of avant-garde arts. That is, indeed, the widely accepted view of the double erosion of artistic and political activism in the mid-1970s. This narrative of closure also highlights two events as its major catalysts: the spectacular World's Fair of 1970 (Expo 70) and the Asama Sansō Incident, the infamous standoff between the ultra-Left student group United Red Army and the police force in 1972. The first is said to signal the cooptation of avant-garde artists, and the second the self-destructive violence of militant student activists.

This narrative, however, has become something of a cliché. I therefore wish to step back and provide a more nuanced picture by considering the loosening of the bonds between avant-garde cinema and news media in relation to Expo 70 and the Asama Sansō Incident. While it is tempting to conclude that filmmakers such as Matsumoto, Oshima, Wakamatsu, and Adachi were disillusioned by the defeat of student activism or coopted by the lure of corporate and state sponsorship (or both), such a reading would overlook the relations among news media, avant-garde cinema, and street politics that informed their works during the 1960s and early 1970s. Instead of simply accepting the above narrative, it would be more productive to ask how these relations themselves had changed in the 1970s and how Expo 70 and the Asama Sansō Incident were implicated in these changes.

MONUMENTALIZING EVENTS: EXPO 70 AND THE ASAMA SANSŌ INCIDENT

To begin with, if Expo 70 and the Asama Sansō Incident were key watershed moments, what connects these seemingly dissimilar events to one another? Expo 70 in Osaka was the pinnacle of extravagant technological display and the spectacular celebration of moving-image media. It inherited a propensity toward expanded cinema experiences via the gigantic multiscreen projections and immersive audiovisual environments already featured at Expo 67 in Montréal.[1] Like Expo 67, this event allowed many artists and corporations to showcase the latest imaging and sound technologies with a utopian bent toward the future (the official slogan for the event was "Progress and Harmony for Mankind"). It was also a massive state project led by the Liberal Democratic Party cabinet, which aimed to boost Japan's international prestige and its growing economy. A record-breaking number of people—more than 64 million—visited Expo 70 in six months. In addition to seventy-seven national pavilions, there were thirty corporate pavilions, including those of major Japanese electrical and electronics companies (Toshiba, Sanyo, Hitachi, Panasonic, Ricoh, Fuji Electric, and IBM Japan).[2] As in the case of the Tokyo Olympics in 1964, the government pushed for large-scale constructions of infrastructure and urban development around the expo site. As Marilyn Ivy observes, "Expo '70 had a great impact on the national economy, particularly on the transportation infrastructure. One out of every two Japanese visited Osaka exposition, using the *shinkansen* (the so-called bullet train), expanded local railway lines, and the improved national highway network."[3] Preparation for the event accelerated the nationwide drive toward urban development and restructuring. After the World's Fair ended, its site was made into a commemorative park. In short, it was both a monumental and a monumentalizing project.

The successful execution of Expo 70 was, however, inseparable from the tight management of visitors' on-site movements. In addition to the construction of new transportation infrastructures such as a monorail, a moving sidewalk, and extended highways, the preparation for Expo 70 involved the invention of new security strategies. Hundreds of security guards, recruited from police forces as well as private-security companies, were trained specifically for this event, and a new centralized computer system was deployed to control and monitor the smooth circulation of visitors between and within pavilions.[4] Importantly, the vigilant policing of pedestrian traffic at Expo 70 depended on the strict separation of exhibition space from the space of everyday activities. In particular, the spectacles of Expo 70 were carefully cut off from the spectacles of protests and performances unfolding on the streets. The sense of gigantic monumentality generated by Expo 70 was predicated on the efficient management of crowds and the constant surveillance of the enclosed exhibition space, presented as a site of the utopian future, but not of the immediate present. The successful display of technologically enhanced spectacles at Expo 70 was thus made possible by their confinement to the enclosed and regulated space of exhibition.

To put it differently, Expo 70 imposed a sense of monumentality by carefully separating the enclosed exhibition site from the open space of urban streets; it operated through a process of *spatial* monumentalization. If spatial monumentality was key to Expo 70, the Asama Sansō Incident was marked by a *temporal* process of monumentalization. According to Adachi, the Asama Sansō Incident "was a collaborative show that television and the state organized and presented as a form of 'national event' in which state power rescued the nation from a 'social disaster.'"[5] Arguably, the colossal stature of the Asama Sansō Incident as a media event derives from its status as a prolonged publicity strategy undertaken by the state authorities. Television also played a key role in this widely mediatized hostage crisis, started by young militant student activists from the ultra-Left United Red Army faction.

On 19 February 1972, five United Red Army activists took a lodgekeeper's wife as hostage and barricaded themselves inside the lodge. The United Red Army faction had been formed in the aftermath of a failed protest against the renewal of the Japan-U.S. Security Treaty in 1970 and the subsequent massive crackdown on militant student activism. Its hostage crisis thus did not draw sympathy from the general public. Although the United Red Army's totalitarian structure and its intrafactional violence, including the lynching of its own members, were revealed only days after the event, the dramatic showdown of the Asama Sansō Incident symbolically drew the curtain on the New Left student movement. It is, in this regard, the final media event that marked the end of the so-called season of politics.

To be sure, most televised media events solicit a sense of collective participation and many of the high-profile media events in Japan had interpellated the audience as national subjects, but the Asama Sansō Incident was particularly effective in aligning the position of the reporter and the audience with that of the state. The axis of identification was different in this case from Kim Hiro's hostage crisis, the media event in which many of the reporters and viewers initially positioned themselves on the side of the hostage-taker. Writing in July 1972, five months after the event, Nakahira argues that the Asama Sansō Incident transformed the semiotic function of live news from a fleeting "document" of the immediate present to an enduring "monument" of history.[6] The hostage crisis started on 19 February and ended on 28 February, with an unprecedented ten-hour marathon of live broadcasting of the final showdown between the police and armed student activists. An astonishing 98.2 percent of viewers in the Tokyo metropolitan area watched live coverage of the event.[7]

In Nakahira's view, the prolonged coverage of the ten-day Asama Sansō Incident changed the nature of the news report, as the unchanging image of the crime scene—the exterior view of the mountain lodge appearing daily on the television news—slowly gained the symbolic value of a historic monument. Precisely because the media was unable to enter (unlike in the case of Kim Hiro's hostage crisis), its reportage had to rely largely on a single long shot of the mountain lodge. The lack of drama was compounded by the use of a fixed camera position from which the news camera recorded the unchanging façade of the building. In so doing, the media elevated this ordinary building to an edifice endowed with the aura of monumentality over the course of the event.[8] Since the images daily broadcast on television were so persistent and unchanging, they began to impose sentiments other than journalistic sensations of actuality.

By virtue of being repeated over and over, the image of the mountain lodge began to demand moral judgment from its viewer. In the eyes of television viewers sitting in their living room, the "brutality of the suspects" became more obvious on the second day than on the first day, and on the third day than on the second day. The police attack on the barricaded lodge was carried out precisely when the commonsensical morality of the ordinary citizens tipped over, and they deemed that shooting to kill suspects was acceptable. I believe that the police authority carefully calculated the timing of its attack, taking into consideration this shift [in the public sentiment]. In the end, all the television stations collaborated with the state authority in this project through their production of the image.[9]

The sensations of actuality and immediacy were thus overshadowed by the timeless impression of moral judgment, which in turn allowed the viewers to collectively identify with the enduring presence of the state authorities. Nakahira's observation that the monumentalizing force of the unchanging image became stronger than the evidential force of the live news explains why this media event occupies such a privileged position in the historiography of postwar Japan. While the iconography of occupied buildings is a recursive one during the season of politics—from the occupied clock tower of the Yasuda Auditorium at the University of Tokyo, where student activists fought riot police, to the balcony of the Ichigaya Headquarters for Japan's Self-Defense Forces, where Mishima staged his coup d'état—no other edifice from the 1960s and 1970s takes on the same ominous quality. The mountain lodge of the Asama Sansō Incident became a memorial monument on which the death of the militant student movement was inscribed.

Certainly, this sense of monumentality derives partly from its retroactive positioning as a decisive turning point in the history of the New Left student movement. However, Nakahira's assertion that it functioned simultaneously as news and as commemoration—an actual event taking place in the present and a memento of the passing era—suggests a crucial change in the public reception of this media event, as it took place. Its status as a media event was inseparable from the viewing public's already formed desire to bury and memorialize student activism, a desire to treat it as a thing of the past. It is crucial that by 1972 the New Left student movement had escalated its intrafactional conflicts and some of the radical factions resorted to violent guerrilla tactics. The collective desire to bury the present in the tomb of history seemed to have overturned the journalistic sensation of actuality, a sensation that derives from the thrill of witnessing a crisis unfolding in front of the camera. In other words, the season of politics that paraded the mediatized images of barricades, hijackings, hostage crises, and bombings no longer commanded attention from the public as it had a few years before.

Expo 70 and the Asama Sansō Incident thus signal two separate but complementary moments. To put it schematically, these events embody a shift from *actuality* to *monumentality* as the central attraction and impression of mediated spectacles. The technologically enhanced spectacles of Expo 70 and the televised spectacle of the Asama Sansō Incident have the same quality of being monumental more than actual, albeit the former works on the spatial register while the latter works on the temporal register. Nevertheless, both events convey an enduring sense of magnitude that folds the immediate present into an archive of history, rerouting the force of the spectacle from the open space of the streets to the enclosed space of the symbolic edifices. The withering of actuality in these mediatized spectacles corresponds to the concurrent shift in the cinema of actuality and to the double disappearance of political and artistic activities from urban space. The sensation of actuality was withering in the field of avant-garde filmmaking, just as the force of the spectacle that once mobilized to counter the workings of the existing police order started to diminish on the level of street politics. The cinema of actuality that kept its proximity to the media and exposed its complicity with the police order through reflexive appropriations of news and media events thus reached an impasse and met its end as the relation between the spectacle and the streets was radically reconfigured.

SEPARATING THE SCREEN AND THE STREETS

The cinema of actuality had a strong affinity with street politics. The movie theater, for example, was often imagined to be an extension of the streets rather than a place where one escaped from reality. The 1968 trailer that Adachi directed for Oshima's *Death by Hanging* nicely sums up the contiguity between the movie theater and the streets. Facing the camera, Oshima makes a direct appeal to the spectator, who is presumably watching the trailer at one of the Art Theatre Guild's theaters: "This is an art theater. But we are not making art. You should also not regard this place as a theater. We made this film just like the way we work or protest on the streets. . . . I hope watching this film itself will become a form of action for you."[10] In this explicit plea to the audience, Oshima and Adachi compare the very act of watching a film inside the theater to the act of protesting and performing on the streets. These actions become exchangeable through the equation of politics and expressive acts. Oshima, in conversation with Mishima, argued that politics is an expressive act much akin to art. In 1968, the conception of filmmaking and film viewing as forms of political action was clearly operative. The screening movement of Wakamatsu and Adachi's *The Red Army/PFLP* was literally driven by this view as they tried to link the circuit of production, distribution, and reception of the film to a series of direct actions staged by guerrilla fighters. Similarly, films such as Oshima's *Diary of a Shinjuku Thief*, Matsumoto's *Funeral Parade of Roses*, and Wakamatsu's *Season of Terror* made it clear that the diegetic world presented on the screen was not only contemporaneous to the spectator, but also contiguous to the world just outside the door of the theater.

The emphasis on the contemporaneity and the spatial contiguity between the screen, theater, and streets is indeed a hallmark of Japanese avant-garde films from the 1960s and early 1970s. Consider, for example, Terayama Shūji's ATG film *Throw Away Your Books, Rally in the Streets* (*Sho o suteyo machi e deyou*, 1971). The film opens with an empty black screen. We hear production-crew noise and the humming sound of a film projector. After a while, the young male actor who plays the protagonist appears. He looks straight at the camera and asks, "What are you doing? Nothing will start if you just sit in the darkness inside the movie theater. The inside of the screen is always empty. Everybody gathered here is tired of waiting around like you: 'Isn't there something fun?'" At this point, the actor lights a cigarette. "The difference between here and there is that you are not allowed to smoke, but I'm free to do so." The use of shifters ("you," "here," "there") and the present tense in this playful address to the viewer both affirms and negates the contiguity between the screen space and the space of the auditorium.[11]

Like Terayama, who reflexively addresses the anticipatory state of waiting in the theater, Okabe Michio opens his experimental film *Crazy Love* (*Kureijii rabu*, 1968) with a static long shot taken from the viewpoint of the spectator sitting inside the movie theater. Directly located in front of the screen, still draped with a curtain, the shot presents the hustle and bustle of the theater before the film starts. This self-referential inclusion of the theater is an extension of another recurrent motif in films from the 1960s: the reflexive presentation of the production process. Oshima and Matsumoto include documentary footage of themselves or their own crews shooting the film in *Diary of a Shinjuku Thief* and *Funeral Parade of Roses*, positioning filmmaking itself as an event akin to street performance. Paralleling filmmaking and performance becomes literal in Terayama's third ATG film, *Pastoral: To Die in the Country* (*Den'en ni shisu*, 1974). In a manner reminiscent of Imamura Shōhei's film, *A Man Vanishes* (*Ningen jōhatsu*, 1967), which blurs the boundary between fiction and nonfiction, the ending scene of *Pastoral* shows the destruction of the set that was pitched on the street of Shinjuku. As the protagonist and his mother sit in silence and the credits start to roll, the walls of the set are taken away and the busy street scene of Shinjuku (where Art Theatre Shinjuku Bunka and Theatre Scorpio were located) is revealed. This sequence encapsulates the spirit of 1960s avant-garde filmmaking, especially the one associated with the alternative film culture around the Art Theatre Guild and Theatre Scorpio. During this period, films emphasized the contiguity between the screen, theater, and streets.

A number of other experimental filmmakers and intermedia artists similarly emphasized this type of contiguity. *Switch*, a conceptual intermedia work by Azuchi Shūzō Gulliver (who appears in Okabe's *Crazy Love*), is a case in point. The film *Switch* is said to consist of a long take of a light switch. Emphasizing the contiguity of screen space and the space of the theater, the lights inside the screening space were turned at the same moment in the film when a hand reached into the frame and flipped the switch. In his discussion of *Switch*, published in the February 1969 issue of *Kikan Firumu* (Film quarterly) dedicated to the issues of expanded cinema, Matsumoto argues that Gulliver's work refuses completion by performatively opening up the situation presented on the screen to the situation outside it.[12] To be sure, this kind of intermedial performance was not limited to Azuchi Gulliver but was generally on the rise in the late 1960s.

Complementary to *Switch*, in extending the screen space into the screening, is the experiment with a closed-circuit television staged on the fourth day of the symposium "EXPOSE·1968." Using the video system provided by Sony, the art critic Tōno Yoshiaki and the Hi Red Center artist Takamatsu Jirō delivered live presentations via a closed-circuit television monitor (figure C.1). As they sat in an adjacent room

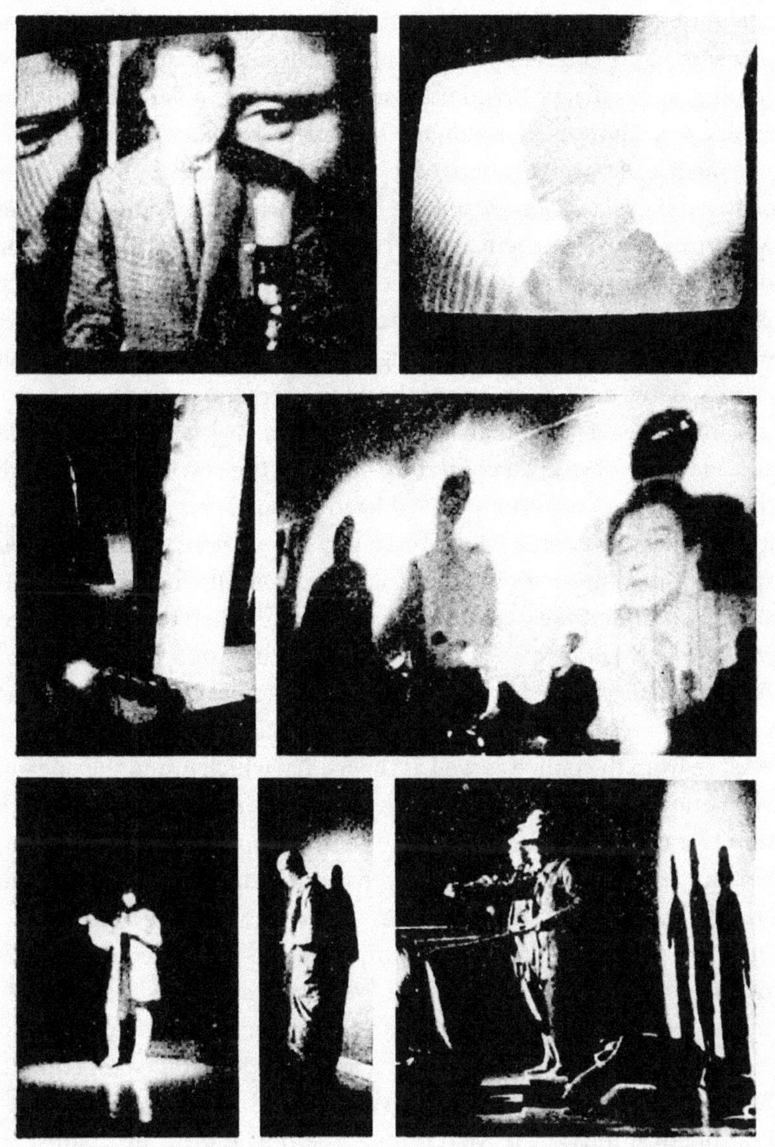

Conc1. A special report on "EXPOSE·1968" showing performances by symposium participants. In *Dezain Hihyō* (July 1968), 72.

and presented their reports on the symposium, their performance was transmitted on a monitor set in the auditorium. This playful mimicry of television highlighted the compound sensations of spatial distance and temporal immediacy.[13] While the spectators were aware that the presenters were in the next room, the separation between viewer and performance nevertheless generated a sense of distance. If Gulliver's *Switch* collapsed the distance between the filmed performance and the screening environment, the event at "EXPOSE·1968" deliberately created a distance between the live performance and the screening environment by inserting the mediation of the video camera and the monitor. Both experiments, however, equally highlight and play with the proximity and distance between the screen space and the screening space.

In the case of Wakamatsu's *Ecstasy of the Angels* (*Tenshi no kōkotsu*, 1972), the perceived contiguity between the screen space and the screening space became a point of heated controversy. Made one year after *The Red Army/PFLP*, the film *Ecstasy of the Angels* features a group of student revolutionaries who break away from the main organization in order to undertake guerrilla bombings of a police station and other symbolic landmarks in Tokyo. On the eve of Christmas 1971, just before *Ecstasy of the Angels*'s scheduled premiere, an actual bombing took place at the very Shinjuku police station bombed in the film. Due to heavy pressure from the police as well as the media, which found the uncanny reverberation between the film and the actual incident suspicious, the film's release was postponed. In the meantime, the Asama Sansō Incident happened, which further delayed the scheduled release of the film. Kuzui Kinshirō, then manager of Art Theatre Shinjuku Bunka, notes, "On February 17 the [United Red Army] leaders Mori Tsuneo and Nagata Yōko were arrested. As the United Red Army started a shootout with the police on February 19, the call to cancel the screening of *Ecstasy of the Angels* became even more intense, as the critics lumped together the film with the United Red Army."[14] While the film was finally screened, at Shinjuku Bunka on 11 March 1972, the police pressure against the film's release in the wake of the Asama Sansō Incident indicates the anxiety surrounding the perceived contiguity between the events on the screen and the events on the streets. The film's proximity to contemporary reality was considered to be dangerous and to hold the potential to disrupt the public order, as if a mere incitement for insurrection *on-screen* would be actualized *on the streets*.

The high-handed police intervention in this case also points to another important historical circumstance: the heightened policing of the streets. In fact, the seemingly isolated case of the *Ecstasy of the Angels* controversy—wherein the spectacle unfolding inside a movie theater had to be separated from the spectacle unfolding on the streets—reflects a more general drive toward the intense management and securitization of urban space at the beginning of the 1970s. The controversy around *Ecstasy of the Angels* proved to be a symbolic moment that exemplified the increasingly enforced separation between cinema and actuality. In order to fully grasp the historical significance of the decline of the cinema of actuality, we must hence look at the shift in governmental control over urban space, a control that manifested itself through the process of criminalizing certain street activities on one hand, and through the process of isolating spectacles within the safely guarded space of exhibition as demonstrated by Expo 70 on the other.

POLICING URBAN SPACE

One of the most significant examples of the governmental control of urban space is the police crackdown on the "folk guerrilla" movement that was gathering thousands of youths and musicians around Shinjuku Station's West Exit Underground Square in 1969. Completed in September 1966, the square was designed as a commercial center adjacent to Shinjuku Station, where several railways converged. During 1969, the square was periodically occupied by peaceful protesters, who gathered and played folk music to express their dissent on every Saturday evening. The media referred to youths who used music as an instrument of political dissent as "folk guerrillas." The folk guerrilla movement gained momentum over the course of 1969. On 17 May, the metropolitan police sent more than 250 members of its riot squad to clear the square's space of assembly, an act that garnered wide media attention because of the riot squad's considerably heavy-handed treatment of the folk guerrillas. The following week's folk guerrilla assembly attracted a crowd of more than 5,000 and continued to attract thousands of people every week thereafter. Although the riot police again stormed the square on 28 June, shooting tear gas and arresting attendees, the protesters and musicians returned to the square the following week.

Then, on 19 July, the metropolitan police sent more than 2,500 riot police to take over the square from the protestors and musicians.[15] This forced evacuation of the West Exit Underground Square was, moreover, accompanied by a strategic renaming of the space. On 18 July, two major railway companies, Odakyū and Keiō, changed all directory signs that read "Nishiguchi Chika Hiroba" (West Exit Underground Square) to "Nishiguchi Chika Tsūro" (West Exit Underground Passageway). The reason for this renaming was simple, yet significant: it allowed police to arrest any and all who gathered and stayed immobile in this place that was no longer a *square*, but rather a *passageway*. Calling the space a passageway enabled the police to apply traffic laws that regulated the movement of people in a given area. In short, since the square was now a passageway or street, pedestrians could no longer *assemble* there, but had to *pass through*.[16] Thus the railway companies created a space of forced mobility and controlled movement in concert with the metropolitan police. This collaboration between corporations and the police to regulate public movement with the aim of suppressing dissent anticipated the tight management and surveillance of the exhibition space of Expo 70 in the following year.

Ironically, before the renaming of the West Exit Underground Square, the organizers of Expo 70 appropriated the notion of open public space by designating the central building of its exhibition site "Festival Square" (*Omatsuri hiroba*). The Festival Square was designed by young architect Isozaki Arata in collaboration with the internationally renowned architect Tange Kenzō, who worked on a number of state projects, including the Hiroshima Peace Center, the Yoyogi National Gymnasium (built for the Tokyo Olympics), and the Tokyo Metropolitan Government Building. The Festival Square was used to showcase main attractions and artistic performances staged by avant-garde artists, such as the group Gutai. The Festival Square also housed the Tower of the Sun, the iconic artwork by the avant-garde artist Okamoto Tarō. In spite of its pretension to openness, the Festival Square at Expo 70 was an enclosed space, not completely open to the public in the way the West Exit Underground Square at Shinjuku Station had been before being renamed. Only the visitors who paid the entrance fee were allowed to enter the Festival Square.

The selective and regulated access to an ostensibly democratic open space exercised at Expo 70 has its counterpart in the establishment of vehicle-free zones, also known as the "Pedestrian Paradise" (*Hokōsha tengoku*), in a number of districts in Tokyo, including Shinjuku, in 1970. Traffic regulations that apply to the Pedestrian Paradise prohibit staging performances, live-music concerts, demonstrations, petitions, filming, and other activities not sanctioned by the police. Put differently, the establishment of the Pedestrian Paradise further prevented student activists and artists from appropriating urban streets as their theater and expressing political dissent there. The transformation of the West Exit Underground Square, a place for spontaneous assemblies and collective protests, into the West Exit Underground Passageway, a space managed by traffic police officers, is thus an important harbinger of the controlled space of freedom exemplified by the Pedestrian Paradise and Expo 70.

The Pedestrian Paradise is indeed a peculiar urban form, one that promises a temporary liberation from traffic rules sanctioned by the state. Its appearance in 1970 suggests that the rhetoric of liberation that had been central to political and artistic movements of the 1960s had been turned against them, effectively foreclosing any attempt to freely appropriate streets for staging politico-artistic spectacles. The Pedestrian Paradise is a superficially "liberated zone" granted by the government instead of being democratically gained by the people.[17] Moreover, the government created this space not out of benevolence, but rather as a strategy for controlling potential dissidents. Establishment of the Pedestrian Paradise was part of the larger effort to purge protesters and rebellious youths from the streets of Tokyo. This cunning application of traffic laws to control protesters echoes the similarly preemptive strategy of demolishing stone pavements in cities and replacing them with asphalt in the 1960s. Tokyo's sidewalks had been paved with concrete blocks, but because student protesters would break the blocks and transform them into instant "weapons," the government decided to redo all the sidewalks with asphalt.[18] The covering of urban streets with asphalt was yet another governmental strategy of prevention.

The setting up of the Pedestrian Paradise was, however, not only a security measure, but also an economic project. It was presented as a safe haven where families could spend time together and shop without distractions in the department stores. As the historian KuroDalaiJee puts it, the so-called liberated zone of the Pedestrian Paradise is an "Expo-like space" devoid of traffic accidents, guerrilla attacks, and demonstrations.[19] It is a space open to docile citizens and potential consumers, but closed off to protesters and street performers. The establishment of the Pedestrian Paradise in the exact same year as Expo 70 and the renewal of the Japan-U.S. Security Treaty indicates how seemingly disparate issues—urban beautification, economic development, and security—are in fact closely related. Indeed, the regulated movement of pedestrians in urban space, the financial investment in extravagant exhibitions of the latest technologies and intermedia artworks, and the policing of antiestablishment movements on the premise of public security are different manifestations of the same economic logic of governmentality.

As evident in the discourse of fūkeiron and its critique of state power, the issue of governmentality was central to urban planning in 1960s and 1970s Japan. Urban planning as it developed in postwar Japan is intertwined with the governmental techniques that aim to shape, guide, and affect conducts of individuals, and it works in concert with regulatory activities that administer and manage the security, productivity, and health of the population. In the development of new traffic regulations, such as the Pedestrian Paradise, the same economic rationality is at work. It is this governmental rationality that informs institutional practices and police procedures that target the population (disease control, biometrics, education reform, and so on) under the guise of liberal (and neoliberal) democracy. The regulatory mechanisms that target the collective life of the population are in no way opposed to individuating techniques of discipline.[20] Rather, the macroeconomic management of the population goes hand in hand with the microeconomic management of the individuals. The government is "a 'contact point' where techniques of domination—or power—and *techniques of the self* 'interact.'"[21]

The renaming of the West Exit Underground Square, the establishment of the Pedestrian Paradise, and the asphalt coating of all the major sidewalks in Tokyo similarly operate through a convergence of governmental techniques. The governmental control that links up these three urban projects is antitheatrical insofar as it forecloses the possibility of turning the streets into a temporary theater of political dissent. Pedestrians are expected to walk through the square without stopping or are encouraged to shop while walking in the artificially liberated zones. In the name of security these projects of urban planning preemptively exclude the very possibility of displaying political dissent on the streets. The operation of governmental control here differs from more clearly repressive acts (e.g., beating protesters or throwing tear-gas canisters into a crowd). This form of control is subtler, and solicits the voluntary submissions of those who are targeted.

MOVING AWAY FROM ACTUALITY

It is noteworthy that this increased governmental control over urban space accompanied the enclosure of technologically enhanced spectacles within monumental pavilions at Expo 70 and the enforced separation of the film screen from the streets (exemplified by the *Ecstasy of the Angels* controversy). The closing down of Theatre Scorpio and Art Theatre Shinjuku Bunka coincided with the mounting efforts to police urban space, especially the streets. Commenting on the 1973 experimental play "Why Don't You Cry, Cry for 1973?," directed by Ninagawa Yukio and written by Shimizu Kunio—two leading figures representative of the underground theater culture formed around Theatre Scorpio—Kuzui recalls how he felt a foreboding sense of the end of an era: "I thought it would no longer be possible to write a drama of youths based on the themes of city, revolution, and struggle. . . . Before you could step outside the theater and find the exact same situation on the street as one on the stage. But suddenly, I realized that the time has changed and the mood of cynicism permeated; the city itself had changed."[22] Kuzui's comment about the changing atmosphere of Shinjuku resonates with the disappearance of topical journalistic references—and with them the sensations of actuality—from the work of filmmakers who generated the cinema of actuality.

For instance, around 1974, when Adachi left Japan to work for the Popular Front for the Liberation of Palestine, Wakamatsu's work started to lose its critical edge. As Hirasawa Gō observes: "After Adachi's departure to Palestine, which coincided with the loss of momentum in student activism, Wakamatsu who kept close ties to activism faced some difficulties [and struggled to make films]. But this situation was not limited to Wakamatsu alone. Instead, it was common to all the filmmakers who actively grappled with actual issues in the 1960s."[23] Indeed, Matsumoto's and Oshima's films also started to lose a journalistic sense of urgency and immediacy in the 1970s. The first to turn away from the immediate present was Matsumoto. His film *Pandemonium* (*Shura*, 1971), set in the 1820s, is an appropriation of a kabuki play by the nineteenth-century playwright Tsuruya Nanboku and presents an intense narrative of private vengeance and betrayal. Coming after *Funeral Parade of Roses*, which playfully appropriated the televisual logic of liveness and incorporated street performances, Matsumoto's turn toward the premodern past is a clear break from journalistic actuality.

Suggestively, Roland Domenig points out the general mutation in the ATG-funded film productions around this time: "After 1972, political topics faded into the background. It is possible to identify two strands of escapism in ATG's films: an escape from urban to more rural settings and an escape into the past."[24] Oshima is exemplary in this regard. Disbanding his production company Sōzōsha after the making of *Dear Summer Sister* (1972), he also turned away from the present and retreated into the distant past. His next film, *In the Realm of the Senses* (1976), is set in the 1930s and depicts an intensely claustrophobic space of erotic seclusion in which the film's lovers isolate themselves. Considering Oshima's earlier commitment to journalistic engagement with the present and the contiguity between the screen space and the streets, *In the Realm of the Senses* signals that the era of his actuality-based filmmaking has ended.

However surprising it may seem, Matsumoto's and Oshima's disengagement from actuality is also part of a larger shift in Japanese independent filmmaking. Represented by the work of filmmakers and video artists such as Hara Kazuo, Suzuki Shiroyasu, Kawanaka Nobuhiro, and Idemitsu Mako, the 1970s was characterized by an increasingly *inward* turn to the realm of private visions, away from the realm of collective struggle. The activist mode of collective productions was replaced by the artisanal mode of solitary productions, giving rise to the "private film" (*kojin eiga*).[25] The associated group of filmmakers and video artists preferred a solitary mode of image-making to a collective one. While Iimura Takahiko, Ōbayashi Nobuhiko and Kawanaka's works from the 1960s had already given rise to the artisanal mode of filmmaking that emphasized the private vision of these filmmakers, the private film as a category took hold in the 1970s as political avant-garde filmmaking started to lose its momentum.

The publication of Kawanaka's book *Eiga: Nichijō no jikken* (Cinema: Everyday experiments) in 1975 is significant in this light. Kawanaka emphasizes what he calls "the private gaze" of the filmmaker. Using the twin notions of the private gaze and the private film, Kawanaka discusses an array of experimental works by Japanese filmmakers and video artists (e.g., Matsumoto, Iimura, Ōbayashi, and Hagiwara Sakumi) alongside works by North American filmmakers (e.g., Maya Deren, Jonas Mekas, Stan Brakhage, Hollis Frampton).[26] In spite of Kawanaka's earlier involvement in the anti-Expo 70 protest actions and the activities of the Japan Filmmakers Cooperative, which inherited the underground spirit of the film culture formed around Theatre Scorpio, his film criticism in *Cinema* is surprisingly formalist and disengaged from the political critique that characterized the writings of those associated with the cinema of actuality. Nevertheless, it is with this very same Kawanaka that Matsumoto formed the first Japanese video-art collective, Bideo Hiroba (Video Commons) in 1972. Matsumoto's prolific involvement in the emergent field of video art that accompanied the rise of private films indicates that his turn to video art also coincided with his turn away from journalistic actuality and street politics. The prominence of self-referentiality and formalist repetition in many of his video artworks from this period suggests an increasing enclosure of the image onto itself. That is, the images on screen become both temporally and spatially separated from the world outside the screen, often retreating inside the sanctioned space of museums and galleries.

These tendencies appear in Matsumoto's early report on the burgeoning situation of video art in Japan (presented at the "International Open Circuits" conference at the Museum of Modern Art in January 1974), wherein he emphasizes the recursive feedback mechanism of video. Video for Matsumoto is first and foremost a medium that generates its own "communication environment" through the mutual participation of the artist and the audience in an enclosed circuit of information. Although Matsumoto positions video in relation to television—he called it "another television"—the strength of this medium for him lies in its kinetic, hallucinatory, and ecstatic effects: "Video for me is becoming an attractive medium not only because of its uniquely processual nature based on its feedback mechanism, but also because it enables me, at a very personal level, to throw myself into my internal world."[27]

This personal and formalist turn toward video technology is epitomized in Matsumoto's participation in Expo 70. While his participation in the event is often narrated as Matsumoto's sell-out moment, it should be seen as a continuation of his growing interest in the medium of video and the realm of private vision on the one hand, and his increasing distance from politics and the street on the other. The kinetic, hallucinatory, and ecstatic effects Matsumoto identifies with video both encapsulate the appeal of this new technology for him and underscore his move toward the creation of a closed, immersive intermedia environment.

Matsumoto's contribution to Expo 70 indicates how his ongoing interest in intermedia converged with his growing interest in the enclosed environment of communication detached from street politics. Pitched as the festival of "environmental art," Expo 70 paraded a number of spectacular media projects that emphasized enclosure. Matsumoto's intermedia artwork *Space Projection Ako*, set inside the Textile Pavilion designed by graphic artist Yokoo Tadanori is one of them. For filmmakers and artists who participated, this festival provided a perfect opportunity to experiment with the latest imaging and sound technologies, and thus allowed them to push the practice of intermedia further into the realm of environmental art.[28] For someone like Matsumoto, who had been theorizing the image beyond the narrow confines of narrative cinema, and exploring boundary-crossing experiments with avant-garde musicians and performers, participation in Expo 70 was logical and, in effect, timely.

The Japanese avant-garde filmmakers' collective investment in the intermedial potentials of the image significantly expanded the conceptual horizon of cinema in the 1960s. This decade saw the rise of intermedia and expanded cinema, as well as an intense politicization of the image as spectacle generated by the news media. This decade also saw television liberate the image from the darkness of the movie theater, and the movie theater in turn open itself up to the streets. The images began to multiply, circulate, and manifest in different media types. The cinema of actuality emerged out of this historical milieu as its practitioners appropriated journalistic images, news, and media events as critical means of intervening into the immediate present. The advent of the cinema of actuality, understood in this context, was thus contemporaneous to the season of image politics, during which the spectacles staged on the streets became contiguous with the spectacles that unfolded on the screen.

However, the outward movement of the image was funneled back into a new space of confinement in the 1970s, as filmmakers and artists began to disengage from street politics and the streets became a primary target of urban policing. It was then that experimental films and video artworks retreated into the enclosed spaces of exhibition, such as the pavilions at Expo 70, art galleries, and museums. In the meantime, the state and corporations combined forces to inexorably drive protesters and performers off the streets; the implementation of the Pedestrian Paradise and other mechanisms of governmental control over urban space attest to this concerted effort. At the same time, the state and the news media also engaged in heavy policing of the perceived contiguity between activist violence on the screen and that on the streets, as evident in the controversy surrounding *Ecstasy of Angels*. The forced separation of cinematic spectacles from street politics resulted in the further withering of actuality in political avant-garde filmmaking. Added to the diminishing sense of actuality in cinema was the monumentalizing effort by the state and the news media to bury the 1960s as a memory of the past, an effort exemplified by the monumental media event of the Asama Sansō Incident.

All these elements indicate significant structural transformations taking place in the wider media environment wherein the urban space of the streets and the mediated image space of the spectacle were set apart. The decline of the cinema of actuality both reflects and embodies this process of transformation. A sense of actuality continued to diminish in Japanese cinema from the 1980s onward. While it is true that the narrative films of contemporary filmmakers such as Aoyama Shinji and Kore-eda Hirokazu often draw attention to the proximity between cinema and news media, these works do not possess the sense of proximity to street politics that characterized the cinema of actuality during the 1960s and early 1970s.

However, as actuality and the proximity to street politics diminish in cinema, other media forms seem to have revived them. For instance, the political and social movements of the twenty-first century's opening decade have often reclaimed streets as a space of direct action and drawn on a number of media activists and artists who appropriate the real-time news updates, blog entries, and Twitter feeds that circulate the Internet. With the proliferation of social media and various mobile smart devices, the sensations of actuality that once emanated from the television and film screen are returning, albeit in different forms. The old desire to link what unfolds on the screen with actions on the streets is again on the upsurge. The lure of actuality is perhaps alive and even more prominent among Internet-based media activists. In our current media environment, in which convergence rather than intermedia is the reigning logic, we remain fascinated by global media events that stir the sensations of actuality, and we remain invested in the transformation of those events into monumentality, as we struggle to make sense of the present in relation to history. The cycle of actuality and monumentality that emerged in 1960s and 1970s Japan is far from over, in spite of changes in media platforms and our experiences of time.

notes

INTRODUCTION

1 Mishima Yukio and Oshima Nagisa, "Mishima Yukio / Oshima Nagisa: Fashisuto ka kakumeika ka" [Mishima Yukio / Oshima Nagisa: Fascist or revolutionary?], *Eiga Geijutsu* [Film art] 16.1 (January 1968): 23–34.

2 Satō Takumi, "Terebi ga utsushita 'hanran'" [The revolt captured on television], in *1968 nen ni nihon to sekai de okotta koto* [Events that took place in Japan and the world in 1968] (Tokyo: Mainichi Shinbunsha, 2009), 39.

3 On the historical role of early cinema as a "visual newspaper," see Charles Musser, *The Emergence of Cinema: The American Screen to 1907* (Berkeley: University of California Press, 1990); and Lee Grieveson, *Policing Cinema: Movies and Censorship in Early-Twentieth-Century America* (Berkeley: University of California Press, 2004). On the cinematic appropriation of the news reports on the Russo-Japanese War (1904–1905) and the production of "fake documentary" films based on these reports, see Komatsu Hiroshi, "Some Characteristics of Japanese Cinema before World War I," trans. Linda C. Ehrlich and Yuko Okutsu, in *Reframing Japanese Cinema: Authorship, Genre, History*, ed. Arthur Nolletti Jr. and David Desser (Bloomington: Indiana University Press, 1992), 229–58.

4 Mediatization is not a transparent process of mediation but a process of codification wherein an event as it is reported or covered by the mass media is delimited or depotentialized. I use the term *mediatization* in the sense used by Jean Baudrillard in his critique of the depoliticizing effects of the media coverage of the events of May '68. "What is mediatized is not what comes off the daily press, out of the tube, or on the radio: it is what is reinterpreted by the sign form, articulated into models, administered by the code (just as the commodity is not what is produced industrially, but what is

mediatized by the exchange value system of abstraction)." Jean Baudrillard, "Requiem for the Media," in *For a Critique of the Political Economy of the Sign*, trans. Charles Levin (St. Louis: Telos, 1981), 175–76.

5 David Desser's seminal work, *Eros Plus Massacre: An Introduction to the Japanese New Wave Cinema* (Bloomington: Indiana University Press, 1988), defines the Japanese New Wave as a body of "films produced and/or released in the wake of Oshima's *A Town of Love and Hope*, films which take an overtly political stance in a general way or toward a specific issue, utilizing a deliberately disjunctive form compared to previous filmic norms in Japan" (4). While Desser's analysis of the New Wave as an "avant-garde artistic movement" is useful, his definition of the New Wave presupposes the autonomy of film history and cinema's independence from other media forms such as television and photography. His is hence a strictly film-historical perspective, which locates an internal rupture—formal and thematic—within the already circumscribed boundary of Japanese cinema. My approach differs from Desser's on two points. First, the films I discuss in this book do not stand in for the general category of the New Wave cinema. Second, I approach this unique moment in the history of filmmaking in Japan from the media-historical perspective that takes into consideration parallel events happening in the adjacent fields of cinema, photography, and journalism.

6 In using the term *political avant-garde*, I gesture toward the discursive nexus between the theorization of cinema as a political form and the practice of avant-garde filmmaking that we find in D. N. Rodowick's seminal work on political modernism, *The Crisis of Political Modernism: Criticism and Ideology in Contemporary Film Theory* (Berkeley: University of California Press, 1988). My use of the term *political avant-garde* also draws on Peter Wollen's analysis of the avant-garde tradition that inherits the language of Marxism and operates on the periphery of the commercial system. See Peter Wollen, "The Two Avant-Gardes," in *Readings and Writings: Semiotic Counter-Strategies* (London: Verso, 1982), 92–104.

7 The ATG started as an association of ten movie theaters committed to the distribution and exhibition of "art films" as opposed to commercial program pictures and Hollywood films. The idea to establish the ATG originated in the activities of a group of cinephiles and cinéastes named Nihon Aato Shiataa Undō no Kai (Japanese Association for an Art Theatre Movement), which promoted the establishment of noncommercial theaters exclusively devoted to the presentation of art films. In addition to distributing and exhibiting art films—most of which were independently produced foreign films—at ATG-owned movie theaters, the Art Theatre Guild also started to produce films made by independent Japanese filmmakers, including young directors such as Imamura Shōhei, Oshima Nagisa, Matsumoto Toshio, Yoshida Kijū, Hani

Susumu, and Kuroki Kazuo, who were already making films on the periphery of the industry. For more information on the history of the ATG, see Satō Tadao, *ATG eiga o yomu: 60 nendai ni hajimatta meisaku no aakaibu* [Reading ATG films: An archive of classics that started in the 1960s] (Tokyo: Firumu Aato-sha, 1991); and Ushida Ayami, *ATG Eiga + Shinjuku* [ATG films + Shinjuku] (Tokyo: D-bungaku Kenkyūkai, 2007).

8 Fujioka Atsuhiro, "Kindaika suru toshi no eiga kankyaku" [The Film Spectators of Modernizing Cities] in *Eigagaku teki sōzōryoku* [The Imagination of Film Studies], ed. Katō Mikirō (Tokyo: Jinbunshoin, 2006), 33. These newspaper conglomerates largely controlled newsreel production, except during wartime, when the government consolidated all the production companies into a single corporation (Nippon News) under the 1939 Film Law, and during the immediate postwar years (1945–52), when film production was subjected to the military censorship of the Allied occupation forces. For an analysis of wartime film production in relation to state policies, see Peter B. High, *Imperial Screen: Japanese Film Culture in the Fifteen Years' War, 1931–1945* (Madison: University of Wisconsin Press, 2003). For an illustrated account of newsreels produced by Nippon News, see Kitajima Noboru, *Nippon nyūsu eigashi: Kaisen zen'ya kara shūsen chokugo made* [Film history of Nippon News: From the eve to the wake of the war] (Tokyo: Mainichi Shinbunsha, 1977). For a study of the culture of censorship and Japanese cinema in the occupation era, see Kyoko Hirano, *Mr. Smith Goes to Tokyo: Under the American Occupation, 1945–1952* (Washington: Smithsonian Institution Press, 1992).

9 See Mitsunobu Sugiyama, "Media and Power in Japan," in *De-Westernizing Media Studies*, ed. James Curran and Myung-Jin Park (London: Routledge, 2000), 192: "What is particularly interesting concerning Japan's television broadcasts is that all four of the Tokyo-based key stations enjoy close relationships with Japan's prominent national newspapers: TBS with the *Mainichi*, Nippon Television (NTV) with *Yomiuri*, Fuji Television (CX) with the *Sankei*, and TV Asahi (ANN) with *Asahi*. Even *Nikkei* is tied-up with Tokyo's local station, TV Tokyo (TN)."

10 Matsui Shigeru, "Tōno Yoshiaki no terebiteki na . . ." [Tōno Yoshiaki's televisual . . .] (paper presented at the Yebisu film festival at Tokyo Metropolitan Museum of Photography, Tokyo, Japan, 11 February 2011). Matsui Shigeru argues that the fervent interest in McLuhan exhibited by Japanese art critics such as Tōno Yoshiaki was a continuation of Japanese art discourse's engagement with mass-communication theory, which social psychologists and sociologists associated with the study group Shisō no Kagaku (such as Shimizu Ikutarō and Tsurumi Shunsuke) had introduced in the 1950s. This interest in mass communication and mass media, especially television, also informs some of the activities of postwar avant-garde collectives, such as

Kiroku Geijutsu no Kai, which brought together leftist intellectuals including Hanada Kiyoteru. I want to thank Marc Steinberg for noting that the McLuhan boom preceded the translation of *Understanding Media*.

11 Noël Burch, *To the Distant Observer: Form and Meaning in the Japanese Cinema*, revised and edited by Annette Michelson (Berkeley: University of California Press, 1979), 13.

12 See Mitsuhiro Yoshimoto, "Japanese Cinema in Search of a Discipline," in *Kurosawa: Film Studies and Japanese Cinema* (Durham: Duke University Press, 2000), 8–49.

13 See Stephen Heath, "Narrative Space," *Screen* 17.3 (1976): 19–75; and Noël Burch, "Oshima Nagisa," in *To the Distant Observer: Form and Meaning in the Japanese Cinema*, revised and edited by Annette Michelson (Berkeley: University of California Press, 1979), 325–44.

14 This scarcity of attention paid to Japanese filmmakers' theorization of cinema outside Japan is epitomized by the lone publication of *Cinema, Censorship, and the State: The Writings of Nagisa Oshima* (1992). This book was to remedy the situation in which, as Annette Michelson put it, "little or none of Japan's critical or theoretical production" was available to English-language readers. See Annette Michelson, "Introduction," in *Cinema, Censorship, and the State: The Writings of Nagisa Oshima*, by Oshima Nagisa, edited by Annette Michelson, translated by Dawn Lawson (Cambridge: MIT Press, 1992), 4. My book will by no means solve this problem in its entirety, but it intends to fill in this disciplinary lacuna. In this regard, I share the commitment to archival research on Japanese film theory and criticism that is found in the recent works of Aaron Gerow, such as his *Visions of Japanese Modernity: Articulations of Cinema, Nation, and Spectatorship, 1895–1925* (Berkeley: University of California Press, 2010), and in Abé Mark Nornes's *Forest of Pressure: Ogawa Shinsuke and Postwar Japanese Documentary* (Minneapolis: University of Minnesota Press, 2007) and *Japanese Documentary Film: The Meiji Era through Hiroshima* (Minneapolis: University of Minnesota Press, 2003).

15 Nakahira Takuma, "Kiroku to iu gen'ei: Dokyumento kara monyumento e" [The document called illusion: From document to monument], in *Mitsuzukeru hate ni hi ga . . .* [Fire, at the horizon to which I gaze . . .] (Tokyo: Osiris, 2007), 236. The essay was originally published in the July issue of *Bijutsu Techō* in 1972.

16 See Daniel Boorstin, *Gen'ei no jidai: Masukomi ga netsuzō suru jijitsu* [The age of the image: Mass media's fabrication of facts (original title: The image: Or what happened to the American dream)], trans. Gotō Kazuhiko and Hoshino Ikumi (Tokyo: Tokyo Sōgensha, 1964).

17 Nakahira, "Kiroku to iu gen'ei," 224.

18 Debord writes, for instance, "reality erupts within the spectacle, and the spectacle is real." See Guy Debord, *The Society of the Spectacle*, trans. Donald

Nicholson-Smith (New York: Zone, 1995), 14. On Debord's definition of the spectacle and its historical relation to television, see Jonathan Crary, "Spectacle, Attention, Counter-Memory," *October* 50 (autumn 1989): 96–107. For Rancière's critique of Debord, see Jacques Rancière, *The Emancipated Spectator*, trans. Gregory Elliott (London: Verso, 2009).

19 As Peter Hallward argues, for Rancière the state of separation between the spectator and the spectacle is empowering precisely when it is used to *stage* the gap between equality and inequality. Rancière's conception of politics is a form of "theatrocracy" based on this "inversion of a Platonic position." See Peter Hallward, "Staging Equality: Rancière's Theatrocracy and the Limits of Anarchic Equality," in *Jacques Rancière: History, Politics, Aesthetics*, ed. Gabriel Rockhill and Philip Watts (Durham: Duke University Press, 2009), 142. Distrustful of appearance, simulacra, and mimesis, Plato scorned theater as a source of duplicity, since actors who speak in the name of another and could be two things at once defy the policing order of keeping everyone in their designated place (Hallward, "Staging Equality," 143–44). While politics understood in this antimimetic tradition is first and foremost grounded in the orderly distribution of one's social function or occupation, genuine political activity according to Rancière, in contrast, "is whatever shifts a body from the place assigned to it or changes a place's destination." See Jacques Rancière, *Disagreement: Politics and Philosophy*, trans. Julie Rose (Minneapolis: University of Minnesota Press, 1999), 30. This dislocation of the body from its designated place is what brings about the disruptive and emancipatory effects of genuine political action.

20 See, for instance, Georges Didi-Huberman, *Confronting Images: Questioning the Ends of a Certain History of Art*, trans. John Goodman (Pennsylvania: Pennsylvania State University Press, 2005); Jacques Rancière, *The Future of the Image*, trans. Gregory Elliott (London: Verso, 2007); Anne Friedberg, *The Virtual Window: From Alberti to Microsoft* (Cambridge: MIT Press, 2006); Jean-Luc Nancy, *The Ground of the Image*, trans. Jeff Fort (New York: Fordham University, 2005); Marie-José Mondzain, *Image, Icon, Economy: The Byzantine Origins of the Contemporary Imaginary*, trans. Rico Franses (Stanford: Stanford University Press, 2005); W. J. T. Mitchell, *Picture Theory: Essays on Verbal and Visual Representation* (Chicago: University of Chicago Press, 1994); W. J. T. Mitchell, "What Is an Image?," *New Literary History* 15.3 (spring 1984): 503–37; and Sunil Manghani, Arthur Piper, and Jon Simons, eds., *Images: A Reader* (London: Sage, 2006).

21 On the concept of remediation, see Jay David Bolter and Richard Grusin, *Remediation: Understanding New Media* (Cambridge: MIT Press, 1999); and on the concept of artifactuality, see Jacques Derrida and Bernard Stiegler, *Echographies of Television: Selected Interviews*, trans. Jennifer Bajorek (Cambridge: Polity, 2002).

CHAPTER 1

1 The screening was phenomenally successful, which led the ATG to subsequently fund Oshima's acclaimed narrative film, *Death by Hanging* (*Kōshikei*, 1968).

2 KuroDalaiJee, *Nikutai no anaakizumu: 1960 nendai Nihon bijutsu ni okeru pafōmansu no chikasuimyaku* [Anarchy of the body: Undercurrents of performance art in 1960s Japan] (Tokyo: Grambooks, 2010), 217.

3 Ibid., 72. KuroDalaiJee offers a meticulously researched account of various performance-based intermedia events in the 1960s, most of which involve border-crossing collaborations among underground performance artists, noise musicians, and experimental filmmakers. As exhaustive as his list of intermedial events is, however, his analysis of the "intermedia" is also constrained by his art-historical perspective, which privileges the centrality of performance art. In contrast, a much more nuanced and insightful film-historical approach to the issues of intermedia is offered by the work of Julian Ross. See Julian Ross, "Projection-Performances: The Degree of Intermediality in the Japanese Expanded Cinema of the 1960s and 1970s," paper presented at the symposium "Visual Underground: Theatre Scorpio and Japanese Experimental Cinema of the Sixties," Montreal, Canada, 17 September 2011. Dick Higgins's "intermedia chart" also lists multiple arts, including cinema, performance, sound poetries, concrete poetry, happenings, performance art, conceptual art, mail art, dance theater, graphic music notations, action music, and so on. See Dick Higgins, "Intermedia," *Leonardo* 34.1 (2001): 49–54. For a concise definition of intermediality, see Livia Monnet, "Towards the Feminine Sublime, or the Story of a 'Twinkling Monad, Shape-shifting across Dimension': Intermediality, Fantasy, and Special Effects in Cyberpunk Film and Animation," *Japan Forum* 14.2 (2002): 225–68.

4 Tone Yasunao, "Geijutsu no chikaku hendō: EXPO kara hippii made" [Tectonic movements in art: From EXPO to hippies], quoted in KuroDalaiJee, *Nikutai no anaakizumu*, 72.

5 Ichiyanagi Toshi, "Gendai eiga jōkyō jiten" [Encyclopedia of the situation of contemporary cinema], *Kikan Firumu* [Film quarterly] 13 (December 1972), 105.

6 For instance, Noël Burch devotes only one paragraph to the analysis of the film *Band of Ninja* in his landmark study of Japanese cinema, *To the Distant Observer*, 332–33. Surprisingly, however, there is no analysis of *Band of Ninja* in Maureen Turim's otherwise comprehensive study of Oshima's work, *The Films of Oshima Nagisa: Images of a Japanese Iconoclast* (Berkeley: University of California Press, 1998). Similarly, David Desser's study of New Wave cinema, *Eros Plus Massacre*, does not discuss *Band of Ninja*, though Desser, too, devotes many pages to the analysis of Oshima's films from the 1960s. Donald Richie briefly discusses *Band of Ninja* in relation to manga and anime

in *A Hundred Years of Japanese Film: A Concise History, with a Selective Guide to Videos and DVDs* (Tokyo: Kodansha International, 2001), 249. A brief discussion of the film also appears in Oshima's *Cinema, Censorship, and the State*, 134.

7 Kohso Iwasaburō suggests that the anti-auteurist look of *Band of Ninja*—which negates the individuality of the artist—resonates with the film's emphasis on the anonymity of the "people." See Kohso Iwasaburō, "Kaikisuru chika minshū: Shirato Sanpei kara Oshima Nagisa ni nagarerumono" [The return of the underground people: What Runs from Shirato Sanpei to Oshima Nagisa], *Eiga kantoku Oshima Nagisa* [Director Oshima Nagisa], included in *Oshima Nagisa 1*, DVD box (Tokyo: Kinokuniya Shoten, 2008), 59.

8 Oshima Nagisa, "Seisaku nooto bassui" [Excerpts from production notes], in *Oshima Nagisa: 1968* (Tokyo: Seidosha, 2004), 8.

9 Ibid.

10 Oshima uses an exaggerated expression, *kūzen zetsugo* ("unparalleled" or "unheard of"), to describe his methodology. See Oshima, "Seisaku nooto bassui," 4.

11 Bolter and Grusin, *Remediation*, 55–56. While I borrow the term *remediation* from Bolter and Grusin, I diverge from their analyses in bypassing the problematic of transparency. Nonetheless, I do follow their formulation of remediation as the "mediation of mediation" (56), and this is the sense of remediation that I use in this book.

12 Burch, *To the Distant Observer*, 333.

13 For the particular economy of motion linking limited animation, manga, and character-based commodities, see Marc Steinberg, *Anime's Media Mix: Franchising Toys and Characters in Japan* (Minneapolis: University of Minnesota Press, 2012). For in-depth theoretical analyses of the historical development of Japanese animation and techniques of limited or limited full animation, see Thomas Lamarre, *The Anime Machine: A Media Theory of Animation* (Minneapolis: University of Minnesota Press, 2009).

14 Oshima Nagisa, "'Ninja bugeichō' no kao" [The face of *Band of Ninja*], *Art Theater* 47 (February 1967): 12–13.

15 Kashihon Mangashi Kenkyūkai, ed., *Kashihon manga Returns* [Rental comics return] (Tokyo: Poplar, 2006), 22.

16 Quoted in Yomota Inuhiko, *Shirato Sanpei ron* [On Shirato Sanpei] (Tokyo: Sakuhinsha, 2004), 11. Shirato's work, such as *Band of Ninja* and *The Legend of Kamui*, found a particularly large readership among leftist student activists and intellectuals in the 1960s.

17 Yomota Inuhiko, *Manga genron* [Principles of manga] (Tokyo: Chikuma Shobō, 1999), 138. Straddling the figural space of the drawing and the semiotic space of the narrative (which the contour of word bubbles most visibly separates), graphic onomatopoeias in the comic are elements that cannot be completely severed from drawings.

18 A few of the comic panels filmed in this sequence appear to be redrawn by Shirato or his assistant, since their compositions are slightly different from the published version of *Band of Ninja*. Oshima notes that some of the original drawings were missing, and he had to ask Shirato to redraw them. See Oshima, "'Ninja bugeichō' no kao," 12.

19 One of the voice-overs takes the persona of a little boy named Yunbogi, and narrates a heart-wrenching story of child neglect and poverty. The narrative of Yunbogi is taken from a widely acclaimed diary written by a ten-year-old Korean boy. Oshima borrows passages from the book and combines them with poetic commentary on the resilience of the Korean people in the wake of the Korean War.

20 The film's affirmative reference to the April Revolution, the famous student uprising that overthrew the dictatorial South Korean regime in 1960, is clearly an extension of Oshima's view on the international scope of leftist, anticolonial activism. Oshima had consistently referenced Korea in relation to the legacy of Japanese colonialism and to the force of postwar leftist activism since *Cruel Story of Youth* (*Nihon no yoru to kiri*, 1960), a film that includes newsreel footage reporting on the April Revolution. Oshima's acclaimed television documentary *Forgotten Soldiers* (*Wasurerareta kōgun*, 1963) addressed the lasting injustices suffered by ethnic Korean minority veterans who served in Japan's imperial army. His next television documentary, *A Monument to Youth* (*Seishun no hi*, 1964), turns to the aftermath of the April Revolution, focusing on the life story of a female student activist who subsequently became a prostitute to support her family. As Maureen Turim suggests, both *Forgotten Soldiers* and *A Monument to Youth* address the history of South Korea since the end of Japan's occupation in 1945 by anchoring the narratives to personal chronicles. See Turim, *The Films of Oshima Nagisa*, 223. Oshima's extended engagement with Korea continued in *Death by Hanging* (*Kōshikei*, 1968) as well as in *Three Resurrected Drunkards* (*Kaettekita yopparai*, 1968).

21 For an insightful analysis of the psychic effects of Marker's use of photograms, as well as the devices of dissolve and fade in *La Jetée*, see Réda Bensmaia, "From the Photogram to the Pictogram: On Chris Marker's *La Jetée*," *Camera Obscura* 24 (1990): 139–61.

22 Oshima, *Oshima Nagisa: 1968*, 86.

23 Oshima quoted in Matsumoto Toshio, *Hyōgen no sekai* [The world of expression] (Tokyo: San'ichi Shobō, 1967), 233.

24 Matsumoto Toshio, "Documentarists of Japan # 9: Matsumoto Toshio," Yamagata International Documentary Film Festival, Documentary Box, http://www.yidff.jp/docbox/9/box9-2-e.html.

25 Matsumoto, *Hyōgen no sekai*, 273.

26 Matsumoto Toshio, "Hyōgen keishiki no jikken" [Experiments in forms of

expression], in *Gendai eiga jiten* [Contemporary encyclopedia of cinema], ed. Okada Susumu, Sasaki Kiichi, Satō Tadao, and Hani Susumu (Tokyo: Bijutsu Shuppansha, 1967), 155.

27 Oshima uses the expression "opinion leader" in his pointed criticism of Matsumoto's failure as a leader of various "movements" (*undō*, alternately translated as "activism"). See Oshima Nagisa, "Shura to shutai = Matsumoto Toshio," in *Dōjidai sakka no hakken* [Discovery of contemporary auteurs] (Tokyo: San'ichi Shobō, 1978), 111–32; and Oshima Nagisa, *Oshima Nagisa: 1960* (Tokyo: Seidosha, 1993), 34.

28 It is important to note that the formation of Eiga to Hihyō no Kai happened before "New Wave" filmmaking emerged, indicating that there was already an intellectual movement that paved the way for the emergence of a new kind of filmmaking.

29 The film journal *Eiga Hihyō* was discontinued in 1959, but revived in 1970. Publication of this second cycle of *Eiga Hihyō* ended in 1973. In order to distinguish these two cycles of publication, I indicate the first cycle as *Eiga Hihyō I* and the second cycle as *Eiga Hihyō II*.

30 Nornes, *Forest of Pressure*, 19.

31 Matsuda Masao notes how the work of Hanada influenced both Matsumoto and Oshima in the early stage of their filmmaking careers: "While Oshima quickly pulled away from the gravitational force of Hanada, Matsumoto remained under the influence of Hanada's theorization of the avant-garde art for a while." Matsuda Masao, "Magazine and Book Check," in *Andaaguraundo firumu aakaibusu* [Underground film archives], ed. Hirasawa Gō (Tokyo: Kawade Shobō, 2001), 125.

32 In this regard, 1960 was a year of great importance, as Matsumoto came to Oshima's support when his most controversial film *Night and Fog in Japan* (*Nihon no yoru to kiri*) was immediately shut down on its release. *Night and Fog in Japan* was Oshima's fourth feature at the Shōchiku Studio. The film daringly touched on the then topical political issue of the U.S.-Japan Security Treaty (ANPO) and offered an insightful critique of left-wing student activism. After merely four days of screening, the Shōchiku Studio pulled the film from circulation.

33 Abé Mark Nornes notes how this immanent critique of the Left took a distinct form of anti-Stalinism. See his *Forest of Pressure*, 22. Matsumoto and Oshima often use the phrase *Yoyogi-ha* to describe those whose ideological position resonates with the Japanese Communist Party. Matsumoto and Oshima thus resonated with the New Left student activists who regarded themselves as anti-*Yoyogi-ha*.

34 While Nornes translates the title of Matsumoto's book, *Eizō no hakken*, as *Discovering the Image*, in his excellent book, *Forest of Pressure*, I prefer to use a more literal translation, *Discovery of the Image*.

35 Matsuda, "Magazine and Book Check," 125.

36 Oshima Nagisa, "Sengo nihon eiga no jōkyō to shutai" [Situation and subject in postwar Japanese cinema], in *Sengo eiga: Hakai to sōzō* [Postwar cinema: Destruction and creation] (Tokyo: San'ichi Shobō, 1963), 204–5.

37 Oshima Nagisa, *Dōjidai sakka no hakken* [Discovery of contemporary auteurs] (Tokyo: San'ichi Shobō, 1978), 127. While Oshima's book, *Sengo eiga*, was published a few months before Matsumoto's *Eizō no hakken*, the influence the latter had over their generation and younger generations of filmmakers and critics was wider. Abé Mark Nornes notes, "When Matsumoto's writings were collected in the book *Eizō no Hakken* (*Discovering the Image*), they quickly became a bible for the new cohort of artists and spectators" (*Forest of Pressure*, 21).

38 Matsumoto also used the expression *neo-documentarism* to describe his method of avant-garde documentary filmmaking. See Matsumoto Toshio, "Zen'ei kiroku eiga no hōhō ni tsuite" [On the method of avant-garde documentary film], *Kiroku Eiga* [Documentary film] 1 (May 1958): 6–11. This essay was collected in his book, *Eizō no hakken* (1963), under a new title, "Zen'ei kiroku eiga ron" [A theory of avant-garde documentary film].

39 For a comprehensive analysis of the Japanese surrealist movement, see Miryam Sas, *Fault Lines: Cultural Memory and Japanese Surrealism* (Stanford: Stanford University Press, 1999). Matsumoto also acknowledges the influence of surrealism and Russian formalism in his interview with Aaron Gerow. Matsumoto Toshio, "Documentarists of Japan # 9: Matsumoto Toshio," Yamagata International Documentary Film Festival, Documentary Box, http://www.yidff.jp/docbox/9/box9-2-e.html.

40 Matsumoto Toshio, "Katachi ni naranai katachi e no mosaku" [Exploration of a form without form], *Kiroku Eiga* [Documentary film] 54 (May 1963), 28.

41 In his relentless critique of the wartime complicity between documentary filmmakers and the state, and in his commitment to the affirmation of the filmmaker's "subjectivity" (*shutaisei*), Matsumoto was again in agreement with Oshima. Both filmmakers acknowledge the influence of the war-responsibility debates generated by literary critics such as Yoshimoto Takaaki.

42 Matsumoto, "Zen'ei kiroku eiga no hōhō ni tsuite," 10.

43 Matsumoto, *Eizō no hakken*, 49.

44 See Hanada Kiyoteru, *Avangyarudo geijutsu* [Avant-garde art] (Tokyo: Miraisha, 1954).

45 Matsumoto Toshio, "Kakusareta sekai no kiroku" [Record of the hidden world], in *Eizō no hakken: Avangyarudo to dokyumentarii* [Discovery of the image: Avant-garde and documentary] (Tokyo: San'ichi Shobō, 1963), 79–93.

46 Ibid., 82.

47 Matsumoto's Freudo-Marxism is reminiscent of the work of Frankfurt

School thinkers, in particular the work of Herbert Marcuse whose *Eros and Civilization* (1955) was translated into Japanese in 1958.

48 Abé Mark Nornes provocatively compares Matsumoto's theorization of the uncanny to Althusser's notion of structured absence and the Lacanian abject in his discussion of Matsumoto's essay "Record of the Hidden World," in *Forest of Pressure*, 25.

49 Karl Marx, *A Contribution to the Critique of Political Economy*, ed. Maurice Dobb (New York: International Publishers, 1979), 21.

50 See Hanada Kiyoteru, "Warai neko" [Cheshire cat], in *Hanada Kiyoteru chosakushū III* [Selected works of Hanada Kiyoteru III] (Tokyo: Miraisha, 1964), 218–31.

51 Nornes, *Forest of Pressure*, 26.

52 Matsumoto Toshio, "Hōhō to imeeji" [Method and the image], in *Eizō no hakken: Avangyarudo to dokyumentarii* [Discovery of the image: Avant-garde and documentary] (Tokyo: San'ichi Shobō, 1963), 61.

53 Matsumoto, "Kakusareta sekai no kiroku," 91.

54 It is hard not to detect echoes of these techniques in Matsumoto's own films, in particular *Security Treaty*, in which collage-like treatments of press photographs, drawings, and news footage abound. Matsumoto's "aggressively experimental filmmaking that politicized film style itself" was not well received. See Nornes, *Forest of Pressure*, 21. Matsumoto's fellow critics and filmmakers associated with the journal *Kiroku Eiga* denounced his arty "vanguard elitism" on the premise that the film was incomprehensible for the masses. See, for instance, Kizaki Keiichirō, "Zen'ei eriito no taishū sogai" [Alienation of the masses by the elite vanguard], *Kiroku Eiga* [Documentary film] 24 (January 1962): 24–26.

55 Matsumoto, "Zen'ei kiroku eiga ron," 55.

56 Ibid.

57 Ibid.

58 As Matsumoto recalled later, he was fully aware of the "sacrilegious" implications of cropping and dissecting the photographs taken by the professional photographer. Not surprisingly, Satow resisted Matsumoto's proposed plan at first, though he relented under pressure from TBS television. From the voice-over commentary on *The Song of Stone* included in part 1 of Matsumoto's DVD box set *Matsumoto Toshio jikken eizōshū, 1961–1987* [Toshio Matsumoto experimental film works: 1961–1987] (Tokyo: Uplink, 2005).

59 Matsumoto Toshio, DVD pamphlet included in *Matsumoto Toshio jikken eizōshū, 1961–1987*, 8.

60 André Bazin, *What Is Cinema?*, vol. 1, trans. Hugh Gray (Berkeley: University of California Press, 1967), 169.

61 Ibid.

62 Kurabayashi Yasushi, "Kanōsei no eiga: Takiguchi Shūzō no *Hokusai* shinario to shururearisumu" [The film of possibility: Takiguchi Shūzō's script for *Ho-*

kusai and surrealism], in *Eizō hyōgen no orutanatibu: 1960 nendai no itsudatsu to sōzō* [Alternative cinematic expressions: Transgression and creation in the 1960s], ed. Nishijima Norio (Tokyo: Shinwasha, 2005), 96–120.

63 Teshigahara Hiroshi and his father, Teshigahara Sōfū, founded Sōgetsu Art Center in 1958. For the history of the Sōgetsu Art Center, see "Sōgetsu Aaato Sentaa no Kiroku," Kankō Iinkai, ed., *Kagayake 60 nendai: Sōgetsu Aaato Sentaa no zenkiroku* [The shining 1960s: A complete record of the Sōgetsu Art Center] (Tokyo: Firumu Aato-sha, 2002).

64 Mondzain, *Image, Icon, Economy*, 8.

65 Nancy, *The Ground of the Image*, 1.

66 Roland Barthes, *Image, Music, Text*, trans. Stephen Heath (New York: Hill and Wang, 1977), 32.

67 Didi-Huberman, *Confronting Images*, 27.

68 Matsumoto Toshio, "Saihan ni yosete" [For the reprint], in *Eizō no hakken: Avangyarudo to dokyumentarii* [Discovery of the image: Avant-garde and documentary] (reprint, Tokyo: Seiryū Shuppan, 2005), 244.

69 For an excellent discussion of the *eizō ronsō* in relation to the waning theory of montage and the question of language, see Tomoda Yoshiyuki, "Eizō ronsō aruiwa gengo to eizō ronsō" [The debate on the image or the debate on language and the image], *Eizōgaku/Iconics* 82 (2009): 63–81. For an analysis of this debate in relation to Abé Kōbō's literary work, see the chapter "The Wall of Language and Micropolitics of Perception" in my dissertation, "Refiguring Actuality: Japan's Film Theory and Avant-Garde Documentary Movement, 1950s–1960s" (PhD diss., Brown University, 2009).

70 "'Eizō Geijutsu no Kai' o sōritsu suru ni atatte" [On the occasion of the founding of the Association of Image Arts], *Eizō Geijutsu* [Image arts] 1 (December 1964): 1.

71 "'*Eiga Bunka*' no sōkan ni tsuite" [On the founding of the journal *Film Culture*], *Eiga Bunka* [Film culture] 1 (March 1950): 5–6.

72 Imamura Taihei, *Eiga no me: Moji kara eizō no bunka e* [The eye of cinema: From print culture to image culture] (Tokyo: Kōwadō, 1992), 44. "Kotoba to eizō," the original essay containing this claim, was published in the August 1976 issue of the journal *Bungaku*. Imamura names the philosopher Nakai Masakazu as one of these intellectuals. We also see a consistent application of the word *eizō* written with the character for "reflection" and "projection" in the 1942 publication of *Eiga, hyōgen, keisei* by Nagae Michitarō, who was close to Nakai Masakazu. See Nagae Michitarō, *Eiga, hyōgen, keisei* [Cinema, expression, formation], ed. Makino Mamoru (Tokyo: Yumani Shobō, 2003).

73 Imamura suggests that what he meant by the term *eizō* was the "screen image" (*Eiga no me*, 45). The increased currency of the term *eizō* thus reflects not simply the attention paid to images in general, but more precisely the awareness of these images as technologically produced and mediated.

74 Imamura Taihei, "Eiga to terebi no renzokusei: Atarashii eizō mondai no

minamoto" [The continuity between cinema and television: The root of new problems concerning the image], *Eizō Bunka* [Image culture] 5 (June 1963), 8. Rejecting what he sees as the lofty view of film theorists like Iwasaki Akira and Uryū Tadao, who isolate cinema from television, Imamura argues: "If we approach this situation from the perspective of film theory, it is clear that television and cinema are neither incompatible, nor are they competing mediums. Both are stemming from the same root." This root, according to Imamura, is the image culture, a matrix of all forms of image-based media. This pervasive culture of the image, Imamura contends, is precisely what Balázs predicted in his 1924 classic, *Der sichtbare Mensch* (*The Visible Man*).

75 Matsumoto, *Eizō no hakken*, 244. Matsumoto was the first who started calling himself not filmmaker but "visual artist" (*eizō sakka*).

76 Okada Susumu, "Eizō no ronri to gengo no ronri" [The logic of image and the logic of language], *Gendai geijutsu* [Contemporary art] 3 (1959), 100.

77 Ibid.

78 Tomoda, "Eizō ronsō aruiwa gengo to eizō ronsō," 63.

79 Hani Susumu, *Kamera to maiku: Gendai geijutsu no hōhō* [The camera and microphone: Methods of contemporary art] (Tokyo: Chūōkōronsha, 1960), 56.

80 Abé Kōbō, "Eizō wa gengo no kabe o hakai suruka" [Does the image demolish the wall of language?], in *Abé Kōbō zenshū* [The complete works of Abé Kōbō] (Tokyo: Shinchōsha, 1998), 11:451. Trained in medicine, Abé was particularly drawn to the study of language dysfunction and perceptual disorders caused by the conditions of aphasia, agnosia, and schizophrenia. Also, one of his stable points of reference is the work of the Russian physiologist Ivan Pavlov, whose idea of human language as a second-order signal system he much admired.

81 Abé, "Eizō wa gengo no kabe o hakai suruka," 11:453.

82 Abé, "Jikken eiga no shinario" [A script for an experimental film], in *Abé Kōbō zenshū* [The complete works of Abé Kōbō] (Tokyo: Shinchōsha, 1998), 11:447. The emphasis is mine.

83 Christian Metz, *Film Language: A Semiotics of the Cinema*, trans. Michael Taylor (Chicago: University of Chicago Press, 1991), 44.

84 See Martin Lefebvre, "L'aventure filmologique: Documents et jalons d'une histoire institutionnelle," *Cinémas: Revue d'études cinématographiques* 19.2–3 (2009): 59–100.

85 Okada acknowledges the influence of French film theorists in many places. For a systematic account of his engagement with French film theories, see Okada Susumu, *Eiga gaku kara eizō gaku e* [From film studies to image studies] (Fukuoka: Kyūshū daigaku Shuppankai, 1987). In his essay "Eizō to majutsu ni kansuru josetsu" [An introduction to the image and magic], published in the anthology *Eizō to wa nanika* [What is an image?] (Tokyo: Shashin Dōjinsha, 1966), Okada calls Bazin "a French film critic whom I re-

spect" (11). In the afterword to the book *From Film Studies to Image Studies*, Okada also recollects how his obsession with the image led him to participate in establishing Nihon Eizō Gakkai (Japan Society of Image Arts and Sciences, or JSIAS) in 1974. The JSIAS is currently the largest academic organization dedicated to the study of cinema and media in Japan.

86 Itō Biichi, ed., *Eizō to wa nanika* [What is an image?] (Tokyo: Shashin Dōjinsha, 1966).

87 Okada Susumu, *Gendai eizō ron* [A contemporary theory of the image] (Tokyo: San'ichi Shobō, 1965), 246.

88 This is Oshima's comment on early television spectatorship. Oshima argues that "open-air television" (*gaitō terebi*), which was set in the open space of the street in broad daylight, brought on a fundamental transformation in our perception of the image. See Oshima Nagisa, *Taiken teki sengo eizō ron* [Theorizing postwar film from my experience] (Tokyo: Asahi Shinbunsha, 1975), 238.

89 Matsumoto Toshio, "Ore tachi wa minna *Kichigai Piero* da" [We are all *Pierrot le fou*], *Dezain Hihyō* [Design review] 6 (July 1968), 40.

90 For instance, the 1967 book on Marshall McLuhan edited by Tōno Yoshiaki (one of the co-organizers of "EXPOSE·1968") and others introduces McLuhan's media theory and his interest in the metaphor of mosaic. See Ōmae Masaomi, Gotō Kazuhiko, Satō Tsuyoshi, and Tōno Yoshiaki, eds., *McLuhan sono hito to riron* [McLuhan and his theory] (Tokyo: Daikōsha, 1967).

91 Matsumoto Toshio, "Ekusupandeddo shinema no tenbō" [An observation on expanded cinema], *Eiga no henkaku: Geijutsu teki rajikarizumu towa nanika* [Transformation of cinema: What is artistic radicalism?] (Tokyo: San'ichi Shobō, 1972), 170. See also Akiyama Kuniharu, "Cross-Talk/Intermedia," *Bijutsu Techō* [Art notebook] 311 (April 1969), 100.

CHAPTER 2

1 Matsuda Masao, *Teroru no kairo* [A circuit of terror] (Tokyo: San'ichi Shobō, 1969), 156.

2 Oshima Nagisa, "Shinario ni tsuite" [About the script], *Art Theater* 65 (February 1969), 21. See also Oshima, *Oshima Nagisa: 1968*, 235. While filming this prefigurative riot in June, two cameramen from Oshima's production company, Sōzōsha, were apprehended by the police and asked to surrender the reel recording the scene, but they refused.

3 Satō, *ATG eiga o yomu*, 180.

4 Rancière, *The Emancipated Spectator*, 2.

5 See Hanada Kiyoteru et al., "Akuchuaritii no tame no kadai" [The challenge of actuality], *Bijutsu Hihyō* [Art notebook] 25 (January 1954): 15–31; Masaki Kyōsuke, "Kiroku geijutsu no akuchuarite" [The actuality of documentary

art], *Gendai Geijutsu* [Contemporary art] 1 (1958): 174–81; Noda Shinkichi, "Higenjitsusei no akuchuaritii" [The actuality of nonreality], *Kiroku Geijutsu* [Documentary art] 2.5 (May 1959): 30–34; Haryū Ichirō, "Akuchuaritii to wa nani ka" [What is actuality?], *Shin Nihon Bungaku* [New Japanese literature] 17.3 (March 1962): 170–77; Yoshimoto Takaaki, "Sengo bungaku no genjitsusei: Akuchuaritii wa kanō ka" [The reality of postwar literature: Is actuality possible?], *Bungei* [Literary art] 1.6 (August 1962): 210–20.

6 On the insightful discussion of Japanese surrealists' interest in the notion of actuality, see Sas, *Fault Lines*.

7 For a more detailed discussion of the literary discourse on actuality and its relation to the work of Hanada Kiyoteru, see my dissertation, "Refiguring Actuality."

8 Takiguchi Shūzō—with whom Tosaka Jun interacted through the Materialism Study Group (Yuibutsuron Kenkyūkai) and whose book *Kindai geijutsu* (Modern art, 1938) he helped publish as part of the Materialist Theory series from Mikasa Shobō—is an interesting case in point. Not only does Takiguchi use the notion of actuality in opposition to eternity in a manner comparable to Tosaka in the 1930s, but he also positions his own involvement in surrealism through the notion of actuality, which he aligns with both historical materialism and journalism in an essay and an interview published in the 1960s. See Takiguchi Shūzō, *Korekushon Takiguchi Shūzō* [Takiguchi Shūzō collection], vol. 1 (Tokyo: Misuzu Shobō, 1991).

9 Tosaka Jun, "Ideorogii gairon" [General remarks on ideology], in *Tosaka Jun zenshū* [The collected works of Tosaka Jun] (Tokyo: Keisō Shobō, 1966), 2:118.

10 Tosaka Jun, "Jaanarizumu to tetsugaku no kōshō" [The encounter between journalism and philosophy], in *Tosaka Jun zenshū* [The collected works of Tosaka Jun] (Tokyo: Keisō Shobō, 1966), 4:148.

11 Tosaka Jun, *Nihon ideorogiiron* [On Japanese ideology] (Tokyo: Iwanami Shoten, 1977), 46.

12 Ibid., 48. Emphasis in original.

13 Tosaka, "Jaanarizumu to tetsugaku no kōshō," 4:150.

14 Harry D. Harootunian, *Overcome by Modernity: History, Culture, and Community in Interwar Japan* (Princeton: Princeton University Press, 2000), 132.

15 Wada Yōichi, "Meiji/Taisho ki no jaanarizumuron" [Theories of journalism during the Meiji and Taisho periods], *Shinbungaku Hyōron* [Newspaper studies review] 18 (March 1969): 70–75.

16 Another Marxist critic who evoked *Aktualität* in relation to philosophy is Theodor Adorno. We find a comparable repositioning of philosophy in Adorno's 1931 lecture delivered at the University of Frankfurt, which is aptly titled "The Actuality of Philosophy" ("Die Aktualität der Philosophie"). Like Tosaka, Adorno offers a historical materialist critique of Husserlian phenomenology and Heideggerian ontology for their shared disposition toward

ahistorical approaches to being and reality. See Theodor Adorno, "The Actuality of Philosophy," in *The Adorno Reader*, by Theodor Adorno, edited by Brian O'Connor (Malden: Blackwell, 2000), 29.

17 Esther Leslie, *Walter Benjamin: Overpowering Conformism* (London: Pluto, 2000), ix. See also Sigrid Weigel, *Body-and-Image Space: Re-reading Walter Benjamin* (New York: Routledge, 1996).

18 Tosaka uses these German terms to clarify his ideas. For instance, he argues that academicism (which encompasses the professionalized fields of literature and art for Tosaka) functions in an opposite manner to journalism, and is said to embody the quality of *Unaktualität*. It is characterized, in short, by its *un*-actual engagement with reality. Tosaka Jun, "Shinbun genshō no bunseki" [An analysis of the newspaper phenomenon], in *Tosaka Jun zenshū* [The collected works of Tosaka Jun] (Tokyo: Keisō Shobō, 1966), 3:125.

19 The wide-reaching impact of Hanada's work and his use of the term *actuality* can be seen even in the rise of a debate on the subject of actuality among literary critics at the beginning of the 1960s. The so-called "debate over pure literature" initiated by the literary critic Hirano Ken is a particularly salient example of this. See my analysis of the debate in "Refiguring Actuality."

20 Tamai Goichi, "Kiroku Geijutsu no Kai: Geijutsu undō shōkai I" [The Association for Documentary Art: Introductions of artistic movements I], *Shin Nihon Bungaku* [New Japanese literature] 12.11 (October 1957), 127.

21 While Italian Neorealism and the French *nouvelle vague* clearly influenced the postwar generation of Japanese filmmakers and critics—Hanada included—this influence alone cannot explain the spread of these techniques, which have traditionally been associated with documentary filmmaking. It is important to consider the discursive impact of groups such as Kiroku Geijutsu no Kai.

22 While the main target of Hanada's criticism is Tsumura Hideo, Hanada also questioned and thus implicitly criticized Sasaki Kiichi's and Imamura Taihei's discussions of documentary film, which in turn solicited Imamura's criticism of Hanada. See Hanada Kiyoteru, "Gūzen no mondai" [A question of contingency], in *Hanada Kiyoteru chosakushū* [Selected works of Hanada Kiyoteru] (Tokyo: Miraisha, 1963), 2:27–49; and Sasaki Kiichi, *Geijutsuron nōto II* [Notes on theories of art II] (Tokyo: Gōdōshuppan, 1968), 217–33.

23 Tsumura Hideo, *Zoku eiga to hihyō* [Sequel: Film and criticism] (Tokyo: Koyama Shoten, 1940), 144.

24 For an in-depth analysis of the historical and political context surrounding the Japanese translation of Paul Rotha's *Documentary Film* (1935), see Abé Mark Nornes, "Pōru Rūta: Paul Rotha and the Politics of Translation," *Cinema Journal* 38.3 (Spring 1999): 91–108.

25 Tsumura, *Zoku eiga to hihyō*, 144. These two German words were indiscriminately translated into Japanese using the same word, *genjitsu*, during the

prewar period. It was Tosaka Jun who put an end to the conflation of the two terms—*Wirklichkeit* and *Realität*—from a Marxist point of view. As Harry Harootunian suggests, "For Tosaka, *genjitsu* acted as a code for idealist philosophers who envisaged reality at a higher plane of existence than at the level of mere, actual occurrences of society" (*Overcome by Modernity*, 129). Tosaka thus began using the loanword *akuchuaritii* instead of *genjitsu* in order to attenuate the philosophical baggage of idealism attached to the latter word.

26 In *Kant and the Problem of Metaphysics*, Martin Heidegger warns "not to take the Kantian term 'reality' ['*Realität*'] in the same sense as modern 'epistemology' does, according to which 'reality' ['*Realität*'] means the same as 'actuality' ['*Wirklichkeit*']—which Kant indicates with the terms '*Dasein*' or 'existence' ['*Existenz*']" (61). In other words, while a finite human existence (*Dasein*) pertains to the existing phenomenal world of "actuality," pure reason can transcend the limit of empirical knowledge (derived from the phenomenal world) by means of pure concepts. That is, the analytical power of pure reason tries to "know the supersensible being rationally" by demonstrating the "objective reality" of the conceptual categories, which belong to ontological knowledge and not to empirical knowledge. See Martin Heidegger, *Kant and the Problem of Metaphysics*, 5th edn., trans. Richard Taft (Bloomington: Indiana University Press, 1997), 61.

27 Hanada does not mention Tosaka explicitly and thus this connection is of necessity speculative. However, it is well known that Hanada was an avid reader of Tosaka's work, and it was thanks to Hanada's preservation of Tosaka's books that they were republished after the war. It is therefore likely that Hanada knew of Tosaka's use of the concept of actuality at the time of his writing.

28 In a roundtable discussion held in 1957, Hanada insisted that a clear distinction be made between reality and actuality: "There has been a tendency to contrast reality to actuality; in order to shatter socialist realism we should focus more on the latter aspect of actuality." See Abé Kōbō et al., "Haado boirudo: Genzai no me" [Hardboiled: The eyes of the present], in *Abé Kōbō zenshū* [The complete works of Abé Kōbō] (Tokyo: Shinchōsha, 1998), 7:25.

29 Hanada Kiyoteru, "Eiga kantoku ron" [On film directors], in *Bungakuteki eigaron* [Literary theories of film], ed. Noma Hiroshi et al. (Tokyo: Chūōkōron, 1957), 76.

30 Hanada Kiyoteru, "Shūru-dokyumentarizumu ni kansuru ichi kōsatsu" [On *sur*-documentarism], *Eiga Hihyō* 2.2 (February 1958): 2–5.

31 Matsumoto, "Zen'ei kiroku eiga no hōhō ni tsuite," 9.

32 Ibid.

33 Noda Shinkichi, Matsumoto Toshio, Teshigahara Hiroshi, and Hani Susumu, "Kiroku eiga to geki eiga: Dokyumentarii no hōhō o megutte" [Docu-

mentary film and fiction film: On the issue of the documentary method], *Shin Nihon Bungaku* [New Japanese literature] 16.5 (May 1961): 125–37.

34 See Gabriel Tarde, *L'opinion et la foule* (Paris: Presses Universitaires de France, 1989), 9.

35 Walter Benjamin, "The Storyteller: Reflections on the Works of Nikolai Leskov," in *Illuminations*, trans. Harry Zohn (New York: Schocken, 1969), 90.

36 Tosaka, "Shinbun genshō no bunseki," 3:132.

37 Ibid.

38 For the ideological function of this mode of address and its complex relation to a dialectic of segmentation and flow, see Jane Feuer, "The Concept of Live Television: Ontology as Ideology," in *Regarding Television*, ed. E. Ann Kaplan (Frederick, Md.: American Film Institute, 1983), 12–22.

39 Mary Ann Doane, "Information, Crisis, Catastrophe," in *New Media, Old Media: A History and Theory Reader*, eds. Wendy Hui Kyong Chun and Thomas Keenan (New York: Routledge, 2006), 255.

40 Ibid., 252.

41 For the notion of "theatrical crime" (*gekijōgata hanzai*), and the most notorious case of the 1980s, see Marilyn Ivy, "Tracking the Mystery Man with the 21 Faces," *Critical Inquiry* 23.1 (autumn 1996): 11–36. My narrative of the Kim Hiro Incident is based on information gleaned from *Asahi Shinbun* articles from 21 February to 24 February 1968.

42 Matsumoto Toshio, "Subete no zen'ei eiga no saizensen kara" [From the frontline of all avant-garde films], in *Andaaguraundo firumu aakaibusu* [Underground film archives], ed. Hirasawa Gō (Tokyo: Kawade Shobō, 2001), 25. See also, Matsumoto Toshio, "Purojekushon aato no kadai" [The task of projection arts], in *Eiga no henkaku: geijutsuteki rajikarizumu to wa nani ka* [Transformation of cinema: What is artistic radicalism?] (Tokyo: San'ichi Shobō, 1972), 160.

43 For McLuhan, the newspaper is a mosaic form similar to that of television. See Marshall McLuhan, *Understanding Media: The Extensions of Man* (Cambridge: MIT Press, 1994), 205.

44 Doane, "Information, Crisis, Catastrophe," 253. But unlike newspaper or television, which keep their information segments distinct, *For the Damaged Right Eye* blurs the boundaries by overlapping information-images.

45 Derrida and Stiegler, *Echographies of Television*, 3. Emphasis in the original.

46 Ibid. Emphasis in the original.

47 Oshima, *Oshima Nagisa: 1968*, 206.

48 Ibid., 217.

49 Ibid., 218.

50 On the project of the Third World, see Vijay Prashad, *Darker Nations: A People's History of the Third World* (New York: New Press, 2007). What Fredric Jameson said about North America and Europe also resonates with the turn toward decolonization struggles and minority issues that gripped

the attention of Japanese filmmakers and intellectuals around 1968: "Politically, a first world 60s owed much to third-worldism in terms of politico-cultural models, as in a symbolic Maoism, and, moreover, found its mission in resistance to wars aimed precisely at stemming the new revolutionary forces in the third world." See Fredric Jameson, "Periodizing the 60s," in *The 60s without Apology*, ed. Sohnya Sayres et al. (Minneapolis: University of Minnesota Press, 1984), 180.

51 Matsuda, *Teroru no kairo*, 156–57.

52 Ibid., 222. Matsuda also acknowledges his struggle to embrace his dual identity as a son of an Okinawan mother and a Japanese father.

53 John Lie also compares these two incidents and draws attention to their similarities. See John Lie, *Zainichi (Koreans in Japan): Diasporic Nationalism and Postcolonial Identity* (Berkeley: University of California Press, 2008), 93.

54 Oshima, *Oshima Nagisa: 1968*, 204.

55 Desser, *Eros Plus Massacre*, 155.

56 Turim, *The Films of Oshima Nagisa*, 65.

57 Burch, *To the Distant Observer*, 334.

58 Stephen Heath, *Questions of Cinema* (Bloomington: Indiana University Press, 1981), 65.

59 Indeed, as early as *Cruel Story of Youth* (*Seishun zankoku monogatari*, 1960), we see Oshima's appropriation of then current journalistic materials. The opening credit sequence in *Cruel Story of Youth* consists of a series of black-and-white shots, presenting intricate collages of hand-torn newspaper clippings as the background. At the end of the film, an imprint of the character for "The End" also appears against a background composed of newspaper clippings. Placed at the beginning and the end, the extradiegetic use of these newspapers helps to ground the diegetic setting of the film in the year of its production: 1960. There is also an inserted news film, shot by the Daimai news team, reporting on the April 1960 Student Revolution in Korea, an event that took place less than two months before the film's release in June 1960. The documentary footage of the 1960 May Day protest shot by Oshima's own crew further accentuates the sense of journalistic actuality.

60 In the essay included in the ATG's pamphlet for the film, Takahashi notes that the "script" for this sequence, handed to him by Oshima and Adachi, was completely blank, and thus he had to psychoanalyze Yokoo and Yokoyama on the spot without guidance. See Takahashi Tetsu, "Oshima eiga to bunseki kaunseringu" [Oshima and analytical counseling], *Art Theater* 65 (February 1969): 13–15.

61 Oshima sees the stone thrown on the night of 29 June as a premonition of the countless stones thrown on 21 October, the day of the infamous Shinjuku Riot. See Oshima, "Shinario ni tsuite," 21.

62 Matsumoto Productions, "Bara no sōretsu" [Funeral parade of roses], *Art Theater* 70 (September 1969), 71.

63 Oshima, *Taiken teki sengo eizō ron*, 244.

64 Marshall McLuhan, "Address to Vision 65," in *Essential McLuhan*, ed. Eric McLuhan and Frank Zingrone (New York: Basic, 1995), 221.

CHAPTER 3

1 Wakamatsu Kōji, *Wakamatsu Kōji: Ore wa te o yogosu* [Wakamatsu Kōji: I dirty my hands] (Tokyo: Dagereo Shuppan, 1982), 116.

2 Because of their close association and the importance of Adachi and other Wakamatsu Production members, I will refer in this chapter not to Wakamatsu alone but instead to Wakamatsu Production as the collective agents responsible for the production of these films.

3 Wakamatsu, *Wakamatsu Kōji*, 116.

4 Hiraoka Masaaki, *Angura kikansetsu: Yami no hyōgensha retsuden* [Theses on the institution of the underground: Biographies of artists of the dark] (Tokyo: Magazine Five, 2007), 135. This essay was originally published in a publicity brochure for the film *Sexual Reincarnation* and was subsequently anthologized in Hiraoka's *Umi o miteita Zatouichi* [Zatouichi who was looking at the sea] (Tokyo: Izara Shobō, 1973). While the temporality of the film and the weekly magazine may be *comparable*, they are not the *same*; there is a gap, and this gap is precisely where the politics of Wakamatsu's filmic repetitions of media events reside.

5 Wakamatsu, *Wakamatsu Kōji*, 116. There is a conflicting account. The film is sometimes credited as having been released in 1971, but Wakamatsu notes that it was shown in December 1970.

6 "Kinkyū daitokushū: Mishima Yukio no shi" [The emergency special: The death of Mishima Yukio], *Shūkan Yomiuri* [Yomiuri Weekly] 29.55 (December 1970): 20–21.

7 Donald Richie, *Viewed Sideways: Writings on Culture and Style in Contemporary Japan* (Berkeley: Stone Bridge Press, 2011), 218.

8 Sharon Hayashi, "The Fantastic Trajectory of Pink Art Cinema from Stalin to Bush," in *Global Art Cinema: New Theories and Histories*, ed. Rosalind Galt and Karl Schoonover (Oxford: Oxford University Press, 2010), 48.

9 Suzuki Yoshiaki, *Pinku eiga suikoden: Sono jūninen shi* [The saga of the pink film: Ten years of its history] (Tokyo: Seishinsha, 1983), 12.

10 Eric Shaefer, *"Bold! Daring! Shocking! True!": A History of Exploitation Films, 1919–1959* (Durham: Duke University Press, 1999), 108–9.

11 Ibid., 6.

12 Suzuki, *Pinku eiga suikoden*, 35. This is why Kobayashi's *Flesh Market* (1962), which was produced and distributed by Ōkura Mitsugu, a former *benshi* (narrator) and the founder of the Ōkura Eiga studio, qualifies as the first pink film. Established in 1961, Ōkura Eiga began specializing in the produc-

tion and distribution of pink films and continues to specialize in pornography today. Murai may have also borrowed the term *pink* from its usage in the United States. According to Schaefer, "The adults-only designation, also known as 'pinking' after the color of the Chicago permit that forbade the admission of children to a film," was already in use in the United States before the Second World War (*"Bold! Daring! Shocking! True!,"* 124).

13 Suzuki, *Pinku eiga suikoden*, 14. Eirin—short for Eiga Rinri Kitei Kanri Iinkai (Film Ethics Regulation Control Committee)—was founded by film industry personnel in 1949 during the Occupation. In 1956 the committee extricated itself from the industry and established the self-regulatory rating system, which was run by a third party. It changed its name from Eiga Rinri Kitei Kanri Iinkai to Eiga Rinri Iinkai (which is now translated as Film Classification and Rating Committee) in 2009.

14 Ibid., 15. Like the exploitation film, the pink film is also differentiated from hardcore pornography.

15 Suzuki, *Pinku eiga suikoden*, 26.

16 Oshima Nagisa, "Wakamatsu Kōji: Sabetsu to satsuriku" [Wakamatsu Kōji: Discrimination and carnage], *Eiga Hihyō II* [Film criticism II] 1.1 (October 1970), 104. The term Oshima uses is *onigo* (demon child), which indicates a lack of resemblance between the parent and the child. In order to get the nuance across, I have translated it as "bastard child."

17 Wakamatsu also brought another film, *Okasareta byakui* (*Violated Angels*, 1967), to the Cannes International Film Festival in 1971. These two films were invited to Cannes, together with Oshima's *The Ceremony* (*Gishiki*, 1971).

18 The manga version of *Tomorrow's Joe* was serialized in the weekly magazine *Shūkan Shōnen Magazine*, from 1968 to 1973. While the Yodogō Hijacking Incident was unfolding, the TV anime version of the work went on the air.

19 Oshima, "Wakamatsu Kōji," 105.

20 Matsuda Masao, *Fūkei no shimetsu* [Extinction of the landscape] (Tokyo: Tabata Shoten, 1971), 201.

21 Saitō Ayako, "Adachi eiga to feminizumu" [Adachi's films and feminism], *Jōkyō* [Situations] 3.30 (June 2003), 165.

22 Laura Mulvey, "Visual Pleasure and Narrative Cinema," in *Narrative, Apparatus, Ideology: A Film Theory Reader*, ed. Philip Rosen (New York: Columbia University Press, 1986), 198–209.

23 Sharon Hayashi, "Shikyū e no kaiki: Rokujūnendai chūki Wakamatsu puro sakuhin ni okeru seiji to sei" [Return to the womb: Politics and sexuality in the mid-1960s Wakamatsu Production films], in *Wakamatsu Kōji: Hankenryoku no shōzō* [Wakamatsu Kōji: A portrait of counter-power], ed. Yomota Inuhiko and Hirasawa Gō (Tokyo: Sakuhinsha, 2007), 97.

24 While this is a phrase that Linda Williams uses to analyze Oshima's *In the*

Realm of the Senses, the questions of perversion and sadomasochism that she raises in reading this film are, arguably, equally applicable to some of Wakamatsu's films. See Linda Williams, *Hard Core: Power, Pleasure and the "Frenzy of the Visible"* (Berkeley: University of California Press, 1989), 222.

25 Rancière, *Disagreement*, 28. Rancière's theorization of the police is pertinent to the historical context of the late 1960s. See Kristin Ross, *May '68 and Its Afterlives* (Chicago: University of Chicago Press, 2002). For an excellent analysis of political activism and art in 1960s Japan through the lens of Rancière, see also William Marotti, "Japan 1968: The Performance of Violence and the Theater of Protest," *The American Historical Review* 114.1 (2009): 97–135; William Marotti, *Money, Trains, and Guillotines: Art and Revolution in 1960s Japan* (Durham: Duke University Press, 2013). Rancière also invited Wakamatsu to the conference "Où va le cinéma?: Cinéma et politique," held at the Centre Pompidou in Paris in 2008. Due to a strike at the Centre Pompidou, Wakamatsu was unable to attend. I thank Hirasawa Gō for informing me of this event.

26 Ibid.

27 Ibid., 29.

28 Rancière plays on the double connotation of the French word *partage* ("distribution" or "partition"), which suggests an act of division as well as the sharing of something in common. The concept of partage relates to his concern with equality and his critique of consensus. He writes, for instance, "I call the distribution of the sensible [*le partage du sensible*] the system of self-evident facts of sense perception that simultaneously discloses the existence of something in common and the delimitations that define the respective parts and positions within it. A distribution of the sensible therefore establishes at one and the same time something common that is shared and exclusive parts." See Jacques Rancière, *The Politics of Aesthetics*, trans. Gabriel Rockhill (London: Continuum, 2004), 12. With regard to the ambivalent concept of partition or distribution (*partage*), Étienne Balibar's following observation about the difference between the police and politics in Rancière's work is useful: "Policing, in general, is a matter of demands; it seeks to give everyone a fair share in the distribution of the common good, by authoritarian or contractual procedures. Democratic politics, in contrast, has as its unique criterion the 'share of the shareless': that is, the requirement of equality set off *against* social identity or personal merit." See Étienne Balibar, "What Is Political Philosophy?: Contextual Notes," trans. Catherine Porter and Philip E. Lewis, in *Jacques Rancière: History, Politics, Aesthetics*, ed. Gabriel Rockhill and Philip Watts (Durham: Duke University Press, 2009), 101.

29 Rancière, *Disagreement*, 30.

30 Ibid., 28.

31 Wakamatsu's antipathy toward the police is directly linked to his personal

experience of being imprisoned for a petty crime: "I wanted to take revenge against the police by killing many policemen in my films." Yomota Inuhiko and Hirasawa Gō, "Wakamatsu Kōji intabyū" [Interview with Wakamatsu Kōji], in *Wakamatsu Kōji: Hankenryoku no shōzō* [Wakamatsu Kōji: A portrait of counter-power], ed. Yomota Inuhiko and Hirasawa Gō (Tokyo: Sakuhinsha, 2007), 176.

32 Hirasawa Gō, "Radikarizumu no keizoku: 1970 nendai ikou ni okeru Wakamatsu Kōji ron" [A continuation of radicalism: Wakamatsu Kōji after the 1970s], in *Wakamatsu Kōji: Hankenryoku no shōzō* [Wakamatsu Kōji: A portrait of counter-power], ed. Yomota Inuhiko and Hirasawa Gō (Tokyo: Sakuhinsha, 2007), 159.

33 *Violated Angels* is not the only film to reference this infamous murder case. The German film *Naked Massacre* (*Die Hinrichtung*, a.k.a. *Born for Hell*, 1976), directed by Denis Héroux, is based on the same incident.

34 Burch, *To the Distant Observer*, 352.

35 Ibid.

36 Ibid., 354.

37 Desser, *Eros Plus Massacre*, 104.

38 To the list of films that make direct references to the news media, especially newspapers, we may also add Wakamatsu's most controversial film, *Kabe no naka no himegoto* (Secrets behind the wall, 1965), which was invited to the Berlin Film Festival and was denounced as a "national disgrace" (*kokujoku*) by Eirin. This film also makes ample use of journalistic materials and includes numerous close-ups of actual newspapers and magazine headlines.

39 See Jean-François Lyotard, "Acinema," in *Narrative, Apparatus, Ideology: A Film Theory Reader*, ed. Philip Rosen (New York: Columbia University Press, 1986), 349–59. See also Crary, "Spectacle, Attention, Counter-Memory."

40 Laura Mulvey, *Death 24x a Second: Stillness and the Moving Image* (London: Reaktion Books, 2006), 186. For an insightful discussion of cinema, attention, and economy, see Jonathan Beller, *The Cinematic Mode of Production: Attention Economy and the Society of the Spectacle* (Lebanon, N.H.: University Press of New England, 2006).

41 Tosaka, *Tosaka Jun zenshū*, 3:133.

42 The German word Tosaka frequently uses is *Aktualität*.

43 Benjamin, "The Storyteller," 90. See also Doane, "Information, Crisis, Catastrophe"; Niklas Luhmann, *The Reality of the Mass Media*, trans. Kathleen Cross (Stanford: Stanford University Press, 2000).

44 Tosaka, "Ideorogii gairon," 2:122.

45 Luhmann, *The Reality of the Mass Media*, 19.

46 Roland Domenig, "A Brief History of Independent Cinema in Japan and the Role of the Art Theatre Guild," *Minikomi* 70 (2005), 11.

47 Oshima Nagisa, "Eiga zokusetsu e no chōsen" [A challenge to vulgar beliefs about cinema], in *Sengo eiga: Hakai to sōzō* [Postwar cinema: Destruction

and creation] (Tokyo: San'ichi Shọbō, 1963), 80. This essay was originally published in the magazine *Gendai no Me* in 1961.

48 Wakamatsu Kōji, *Jikō nashi* [No statute of limitations], edited by Koide Shinobu and Kakegawa Masayuki (Tokyo: Waizu Shuppan, 2004), 202.

49 DNA Media, "Mishima Yukio no shi wa, touji dou ronhyō sareta ka" [How Mishima Yukio's death was discussed at the time], in *Mishima Yukio ga shinda hi* [The day Mishima Yukio died], ed. Chūjō Shōhei (Tokyo: Jitsugyō no Nihon Sha, 2005), 19.

50 *Sexual Reincarnation* also references Oshima's *Night and Fog in Japan* (1960), a film which was heavily implicated in the media event of the televised assassination of Asanuma Inejirō. This reference is made explicit by the opening credit sequence, which starts with the scenes of the wedding and by the motif of the marriage between two generations of student activists.

CHAPTER 4

1 "'108 gō' hannin no taiho" [The arrest of criminal no. 108], editorial, *Asahi Shinbun* [Asahi newspaper], 8 April 1969, 5.

2 The New Left Zenkyōtō generation of student activists differentiated themselves from an older hierarchical model of activism, emphasizing "an alternative organizational form that was deliberately horizontal, spontaneous, and participatory." See Patricia Steinhoff, "Student Conflict," in *Conflict in Japan*, ed. Ellis S. Krauss, Thomas P. Rohlen, and Patricia G. Steinhoff (Honolulu: University of Hawaii Press, 1984), 179.

3 Simon Andrew Avenell, *Making Japanese Citizens: Civil Society and Mythology of the* Shimin *in Postwar Japan* (Berkeley: University of California Press, 2010), 110–11.

4 In this incident, 8,500 riot police equipped with 4,000 teargas shells, escorted by 700 armed police cars and three helicopters, stormed the building as the students fought back with Molotov cocktails and projectiles. Mainichi Shinbunsha, *1968 nen gurafiti* [Graffiti of 1968] (Tokyo: Mainichi Shinbunsha, 2010), 97. In July 1969 the Diet also passed the University Control Law, which conferred on the Ministry of Education the power to supersede the university administration in a time of crisis and allowed the police to enter the campus without invitation. On the impact of this law, see Steinhoff, "Student Conflict."

5 At one level, the connotation of eventlessness and the lack of spectacularity associated with the term *landscape* were meant to counter the sentimental, existentialist connotation of the term *situation*, which was popular among New Left student activists in the 1960s. Matsuda, for instance, argues that his rejection of the term *situation* (*jōkyō*) was an implicit critique of the work of the leftist intellectual Yoshimoto Takaaki, who exerted a considerable influence on student radicals. Yoshimoto also emphasized the idea of

autonomy (*jiritsu*). Matsuda, *Fūkei no shimetsu*, 134. See also, Yoshimoto Takaaki, *Jōkyō e no hatsugen* [Addressing the situation] (Tokyo: Tokuma Shoten, 1968).

6 Michel Foucault, "Governmentality," in *The Foucault Effect: Studies of Governmentality*, ed. Graham Burchell, Colin Gordon, and Peter Miller (Chicago: University of Chicago Press, 1991), 87–104.

7 Gilles Deleuze, *Foucault* (Paris: Les Éditions de Minuit, 1986), 36.

8 Hara Masataka (a.k.a. Masato), a co-scriptwriter for Oshima's *The Man Who Left His Will on Film*, indirectly participated in the fūkeiron discourse by writing a pointed criticism of the film. However, his argument, which draws on the phenomenological philosophy of Maurice Merleau-Ponty, veers toward the discussion of "intersubjectivity" and the subject's relation to the world. See Hara Masataka, "Sekai-nai-sonzai no fūkeironteki tenbō" [The landscape theory's perspective on being-in-the-world], *Eiga Hihyō II* [Film criticism II] 1.1 (October 1970): 42–57.

9 On Adachi's career as a filmmaker and an activist, see Adachi Masao, *Eiga/Kakumei* [Cinema/Revolution] (Tokyo: Kawade Shobō Shinsha, 2003).

10 Another remarkable film by Jōnouchi, which conveys the atmosphere of the period, is the experimental *Gewaltopia Trailer* (1969), which playfully mixes documented images of the barricaded campus of Nihon University with remediated footage of classical films such as *The Lost World* (1925), *Nosferatu* (1922), and *King Kong* (1933). The film evokes a sense of imminent revolutionary destruction.

11 Adachi, *Eiga/Kakumei*, 90.

12 Kuzui Kinshirō and Hirasawa Gō, *Yuigon: Aato Shiataa Shinjuku Bunka* [Testament: Art Theatre Shinjuku Bunka] (Tokyo: Kawade Shobō Shinsha, 2008), 149.

13 Oshima's films to which Adachi contributed as a scriptwriter are *Shinjuku dorobō nikki* (*Diary of a Shinjuku Thief*, 1968) and *Kaette kita yopparai* (*Three Resurrected Drunkards*, 1968).

14 Although *A.K.A. Serial Killer* was not officially shown to the public until 1975, the handful of critics and filmmakers who had seen it engaged in a discussion of the film's central focus on landscapes—a discussion and theorization of landscape that came to be known as fūkeiron. The film was not screened in the United States until recently, and the U.S. premiere of the film was made possible by the joint efforts of Japanese scholars such as Hirasawa Gō, who has been working on the theory of fūkeiron, as well as scholars such as Abé Mark Nornes, Aaron Gerow, and Harry Harootunian. The revived interest in *A.K.A. Serial Killer* was prompted, at least in part, by the return of Adachi Masao to Japan from Lebanon in 2000.

15 Oshima Nagisa, "How to Die in the 1970s," commentary included in the DVD *The Man Who Left His Will on Film* (1970).

16 While the term *landscape film* was initially used to describe just two films

(A.K.A. *Serial Killer* and *The Man Who Left His Will on Film*), it has since been applied to other films, such as Hara Masato (a.k.a. Masataka)'s *Hatsukuni shirasumera mikoto* (1973) and Takamine Gō's *Okinawan Dream Show* (*Okinawan doriimu shou* 1971–74).

17 In his analysis of Álvarez's use of dramatic montage, John Mraz writes, "By using the U.S. photos in his dramatic montages, he consciously 'reappropriated' images produced under imperialism, transforming their meaning and 'restoring their truth' by inserting them into a revolutionary cinematic context." See John Mraz, "Santiago Alvarez: From Dramatic Form to Direct Cinema," in *The Social Documentary in Latin America*, ed. Julian Burton (Pittsburgh: University of Pittsburgh, 1990), 136.

18 Fernando Solanas and Octavio Getino, "Towards a Third Cinema," in *Movies and Methods: An Anthology*, ed. Bill Nichols (Berkeley: University of California Press, 1976), 58, emphasis in the original. Glauber Rocha, the leading voice of the Cine Novo movement, also noted, "Only through the dialectic of violence . . . will we reach lyricism." Quoted in Robert Stam, "Beyond Third Cinema: The Aesthetics of Hybridity," in *Rethinking Third Cinema*, ed. Wimal Dissanayake and Anthony R. Guneratne (London: Routledge, 2003), 31.

19 Thomas Waugh, "Beyond *Vérité*: Emile de Antonio and the New Documentary of the Seventies," in *Movies and Methods: An Anthology II*, ed. Bill Nichols (Berkeley: University of California Press, 1985), 237.

20 There was also a series of documentaries made during the May uprising (e.g., *À bientôt, j'espère* by Chris Marker and the SLON [Société Pour le Lancement des Oeuvres Nouvelles] workers' film collective). See Kristin Ross, *May '68 and Its Afterlives* (Chicago: University of Chicago Press, 2002), 33.

21 For a comprehensive and insightful account of the works of Ogawa and Tsuchimoto, see Abé Mark Nornes, "The Postwar Documentary Trace: Groping in the Dark," *Positions* 10.1 (spring 2002): 39–78; and Nornes, *Forest of Pressure*.

22 Paul Rotha, *Documentary Film* (New York: Hastings House, 1952), 70.

23 Michael Renov, *The Subject of Documentary* (Minneapolis: University of Minnesota Press, 2004), 11.

24 Ogawa Shinsuke, *Eiga o toru: Dokyumentarii no shifuku o motomete* [Shooting films: Seeking bliss in the documentary], ed. Yamane Sadao (Tokyo: Satsuma Shobō, 1993), 82.

25 Nornes, "The Postwar Documentary Trace," 52.

26 Matsuda Masao, "Ajitēshon no ne: *Assatsu no mori* san" [The roots of agitation: Praise for *Forest of Pressure*], in *Bara to mumeisha* [A rose and the nameless one] (Tokyo: Haga Shoten, 1970), 215.

27 Oshima Nagisa, "Ogawa Shinsuke: Tōsō to datsuraku" [Ogawa Shinsuke: Fighting and dropping out], *Eiga Hihyō II* [Film criticism II] 1.3 (December 1970), 16.

28 See Noël Burch, "Primitivism and the Avant-Garde," in *Narrative, Apparatus, Ideology*, ed. Philip Rosen (New York: Columbia University Press, 1986), 483–505.

29 Although the reel that includes these views appears to contain a few jerky handheld shots of cityscapes, it primarily consists of fixed-frame shots of highly composed landscapes.

30 Despite the term *landscape* (*fūkei*) used by the scriptwriters of *The Man Who Left His Will on Film*, these images are neither pastoral nor sublime. Strictly speaking, the landscapes in question here are all *urban* landscapes.

31 Noël Burch, *Life to Those Shadows*, trans. and ed. Ben Brewster (Berkeley: University of California Press, 1990).

32 Ibid., 209.

33 Philip Rosen, *Change Mummified: Cinema, Historicity, Theory* (Minneapolis: University of Minnesota Press, 2001), 245.

34 Tom Gunning, "'Primitive' Cinema: A Frame-up? Or the Trick's on Us," *Cinema Journal* 28.2 (winter 1989), 8.

35 John Grierson, "First Principles of Documentary," *Grierson on Documentary*, ed. Forsyth Hardy (London: Faber and Faber, 1966), 146.

36 Rosen, *Change Mummified*, 242–43. Rosen writes: "In its own originary self-definitions, the documentary tradition shares the denigration of preclassical cinema as primitive with its putative other, mainstream fictional filmmaking. If proponents of documentary banished the newsreels that became a secondary mainstream product from their realm, it is all the more clear that actualities could not be admitted. In the 1930s Grierson himself associated actuality films with an outgrown childhood—his own as well as the medium's" (243).

37 Turim, *The Films of Oshima Nagisa*, 101.

38 Ibid., 108.

39 Ibid., 106–7.

40 Hirasawa Gō, "Fūkei, aruiwa fūkeiron o megutte: *Tokyo sensō sengo hiwa ron*" [The landscape, or on the topic of the landscape: On *The Man Who Left His Will on Film*], in *Tokyo sensō sengo hiwa* [The man who left his will on film], booklet in *Oshima Nagisa*, DVD Box 2 (Tokyo: Kinokuniya, 2010), 10.

41 Hara Masato, "*Tokyo sensō* kara *Tokyo fūkei sensō* e" [From the *Tokyo War* to the *Tokyo War of Landscape*], in *Tokyo sensō sengo hiwai* [The man who left his will on film], booklet in *Oshima Nagisa*, DVD Box 2 (Tokyo: Kinokuniya, 2010), 33.

42 Cited in Matsuda Masao, "Misshitsu no teroru" [Terror in the closed chamber], in *Fūkei no shimetsu* [Extinction of the landscape] (Tokyo: Tabata Shoten, 1971), 238.

43 Adachi, *Eiga/Kakumei*, 290.

44 Ibid. At the Kinema Club IV conference (22–26 June 2005), Hirai Gen

also pointed out this intriguing passage in his analysis of Nagayama Norio through the framework of the historical disintegration of the welfare state.

45 Matsuda Masao, “Fūkei to shite no toshi” [City as landscape], in *Fūkei no shimetsu* [Extinction of the landscape] (Tokyo: Tabata Shoten, 1973), 16. The essay was originally published in the April 1970 issue of the journal *Gendai no Me* [Contemporary eye].

46 Matsuda Masao, “Waga rettō, waga fūkei” [My archipelago, my landscape], in *Fūkei no shimetsu* [Extinction of the landscape] (Tokyo: Tabata Shoten, 1973), 92–93.

47 Matsuda Masao, “Fūkei no shimetsu no tame ni” [For the extinction of the landscape], in *Fūkei no shimetsu* [Extinction of the landscape] (Tokyo: Tabata Shoten, 1973), 280.

48 Matsuda Masao, “Misshitsu, fūkei, kenryoku” [Closed chamber, landscape, and the power of domination], in *Bara to mumeisha* [A rose and the nameless one] (Tokyo: Haga Shoten, 1970), 123.

49 W. J. T. Mitchell, “Imperial Landscape,” in *Landscape and Power*, ed. W. J. T. Mitchell (Chicago: University of Chicago Press, 1994), 14.

50 Ibid.

51 Following the lead of John Berger’s *Ways of Seeing* (1972), Cosgrove writes, “Landscape first emerged as a term, an idea, or better still, *a way of seeing* the external world, in the fifteenth and early sixteenth century. It was, and it remains, a visual term, one that arose initially out of renaissance humanism and its particular concepts and constructs of space.” See Denis Cosgrove, “Prospect, Perspective and the Evolution of the Landscape Idea,” *Transactions of the Institute of the British Geographers*, New Series 10.1 (1985), 46.

52 Jean-Louis Baudry, “Ideological Effects of the Basic Cinematographic Apparatus,” in *Narrative, Apparatus, Ideology: A Film Theory Reader*, ed. Philip Rosen (New York: Columbia University Press, 1986), 286–98. See also, Jacques Aumont, “The Variable Eye, or the Mobilization of the Gaze,” in *The Image in Dispute: Art and Cinema in the Age of Photography*, ed. Dudley Andrew (Austin: University of Texas Press, 1997), 238–58.

53 To quote Karatani, “The philosophical standpoint which distinguishes between subject and object came into existence within what I refer to as ‘landscape.’ Rather than existing prior to landscape, subject and object emerge from within it.” See Karatani Kōjin, *Origins of Modern Japanese Literature*, foreword by Fredric Jameson, trans. Brett de Bary (Durham: Duke University Press, 1993), 34.

54 Martin Heidegger, *The Question Concerning Technology and Other Essays*, trans. William Lovitt (New York: Harper and Row, 1977), 132.

55 Matsuda, “Eizō, fūkei, gengo” [The image, landscape, and language], in *Fūkei no shimetsu* [Extinction of the landscape] (Tokyo: Tabata Shoten, 1973), 98–99.

56 Ibid., 102.

57 Ibid., 103.
58 Nakahira, *Mitsuzukeru hate ni hi ga . . .*, 129.
59 Michel Foucault, *Security, Territory, Population: Lectures at the Collège de France 1977–1978*, trans. Graham Burchell, ed. Michel Senellart (New York: Palgrave Macmillan, 2007), 200.
60 Nakahira, *Mitsuzukeru hate ni hi ga . . .*, 127.
61 In an interview Sasaki Mamoru recalls, "One day I looked at a newspaper, and there was a special on Nagayama's arrest. All the routes he traced were indicated in the newspaper. I thought if we only filmed the landscapes that he would have seen, it will become a 'landscape film' that fits what Matsuda was proposing at the time." See Sasaki Mamoru, "Fūkei ga kawaranakereba 'kakumei' wa dekinai" [We cannot have a "revolution" unless landscapes are changed], in *Oshima Nagisa: 1968*, by Oshima Nagisa (Tokyo: Seidosha, 2004), 297.
62 Matsuda, "Waga rettō, waga fūkei," 91. Emphasis in the original.
63 Ibid., 92. Emphasis in the original.
64 For his detailed discussion of the concept of the Third World (as an imaginary space), see Matsuda Masao, "Sien no kūkan" [A space for a personal grudge], in *Fūkei no shimetsu* [Extinction of the landscape] (Tokyo: Tabata Shoten, 1973), 165–82.
65 Matsuda, "Waga rettō, waga fūkei," 92.
66 By extending the metaphor of diagram, Deleuze rearticulates Foucault's understanding of power as the relation of forces operative at a particular historical moment; this relation is akin to "a map, a cartography that is coextensive with the whole social field." See Deleuze, *Foucault*, 34. Emphasis in the original.
67 Edward Branigan, "Subjectivity under Siege: From Fellini's *8 1/2* to Oshima's *The Story of a Man Who Left His Will on Film*," *Screen* 19.1 (spring 1978): 7–40; Burch, *To the Distant Observer*; Desser, *Eros Plus Massacre*. With regard to *The Man Who Left His Will on Film*, Turim writes, "Among Oshima's 'difficult' films, this one stands out as most puzzling" (*The Films of Oshima Nagisa*, 107).
68 Matsuda, "Fūkei no shimetsu no tame ni," 287.
69 Paul Virilio, *Speed and Politics: An Essay on Dromology*, trans. Mark Polizzotti (New York: Semiotext(e), 1986), 14. Emphasis in the original.
70 Foucault, *Security, Territory, Population*, 325.
71 Foucault, "Governmentality," 92–93.
72 Colin Gordon, "Governmental Rationality: An Introduction," in *The Foucault Effect*, ed. Graham Burchell, Colin Gordon, and Peter Miller (Chicago: University of Chicago Press, 1991), 2.
73 Michel Foucault in "The Political Technology of Individuals," quoted in Ben Golder and Peter Fitzpatrick, *Foucault's Law* (London: Routledge, 2009), 48.
74 Foucault, *Security, Territory, Population*, 335.

75 Obinata Sumio, *Nihon kindai kokka no seiritsu to keisatsu* [The birth of the modern Japanese state and the police] (Tokyo: Azekura Shobō, 1992), 60–61.

76 Mitchell Dean, *Governmentality: Power and Rule in Modern Society* (London: Sage, 1999), 20.

77 Foucault writes, "It was through the development of the science of government that the notion of economy came to be recentered on to that different plane of reality which we characterize today as the 'economic,' and it was also through this science that it became possible to identify problems specific to the population; but conversely we can say as well that it was thanks to the perception of the specific problems of the population, and thanks to the isolation of that area of reality that we call the economy, that the problem of government finally came to be thought, reflected and calculated outside of the juridical framework of sovereignty" (*The Foucault Effect*, 99).

78 Gordon, "Governmental Rationality," 2.

79 The security-guard industry also gained popularity in the 1960s through the media's representation. In 1965 the first security-guard firm, Nihon Keibi Hoshō, became the model for a television program entitled *The Security Guard* (*Za gaadoman*). On the historical development of the Japanese security-guard industry, see Tanaka Tomohito, *Keibigyō no shakaigaku* [The sociology of the security-guard business] (Tokyo: Akashi Shoten, 2009).

80 Foucault, *Security, Territory, Population*, 21.

81 Reiko Tomii, "*Geijutsu* on Their Minds: Memorable Words on Anti-Art," in *Art, Anti-Art, Non-Art: Experimentations in the Public Sphere in Postwar Japan 1950–1970*, ed. Charles Merewether and Rika Iezumi Hiro (Los Angeles: Getty Research Institute, 2007), 55.

82 Tsuchiyama Kimie, *Kōdo seichōki "Toshi seisaku" no seiji katei* [Political process of "urban policy" in the high-growth era] (Tokyo: Nippon Hyōronsha, 2007), 64–65. For an insightful analysis of the Discover Japan campaign, see Marilyn Ivy, *Discourses of the Vanishing: Modernity, Phantasm, Japan* (Chicago: University of Chicago Press, 1995).

83 This also indicates the shift from the 1960s—the era of antistate political movements emblematized by the mass protests against the Japan-U.S. Security Treaty (ANPO)—to the 1970s, an era marked by the consolidation of Japan as a postindustrial society and by diffused networks of resistance and subversion. This is where I also locate the symptomatic waning of the centralized mode of imagining political resistance, which had been anchored around the figure of the subject (*shutai*), which had long dominated the political imagination of postwar Japanese intellectuals. The discourse on subjectivity (*shutaisei*)—first articulated in the immediate postwar period by critics and writers associated with the literary journal *Kindai Bungaku*, and perpetuated well into the 1960s by Marxist critics such as Yoshimoto Takaaki—lost its currency by the end of the 1960s. For the discourse on sub-

jectivity, see Victor J. Koshmann, *Revolution and Subjectivity in Postwar Japan* (Chicago: University of Chicago Press, 1996).

CHAPTER 5

1 Adachi Masao, "Zoku·*sōzō* to *hōdō* no kairo: *Sekigun-PFLP: Sekai sensō sengen* jōei undō no tame no nōto" [Sequel: The circuit of *Creation* and *News Reports*: Notes on the screening movement for *The Red Army/PFLP: The Declaration of World War*], *Eiga Hihyō II* [Film criticism II] 3.3 (March 1972), 27.

2 Yomota Inuhiko also compares these two films in his essay "Wakamatsu Kōji, Adachi Masao and the Palestinian Issue" ("Wakamatsu Kōji, Adachi Masao to paresuchina mondai"). See Yomota Inuhiko, *Paresuchina nau: Sensō, eiga, ningen* [Palestine now: War, cinema, and the human] (Tokyo: Sakuhinsha, 2006).

3 Nornes, *Forest of Pressure*, 147.

4 Adachi's writings support this reading. See Adachi Masao, "Waga sensen no saikōchiku no tame ni" [For the reconstruction of my frontline], *Eiga Hihyō II* [Film criticism II] 3.8 (August 1972): 13–23.

5 Brigitte Nacos, *Mass-Mediated Terrorism: The Central Role of the Media in Terrorism and Counterterrorism* (Lanham: Rowman and Littlefield, 2007), 28.

6 Gilles Deleuze and Félix Guattari, *A Thousand Plateaus: Capitalism and Schizophrenia*, trans. Brian Massumi (Minneapolis: University of Minnesota Press, 1987), 81.

7 Gilles Deleuze and Félix Guattari, *Mille plateaux: Capitalisme et schizophrénie* (Paris: Les Éditions de Minute, 1980), 103.

8 Guy Debord and Gil J. Wolman, "Methods of Detournement," in *Situationist International Anthology*, ed. and trans. Ken Knabb (Berkeley: Bureau of Public Secrets, 1981), 9.

9 This instrumental or operational understanding of the medium as a communicative means to disseminate a message is, of course, an antithesis to the aesthetic and art-historical understanding of the medium. For the aesthetic and art-historical conceptions of the medium, see Rosalind Krauss, "Reinventing the Medium," *Critical Inquiry* 25.2 (1999): 289–305.

10 Wakamatsu Production, "Sekigun-PFLP: Sekai sensō sengen" [The Red Army/PFLP: The declaration of world war], *Eiga Hihyō II* [Film criticism II] 3.3 (March 1972), 12.

11 Giorgio Agamben, "Difference and Repetition: On Guy Debord's Films," in *Guy Debord and the Situationist International: Texts and Documents*, ed. Tom McDonough (Cambridge: MIT Press, 2002), 318.

12 Ibid.

13 Ibid., 319.

14 Similarly, most of the militants at the Jerash base in Jordan whom Wakamatsu and Adachi interviewed and lived alongside for two weeks were killed soon after the filmmakers left. Wakamatsu recalls the shock he experienced

the next day, when he returned to Beirut and saw the newspaper headline reporting the attack on the Jerash camp by the joint military forces of Israel and Jordan: "We suddenly understood why the leader of these commandos rushed us to leave the mountain. Perhaps they had information about the attack and therefore tried to save our lives by letting us—ignorant Japanese who didn't even have any escape route—leave the mountain. If we had stayed there with them, we probably would have been killed or captured" (*Jikō nashi*, 60).

15 Adachi, *Eiga/Kakumei*, 387.

16 Jewish prisoners, as Jean-Luc Nancy argues, embodied an antithesis to the super-representation of the Aryan self: "The death camp constitutes the stage on which super-representation plays out the spectacle of the annihilation of what, in its eyes, is non-representation. . . . Auschwitz is a space organized in such a way that Presence itself . . . plays out the spectacle of annihilating what, in principle, is so forbidding to representation" (*The Ground of the Image*, 40).

17 The term *flow* is used by Raymond Williams, whereas the term *segmentation* is from John Ellis. John Fiske succinctly summarizes the connection between the two: "Williams uses the term 'flow' to express this principle [of association], Ellis the term 'segmentation,' and the difference between the two words indicates the difference between the two approaches to what is essentially the same principle, that of association." See John Fiske, *Television Culture* (London: Methuen, 1987), 99. See also Feuer, "The Concept of Live Television"; Raymond Williams, *Television: Technology and Cultural Form* (London: Fontana, 1974); John Ellis, *Visible Fictions: Cinema, Television, Video* (London: Routledge and Kegan Paul, 1982).

18 On this point I part ways with Yomota Inuhiko, who regards the remediated use of televisual images in *The Red Army/PFLP* to be taken "literally" insofar as the film presents news footage on the hijackings carried out by the PFLP and the Red Army as images to be embraced rather than critiqued. But Yomota also argues that the remediation of televisual images in *Here and Elsewhere* is aimed to underscore the film's critique of capitalism (*Paresuchina nau*, 290).

19 Eyal Weizman, "Strategic Points, Flexible Lines, Tense Surfaces, Political Volumes: Ariel Sharon and the Geometry of Occupation," *Philosophical Forum* 35.2 (summer 2004), 229. See also Eyal Weizman, *Hollow Land: Israel's Architecture of Occupation* (London: Verso, 2007).

20 W. J. T. Mitchell calls the landscape of Israel/Palestine "a palimpsest of scar tissue" ("Imperial Landscape," 20).

21 Doane, "Information, Crisis, Catastrophe," 252.

22 Shigenobu Fusako, "Eiga no senyū tachi" [Comrades in cinema], *Jōkyō* [Situations] 4.6, special issue on Adachi Masao (June 2003): 17. Shigenobu was arrested in Osaka in 2000. She was the founder of the Japanese Red

Army (or the Arab Red Army, which is not to be confused with the United Red Army in Japan), which had its basis in the Middle East. She was charged for her alleged involvement in a series of militant direct actions, such as the 1974 takeover of the French embassy in the Hague in the Netherlands.

23 Adachi, *Eiga/Kakumei*, 360.

24 Matsuda Masao, *Fukanōsei no media* [Impossible media] (Tokyo: Tabata Shoten, 1973), 317.

25 Ibid.

26 Adachi Masao, *Eiga e no senryaku* [Strategies for cinema] (Tokyo: Shōbunsha, 1974), 178.

27 Ibid., 143.

28 As Yuri Tsivian notes, Vertov's films, such as *Man with a Movie Camera* (1929), are manifestos written in celluloid: "There are things and images in Vertov's movies that are meant to be read, not just seen." See Yuri Tsivian, "Introduction," in *Lines of Resistance: Dziga Vertov and the Twenties*, ed. Yuri Tsivian (Gemonda: Le Giornate del Cinema Muto, 2004), 14. Godard also explicitly positions his work *Tout va bien* (1972) as a newsreel. See David Sterritt, ed., *Jean-Luc Godard Interviews* (Jackson: University Press of Mississippi, 1998), 61.

29 Deleuze and Guattari, *A Thousand Plateaus*, 83. Emphasis in the original.

30 The order-word operates through redundancy: "The relation between the statement and the act is internal, immanent, but it is not one of identity. Rather it is a relation of *redundancy*. The order-word itself is the redundancy of the act and the statement." Ibid., 79. Emphasis in the original.

31 "Gunpoint" is presented in reverse (as if in the mirror) in anticipation of the incorporeal transformation of the spectator who will cross the screen to join the militant struggle.

32 The red-bus caravan indeed succeeded in mobilizing spectators insofar as some of the participants became revolutionaries themselves. Adachi also underwent a certain transformation—from being a critic-filmmaker to an activist-filmmaker. After the tour fell apart due to internal fighting, Adachi made an effort to resume the caravan, but subsequently left Japan to work as a volunteer cameraman for *Al Hadaf* and to informally assist the PFLP's filmmaking unit in 1974.

33 Adachi, "Waga sensen no saikōchiku no tameni." See also Adachi Masao, "'Hōdō' to 'sōzō' no kairo: *Sekigun-PFLP: Sekai sensō sengen* no tame no nōto" [The circuit of news reports and creation: Notes on *The Red Army/PFLP: The Declaration of World War*], *Eiga Hihyō II* [Film criticism II] 2.10 (October 1971): 14–23.

34 See Adachi, *Eiga e no senryaku*, 137–51. The title "What Is Not to Be Done" playfully reverses the slogan "What to do?" ("Que faire?") used in the film *Vent d'est*, as Adachi presents his vision of activist cinema as a series of antitheses to Godard's vision of political cinema.

35 Ibid.

CONCLUSION

1 For an informative analysis of Expo 67, and its significance to the histories of the multiscreen practice and expanded cinema, see Janine Marchessault, "Multi-Screens and Future Cinema: The Labyrinth Project at Expo 67," in *Fluid Screens, Expanded Cinema*, ed. Janine Marchessault and Susan Lord (Toronto: University of Toronto Press, 2007), 29–51. For an interdisciplinary analysis of Expo 67, see also Rhona Richman Kenneally and Johanne Sloan, eds., *Expo 67: Not Just a Souvenir* (Toronto: University of Toronto Press, 2010).

2 See Hashizume Shin'ya, ed., *Expo '70: Pabirion: Osaka Banpaku kōshiki memoriaru gaido* [Expo 70 pavilions: An official guide to Osaka Expo] (Tokyo: Heibon-sha, 2010).

3 Ivy, *Discourses of Vanishing*, 36.

4 A 2003 television documentary by NHK details the formation and activities of the special security force for Expo 70. See *Project X: Osaka Banpaku shijō saidai no keibi sakusen* [Project X: Osaka Expo: The biggest security operation in history], DVD (Tokyo: NHK Enterprise, 2005).

5 Adachi Masao, "Terebijon wa shin no teki de aruka" [Is television a true enemy?], in *Eiga e no senryaku* [Strategies for cinema] (Tokyo: Shōbunsha, 1974), 170–71.

6 Nakahira, "Kiroku to iu gen'ei," 228. While Nakahira does not reference Foucault in this essay, the notions of "document" (*dokyumento* or *kiroku*) and "monument" (*monyumento* or *kinenhi*) indicate his awareness of Foucault's *L'Archéologie du savoir* (1969), which was translated into Japanese in 1970. Photography and media critics often used the conceptual pairing of document and monument in the early 1970s, although whether they properly understood Foucault's argument about the modern discipline of history is open to debate. For instance, Taki Kōji explicitly refers to Foucault and discusses the transformation of documents into monuments in his essay "Manazashi no atsumi e" [Toward the thickness of the gaze], first published in the photography journal *Asahi Camera* in 1972. See Taki Kōji, *Kotoba no nai sikō: Jibutsu/kūkan/eizō ni tsuite no oboegaki* [Thought without words: A note on things/spaces/images] (Tokyo: Tabata Shoten, 1972).

7 Matsuda, *Fukanōsei no media*, 122.

8 Nakahira, "Kiroku to iu gen'ei," 228.

9 Ibid., 227–28.

10 Adachi, *Eiga/Kakumei*, 516.

11 On the connection between Terayama's films and his involvement in theater, see Steven C. Ridgely, *Japanese Counterculture: The Antiestablishment Art of Terayama Shūji* (Minnesota: University of Minnesota Press, 2010).

12 Matsumoto Toshio, "Mirai to mukiatte iru mono" [Those who face the future], *Kikan Firumu* [Film quarterly] 2 (February 1969): 140–48.

13 "Tokushū: Banpaku to Anpo/EXPOSE·1968 zenkiroku shūroku" [A special on expo and Anpo: A complete record of "EXPOSE·1968"], *Dezain Hihyō* [Design review] 6 (1969), 73. I want to thank Matsui Shigeru for drawing my attention to the centrality of television for Tōno's performance at "EXPOSE·1968."

14 Kuzui and Hirasawa, *Yuigon*, 296.

15 Tsuji Shun'ichirō, *Fōku songu undō: 25 nenme no sōkatsu* [The folk song movement: An overview after twenty-five years] (Tokyo: Shinpūsha, 2001), 48.

16 A remarkable scene of the police forcing pedestrians and protesters to walk appears in the documentary film *Chika hiroba* (1969), directed by Ouchida Keiya. I would like to thank Roland Domenig for introducing me to this rare documentary film. See also Roland Domenig, "Don't Stop! Keep Moving On!: The Kinetics of Shinjuku in 1969," paper presented at the conference "Cultural Geographies of 1960s Japan: Cinema, Music + Arts," University of California, Berkeley, 2012.

17 Ushida Ayami, *ATG Eiga + Shinjuku* [ATG films + Shinjuku] (Tokyo: D-bungaku Kenkyūkai, 2007), 22.

18 In anticipation of the intensifying protest movement against the renewal of the Japan-U.S. Security Treaty, for instance, the metropolitan police officially requested the Ministry of Construction to change most of the stone-paved sidewalks into asphalt in February 1969. See "Anpo no suteishi" [Stones thrown during the Anpo], *Asahi shinbun*, 24 February 1969, 16.

19 KuroDalaiJee, *Nikutai no anaakizumu*, 268.

20 "As for discipline, this is not eliminated together; clearly, its mode of organization, all the institutions within which it had developed in the seventeenth and eighteenth centuries—schools, manufactures, armies, etc.—all this can only be understood on the basis of the development of the great administrative monarchies, but nevertheless, discipline was never more important or more valorized than at the moment when it became important to manage a population" (Foucault, "Governmentality," 102).

21 Graham Burchell, "Liberal Government and Techniques of the Self," in *Foucault and Political Reason: Liberalism, Neo-Liberalism, and Rationalities of Government*, ed. Andrew Barry et al. (Chicago: University of Chicago Press, 1996), 20. Emphasis in the original.

22 Kuzui and Hirasawa, *Yuigon*, 337.

23 Hirasawa, "Radikarizumu no keizoku: 1970 nendai ikō ni okeru Wakamatsu Kōji ron" [A continuation of radicalism: Wakamatsu Kōji after the 1970s], in *Wakamatsu Kōji: Hankenryoku no shōzō* [Wakamatsu Kōji: A portrait of counter-power], ed. Yomota Inuhiko and Hirasawa Gō (Tokyo: Sakuhinsha, 2007), 160.

24 Domenig, "A Brief History of Independent Cinema in Japan and the Role of the Art Theatre Guild," 14.

25 Nornes defines the private film as "a new mode based on the solitary work

of a singular filmmaking subject," as an "artisanal" mode of filmmaking in which "the lone filmmaker oversees the initial conceptualization, the photography, the editing, and even the distribution of his or her work" (*Forest of Pressure*, 131).

26 See Kawanaka Nobuhiro, *Eiga: Nichijō no jikken* [Cinema: Everyday experiments] (Tokyo: Firumu Aato-sha, 1975).

27 Matsumoto Toshio, "Bideo aato tenbō" [An observation on video art], in *Genshi no bigaku* [Aesthetics of hallucination] (Tokyo: Firumu Aato-sha, 1976), 217.

28 For the lineage of the term *kankyō* (environment) in postwar art discourse and its relevance to Expo 70, see Sawaragi Noi, *Sensō to banpaku* [The war and the Expo] (Tokyo: Bijutsu Shuppansha, 2005). See also the special issue of *Bijutsu Techō* (November 1966) that is dedicated to the exhibition "Kūkan kara kankyō e" (From space to environment), which situated the concept of environment at its center.

bibliography

Abé, Kōbō. *Abé Kōbō zenshū* [The complete works of Abé Kōbō]. 30 volumes. Tokyo: Shinchōsha, 1997–2009.

———. "Eizō wa gengo no kabe o hakai suruka" [Does the image demolish the wall of language?]. *Abé Kōbō zenshū* [The complete works of Abé Kōbō], 11:451–54. Tokyo: Shinchōsha, 1998.

———. "Jikken eiga no shinario" [A script for an experimental film]. *Abé Kōbō zenshū* [The complete works of Abé Kōbō], 11:447–50. Tokyo: Shinchōsha, 1998.

Abé, Kōbō, et al. "Haado boirudo: Genzai no me" [Hardboiled: The eyes of the present]. *Abé Kōbō zenshū* [The complete works of Abé Kōbō], 7:21–26. Tokyo: Shinchōsha, 1998.

Adachi, Masao. *Eiga e no senryaku* [Strategies for cinema]. Tokyo: Shōbunsha, 1974.

———. *Eiga/Kakumei* [Cinema/Revolution]. Tokyo: Kawaide Shobō, 2003.

———. "'Hōdō' to 'sōzō' no kairo: *Sekigun-PFLP: Sekai sensō sengen* no tame no nōto" [The circuit of news reports and creation: Notes on *The Red Army/PFLP: The Declaration of World War*]. *Eiga Hihyō II* [Film criticism II] 2.10 (October 1971): 14–23.

———. "Terebijon wa shin no teki de aruka" [Is television a true enemy?]. *Eiga e no senryaku* [Strategies for cinema], 165–74. Tokyo: Shōbunsha, 1974.

———. "Waga sensen no saikōchiku no tame ni" [For the reconstruction of my frontline]. *Eiga Hihyō II* [Film criticism II] 3.8 (August 1972): 13–23.

———. "Zoku *sōzō* to *hōdō* no kairo: *Sekigun-PFLP: Sekai sensō sengen* jōei undō no tame no nōto" [Sequel: The circuit of *Creation* and *News Reports*: Notes on the screening movement for *The Red Army/PFLP: The Declaration of World War*]. *Eiga Hihyō II* [Film criticism II] 3.3 (March 1972): 26–33.

Adorno, Theodor. "The Actuality of Philosophy." *The Adorno Reader*, 23–39. Edited by Brian O'Connor. Malden: Blackwell, 2000.

———. *The Adorno Reader*. Edited by Brian O'Connor. Malden: Blackwell, 2000.

Agamben, Giorgio. "Difference and Repetition: On Guy Debord's Film." *Guy Debord and the Situationist International: Texts and Documents*, ed. Tom McDonough, 313–19. Cambridge: MIT Press, 2002.

Akiyama Kuniharu, "Cross-Talk/Intermedia." *Bijutsu Techō* [Art notebook] 311 (April 1969): 100–126.

Aumont, Jacques. "The Variable Eye, or the Mobilization of the Gaze." *The Image in Dispute: Art and Cinema in the Age of Photography*, ed. Dudley Andrew, 238–58. Austin: University of Texas Press, 1997.

Avenell, Simon Andrew. *Making Japanese Citizens: Civil Society and Mythology of the* Shimin *in Postwar Japan*. Berkeley: University of California Press, 2010.

Balibar, Étienne. "What Is Political Philosophy?: Contextual Notes." Translated by Catherine Porter and Philip E. Lewis. *Jacques Rancière: History, Politics, Aesthetics*, ed. Gabriel Rockhill and Philip Watts, 95–104. Durham: Duke University Press, 2009.

Barthes, Roland. *Image, Music, Text*. Translated by Stephen Heath. New York: Hill and Wang, 1977.

Baudrillard, Jean. "Requiem for the Media." *For a Critique of the Political Economy of the Sign*, trans. Charles Levin, 164–84. St Louis: Telos, 1981.

Baudry, Jean-Louis. "Ideological Effects of the Basic Cinematographic Apparatus." *Narrative, Apparatus, Ideology: A Film Theory Reader*, ed. Philip Rosen, 286–98. New York: Columbia University Press, 1986.

Bazin, André. *What Is Cinema?* Volume 1. Translated by Hugh Gray. Berkeley: University of California Press, 1967.

Beller, Jonathan. *The Cinematic Mode of Production: Attention Economy and the Society of the Spectacle*. Lebanon, N.H.: University Press of New England, 2006.

Benjamin, Walter. *Illuminations*. Translated by Harry Zohn. New York: Schocken, 1969.

———. "The Storyteller: Reflections on the Works of Nikolai Leskov." *Illuminations*, 83–109. Translated by Harry Zohn. New York: Schocken, 1969.

Bensmaia, Réda. "From the Photogram to the Pictogram: On Chris Marker's *La Jetée*." *Camera Obscura* 24 (1990): 139–61.

Bolter, Jay David, and Richard Grusin. *Remediation: Understanding New Media*. Cambridge: MIT Press, 1999.

Boorstin, Daniel. *Gen'ei no jidai: Masukomi ga netsuzō suru jijitsu* [The age of the image: Mass media's fabrication of facts (original title: The image: Or what happened to the American dream)]. Translated by Gotō Kazuhiko and Hoshino Ikumi. Tokyo: Tokyo Sōgensha, 1964.

———. *The Image: Or What Happened to the American Dream?* New York: Atheneum, 1962.

Branigan, Edward. "Subjectivity under Siege: From Fellini's *8 1/2* to Oshima's *The Story of a Man Who Left His Will on Film*." *Screen* 19.1 (spring 1978): 7–40.

Burch, Noël. *Life to Those Shadows*. Translated and edited by Ben Brewster. Berkeley: University of California Press, 1990.

———. "Oshima Nagisa." *To the Distant Observer: Form and Meaning in the Japanese Cinema*, 325–44. Revised and edited by Annette Michelson. Berkeley: University of California Press, 1979.

———. "Primitivism and the Avant-Garde." *Narrative, Apparatus, Ideology*, ed. Philip Rosen, 483–505. New York: Columbia University Press, 1986.

———. *To the Distant Observer: Form and Meaning in the Japanese Cinema*. Revised and edited by Annette Michelson. Berkeley: University of California Press, 1979.

Burchell, Graham. "Liberal Government and Techniques of the Self." *Foucault and Political Reason: Liberalism, Neo-Liberalism, and Rationalities of Government*, ed. Andrew Barry, Thomas Osborne, and Nikolas Rose, 19–36. Chicago: University of Chicago Press, 1996.

Cosgrove, Denis. "Prospect, Perspective and the Evolution of the Landscape Idea." *Transactions of the Institute of the British Geographers* 10.1 (1985): 45–62.

Crary, Jonathan. "Spectacle, Attention, Counter-Memory." *October* 50 (autumn 1989): 96–107.

Dean, Mitchell. *Governmentality: Power and Rule in Modern Society*. London: Sage, 1999.

Debord, Guy. *The Society of the Spectacle*. Translated by Donald Nicholson-Smith. New York: Zone, 1995.

Debord, Guy, and Gil J. Wolman. "Methods of Detournement." *Situationist International Anthology*, ed. and trans. Ken Knabb, 8–14. Berkeley: Bureau of Public Secrets, 1981.

Deleuze, Gilles. *Foucault*. Paris: Les Éditions de Minuit, 1986.

Deleuze, Gilles, and Félix Guattari. *Mille plateaux: Capitalisme et schizophrénie*. Paris: Les Éditions de Minuit, 1980.

———. *A Thousand Plateaus: Capitalism and Schizophrenia*. Translated by Brian Massumi. Minneapolis: University of Minnesota Press, 1987.

Derrida, Jacques, and Bernard Stiegler. *Echographies of Television: Selected Interviews*. Translated by Jennifer Bajorek. Cambridge: Polity, 2002.

Desser, David. *Eros Plus Massacre: An Introduction to the Japanese New Wave Cinema*. Bloomington: Indiana University Press, 1988.

Didi-Huberman, Georges. *Confronting Images: Questioning the Ends of a Certain History of Art*. Translated by John Goodman. University Park: Pennsylvania State University Press, 2005.

DNA Media. "Mishima Yukio no shi wa, touji dou ronhyō sareta ka" [How Mishima Yukio's death was discussed at the time]. *Mishima Yukio ga shinda hi* [The day Mishima Yukio died], ed. Chūjō Shōhei, 18–52. Tokyo: Jitsugyō no Nihon Sha, 2005.

Doane, Mary Ann. "Information, Crisis, Catastrophe." *New Media, Old Media: A History and Theory Reader*, ed. Wendy Hui Kyong Chun and Thomas Keenan, 251–64. New York: Routledge, 2006.

Domenig, Roland. "A Brief History of Independent Cinema in Japan and the Role of the Art Theatre Guild." *Minikomi* 70 (2005): 6–16.

———. "Don't Stop! Keep Moving On!: The Kinetics of Shinjuku in 1969." Paper presented at the conference "Cultural Geographies of 1960s Japan: Cinema, Music + Arts." University of California, Berkeley, 2012.

"'*Eiga Bunka*' no sōkan ni tsuite" [On the founding of the journal *Film Culture*]. *Eiga Bunka* [Film culture] 1 (March 1950): 5–6.

"'Eizō Geijutsu no Kai' o sōritsu suru ni atatte" [On the occasion of the founding of the Association of Image Arts]. *Eizō Geijutsu* [Image arts] 1 (December 1964): 1.

Ellis, John. *Visible Fictions: Cinema, Television, Video*. London: Routledge and Kegan Paul, 1982.

Feuer, Jane. "The Concept of Live Television: Ontology as Ideology." *Regarding Television*, edited by E. Ann Kaplan, 12–22. Frederick, Md.: American Film Institute, 1983.

Fiske, John. *Television Culture*. London: Methuen, 1987.

Foucault, Michel. "Governmentality." *The Foucault Effect: Studies of Governmentality*, ed. Graham Burchell, Colin Gordon, and Peter Miller, 87–104. Chicago: University of Chicago Press, 1991.

———. *Security, Territory, Population: Lectures at the Collège de France 1977–1978*. Translated by Graham Burchell. Edited by Michel Senellart. New York: Palgrave Macmillan, 2007.

———. "What Is Enlightenment?" *The Foucault Reader*, ed. Paul Rabinow, 32–50. New York: Pantheon, 1984.

Friedberg, Anne. *The Virtual Window: From Alberti to Microsoft*. Cambridge: MIT Press, 2006.

Fujioka, Atsuhiro. "Kindaika suru toshi no eiga kankyaku" [The film spectators of modernizing cities]. *Eigagaku teki sōzōryoku* [The imagination of film studies], ed. Katō Mikirō, 30–54. Tokyo: Jinbunshoin, 2006.

Furuhata, Yuriko. "Refiguring Actuality: Japan's Film Theory and Avant-Garde Documentary Movement, 1950s–1960s." PhD diss., Brown University, 2009.

Gerow, Aaron. *Visions of Japanese Modernity: Articulations of Cinema, Nation, and Spectatorship, 1895–1925*. Berkeley: University of California Press, 2010.

Golder, Ben, and Peter Fitzpatrick. *Foucault's Law*. London: Routledge, 2009.

Gordon, Colin. "Governmental Rationality: An Introduction." *The Foucault Effect*, ed. Graham Burchell, Colin Gordon, and Peter Miller, 1–51. Chicago: University of Chicago Press, 1991.

Grierson, John. "First Principles of Documentary." *Grierson on Documentary*, 145–56. Edited by Forsyth Hardy. London: Faber and Faber, 1966.

———. *Grierson on Documentary*. Edited by Forsyth Hardy. London: Faber and Faber, 1966.

Grieveson, Lee. *Policing Cinema: Movies and Censorship in Early-Twentieth-Century America*. Berkeley: University of California Press, 2004.

Gunning, Tom. "'Primitive' Cinema: A Frame-up? Or the Trick's on Us." *Cinema Journal* 28.2. (winter 1989): 3–12.

Hallward, Peter. "Staging Equality: Rancière's Theatrocracy and the Limits of Anarchic Equality." *Jacques Rancière: History, Politics, Aesthetics*, ed. Gabriel Rockhill and Philip Watts, 140–57. Durham: Duke University Press, 2009.

Hanada, Kiyoteru. *Avangyarudo geijutsu* [Avant-garde art]. Tokyo: Miraisha, 1954.

———. "Eiga kantoku ron" [On film directors]. *Bungakuteki eigaron* [Literary theories of film], ed. Noma Hiroshi et al., 65–97. Tokyo: Chūōkōron, 1957.

———. "Gūzen no mondai" [A question of contingency]. *Hanada Kiyoteru chosakushū* [Selected works of Hanada Kiyoteru], 2:27–49. Tokyo: Miraisha, 1963.

———. *Hanada Kiyoteru chosakushū* [Selected works of Hanada Kiyoteru]. 7 vols. Tokyo: Miraisha, 1963–1966.

———. "Shūru-dokyumentarizumu ni kansuru ichi kōsatsu" [On *sur*-documentarism]. *Eiga Hihyō* [Film criticism] 2.2 (February 1958): 2–5.

———. "Warai neko" [Cheshire cat]. *Hanada Kiyoteru chosakushū III* [Selected works of Hanada Kiyoteru III], 218–31. Tokyo: Miraisha, 1964.

Hanada, Kiyoteru, et al. "Akuchuaritii no tame no kadai" [The challenge of actuality]. *Bijutsu Hihyō* [Art notebook] 25 (January 1954): 15–31.

Hani, Susumu. *Kamera to maiku: Gendai geijutsu no hōhō* [The camera and microphone: Methods of contemporary art]. Tokyo: Chūōkōronsha, 1960.

Hara, Masataka. "Sekai-nai-sonzai no fūkeironteki tenbō" [The landscape theory's perspective on being-in-the-world]. *Eiga Hihyō II* [Film criticism II] 1.1 (October 1970): 42–57.

Hara, Masato. "*Tokyo sensō* kara *Tokyo fūkei sensō* e" [From the *Tokyo War* to the *Tokyo War of Landscape*]. *Tokyo sensō sengo hiwa* [The man who left his will on film], booklet in *Oshima Nagisa*, DVD Box 2, 26–38. Tokyo: Kinokuniya, 2010.

Harootunian, Harry D. *Overcome by Modernity: History, Culture, and Community in Interwar Japan*. Princeton: Princeton University Press, 2000.

Haryū, Ichirō. "Akuchuaritii to wa nani ka" [What is actuality?]. *Shin Nihon Bungaku* [New Japanese literature] 17.3 (March 1962): 170–77.

Hashizume, Shin'ya, ed. *Expo '70: Pabirion: Osaka Banpaku kōshiki memoriaru gaido* [Expo 70 pavilions: An official guide to Osaka Expo]. Tokyo: Heibonsha, 2010.

Hayashi, Sharon. "The Fantastic Trajectory of Pink Art Cinema from Stalin to Bush." *Global Art Cinema: New Theories and Histories*, ed. Rosalind Galt and Karl Schoonover, 48–61. Oxford: Oxford University Press, 2010.

———. "Shikyū e no kaiki: Rokujūnendai chūki Wakamatsu puro sakuhin ni okeru seiji to sei" [Return to the womb: Politics and sexuality in the mid-1960s Wakamatsu Production films]. *Wakamatsu Kōji: Hankenryoku no shōzō* [Wakamatsu Kōji: A portrait of counter-power], ed. Yomota Inuhiko and Hirasawa Gō, 95–111. Tokyo: Sakuhinsha, 2007.

Heath, Stephen. "Narrative Space." *Screen* 17.3 (1976): 19–75.

———. *Questions of Cinema*. Bloomington: Indiana University Press, 1981.

Heidegger, Martin. *Kant and the Problem of Metaphysics*. 5th edn. Translated by Richard Taft. Bloomington: Indiana University Press, 1997.

———. *The Question Concerning Technology and Other Essays*. Translated by William Lovitt. New York: Harper and Row, 1977.

Higgins, Dick. "Intermedia." *Leonardo* 34.1 (2001): 49–54.

High, Peter B. *Imperial Screen: Japanese Film Culture in the Fifteen Years' War, 1931–1945*. Madison: University of Wisconsin Press, 2003.

Hirano, Kyoko. *Mr. Smith Goes to Tokyo: Under the American Occupation, 1945–1952*. Washington: Smithsonian Institution Press, 1992.

Hiraoka, Masaaki. *Angura kikansetsu: Yami no hyōgensha retsuden* [Theses on the institution of the underground: Biographies of artists of the dark]. Tokyo: Magazine Five, 2007.

———. *Umi o miteita Zatōichi* [Zatōichi who was looking at the sea]. Tokyo: Izara Shobō, 1973.

Hirasawa, Gō, ed. *Andaaguraundo firumu aakaibusu* [Underground film archives]. Tokyo: Kawade Shobō, 2001.

———. "Fūkei, aruiwa fūkeiron o megutte: *Tokyo sensō sengo hiwa ron*." [The landscape, or on the topic of the landscape: On *The Man Who Left His Will on Film*]. *Tokyo sensō sengo hiwa* [The man who left his will on film], booklet included in *Oshima Nagisa*, DVD Box 2, 10–16. Tokyo: Kinokuniya, 2010.

———. "Radikarizumu no keizoku: 1970 nendai ikō ni okeru Wakamatsu Kōji ron" [A continuation of radicalism: Wakamatsu Kōji after the 1970s]. *Wakamatsu Kōji: Hankenryoku no shōzō* [Wakamatsu Kōji: A portrait of counter-power], ed. Yomota Inuhiko and Hirasawa Gō, 158–74. Tokyo: Sakuhinsha, 2007.

Ichiyanagi, Toshi. "Gendai eiga jōkyō jiten" [Encyclopedia of the situation of contemporary cinema]. *Kikan Firumu* [Film quarterly] 13 (December 1972): 99–152.

Imamura, Taihei. *Eiga no me: Moji kara eizō no bunka e* [The eye of cinema: From print culture to image culture]. Tokyo: Kōwadō, 1992.

———. "Eiga to terebi no renzokusei: Atarashii eizō mondai no minamoto" [The continuity between cinema and television: The root of new problems concerning the image]. *Eizō Bunka* [Image culture] 5 (June 1963): 6–15.

Itō, Biichi, ed. *Eizō to wa nanika* [What is an image?]. Tokyo: Shashin Dōjinsha, 1966.

Ivy, Marilyn. *Discourses of the Vanishing: Modernity, Phantasm, Japan*. Chicago: University of Chicago Press, 1995.

———. "Tracking the Mystery Man with the 21 Faces." *Critical Inquiry* 23.1 (autumn 1996): 11–36.

Jameson, Fredric. "Periodizing the 60s." *The 60s without Apology*, ed. Sohnya Sayres, Anders Stephanson, Stanley Aronowitz, and Fredric Jameson, 178–209. Minneapolis: University of Minnesota Press, 1984.

Karatani, Kōjin. *Origins of Modern Japanese Literature*. Foreword by Fredric Jameson. Translated by Brett de Bary. Durham: Duke University Press, 1993.

Kashihon Mangashi Kenkyūkai, ed. *Kashihon manga Returns* [Rental comics return]. Tokyo: Poplar, 2006.

Kawanaka, Nobuhiro. *Eiga: Nichijō no jikken* [Cinema: Everyday experiments]. Tokyo: Firumu Aato-sha, 1975.

"Kinkyū daitokushū: Mishima Yukio no shi" [The emergency special: The death of Mishima Yukio]. *Shūkan Yomiuri* [Yomiuri Weekly] 29.55 (December 1970): 20–21.

Kitajima, Noboru, ed. *Nippon nyūsu eigashi: Kaisen zen'ya kara shūsen chokugo made* [Film history of Nippon News: From the eve to the wake of the war]. Tokyo: Mainichi Shinbunsha, 1977.

Kizaki, Keiichirō. "Zen'ei eriito no taishū sogai" [Alienation of the masses by the elite vanguard]. *Kiroku Eiga* [Documentary film] 24 (January 1962): 24–26.

Kohso, Iwasaburō. "Kaikisuru chika minshū: Shirato Sanpei kara Oshima Nagisa ni nagarerumono" [The return of the underground people: What runs from Shirato Sanpei to Oshima Nagisa]. *Eiga kantoku Oshima Nagisa* [Director Oshima Nagisa], booklet in *Oshima Nagisa*, DVD Box 1, 56–61. Tokyo: Kinokuniya Shoten, 2008.

Komatsu, Hiroshi. "Some Characteristics of Japanese Cinema before World War I." Translated by Linda C. Ehrlich and Yuko Okutsu. *Reframing Japanese Cinema: Authorship, Genre, History*, ed. Arthur Nolletti Jr. and David Desser, 229–58. Bloomington: Indiana University Press, 1992.

Koshmann, Victor J. *Revolution and Subjectivity in Postwar Japan*. Chicago: University of Chicago Press, 1996.

Krauss, Rosalind. "Reinventing the Medium." *Critical Inquiry* 25.2 (1999): 289–305.

Kurabayashi, Yasushi. "Kanōsei no eiga: Takiguchi Shūzō no *Hokusai* shinario to shururearisumu." [The film of possibility: Takiguchi Shūzō's script for *Hokusai* and surrealism]. *Eizō hyōgen no orutanatibu: 1960 nendai no itsudatsu to sōzō* [Alternative cinematic expressions: Transgression and creation in the 1960s], ed. Nishijima Norio, 96–120. Tokyo: Shinwasha, 2005.

KuroDalaiJee. *Nikutai no anaakizumu: 1960 nendai Nihon bijutsu ni okeru pafōmansu no chikasuimyaku* [Anarchy of the body: Undercurrents of performance art in 1960s Japan]. Tokyo: Grambooks, 2010.

Kuzui, Kinshirō, and Hirasawa Gō. *Yuigon: Aato Shiataa Shinjuku Bunka* [Testament: Art Theatre Shinjuku Bunka]. Tokyo: Kawaide Shobō Shinsha, 2008.

Lamarre, Thomas. *The Anime Machine: A Media Theory of Animation*. Minneapolis: University of Minnesota Press, 2009.

Lefebvre, Martin. "L'aventure filmologique: Documents et jalons d'une histoire institutionnelle." *Cinémas: Revue d'études cinématographiques* 19.2–3 (2009): 59–100.

Leslie, Esther. *Walter Benjamin: Overpowering Conformism*. London: Pluto, 2000.

Lie, John. *Zainichi (Koreans in Japan): Diasporic Nationalism and Postcolonial Identity*. Berkeley: University of California Press, 2008.

Luhmann, Niklas. *The Reality of the Mass Media*. Translated by Kathleen Cross. Stanford: Stanford University Press, 2000.

Lyotard, Jean-François. "Acinema." *Narrative, Apparatus, Ideology: A Film Theory Reader*, ed. Philip Rosen, 349–59. New York: Columbia University Press, 1986.

Mainichi Shinbunsha. *1968 nen gurafiti* [Graffiti of 1968]. Tokyo: Mainichi Shinbunsha, 2010.

Manghani, Sunil, Arthur Piper, and Jon Simons, eds. *Images: A Reader*. London: Sage, 2006.

Marchessault, Janine. "Multi-Screens and Future Cinema: The Labyrinth Project at Expo 67." *Fluid Screens, Expanded Cinema*, ed. Janine Marchessault and Susan Lord, 29–51. Toronto: University of Toronto Press, 2007.

Marotti, William. "Japan 1968: The Performance of Violence and the Theater of Protest." *The American Historical Review* 114.1 (2009): 97–135.

———. *Money, Trains, and Guillotines: Art and Revolution in 1960s Japan*. Durham: Duke University Press, 2013.

Marx, Karl. *A Contribution to the Critique of Political Economy*. Edited by Maurice Dobb. New York: International Publishers, 1979.

Masaki, Kyōsuke. "Kiroku geijutsu no akuchuarite" [The actuality of documentary art]. *Gendai Geijutsu* [Contemporary art] 1 (1958): 174–81.

Matsuda, Masao. "Ajitēshon no ne: *Assatsu no mori* san" [The roots of agitation: Praise for *Forest of Pressure*]. *Bara to mumeisha* [A rose and the nameless one], 212–24. Tokyo: Haga Shoten, 1970.

———. *Bara to mumeisha* [A rose and the nameless one]. Tokyo: Haga Shoten, 1970.

———. "Eizō, fūkei, gengo" [The image, landscape, and language]. *Fūkei no shimetsu* [Extinction of the landscape], 94–109. Tokyo: Tabata Shoten, 1971.

———. *Fukanōsei no media* [Impossible media]. Tokyo: Tabata Shoten, 1973.

———. *Fūkei no shimetsu* [Extinction of the landscape]. Tokyo: Tabata Shoten, 1971.

———. "Fūkei no shimetsu no tame ni" [For the extinction of the landscape]. *Fūkei no shimetsu* [Extinction of the landscape], 270–87. Tokyo: Tabata Shoten, 1971.

———. "Fūkei to shite no toshi" [City as landscape]. *Fūkei no shimetsu* [Extinction of the landscape], 7–21. Tokyo: Tabata Shoten, 1971.

———. "Magazine and Book Check." *Andaaguraundo firumu aakaibusu* [Underground film archives], ed. Hirasawa Gō, 121–30. Tokyo: Kawade Shobō, 2001.

———. "Misshitsu, fūkei, kenryoku" [Closed chamber, landscape, and the power of domination]. *Bara to mumeisha* [A rose and the nameless one], 114–26. Tokyo: Haga Shoten, 1970.

———. "Misshitsu no teroru" [Terror in the closed chamber]. *Fūkei no shimetsu* [Extinction of the landscape], 233–39. Tokyo: Tabata Shoten, 1971.

———. "Sien no kūkan" [A space for a personal grudge]. *Fūkei no shimetsu* [Extinction of the landscape], 165–82. Tokyo: Tabata Shoten, 1971.

———. *Teroru no kairo* [A circuit of terror]. Tokyo: San'ichi Shobō, 1969.

———. "Waga rettō, waga fūkei" [My archipelago, my landscape]. *Fūkei no shimetsu* [Extinction of the landscape], 91–93. Tokyo: Tabata Shoten, 1971.

Matsui, Shigeru. "Tōno Yoshiaki no terebiteki na . . ." [Tōno Yoshiaki's televisual . . .]. Paper presented at the Yebisu film festival at Tokyo Metropolitan Museum of Photography, Tokyo, Japan, 11 February 2011.

Matsumoto, Toshio. "Bideo aato tenbō" [An observation on video art]. *Genshi no bigaku* [Aesthetics of hallucination], 205–18. Tokyo: Firumu Aato-sha, 1976.

———. "Documentarists of Japan # 9: Matsumoto Toshio." Yamagata International Documentary Film Festival. Documentary Box. http://www.yidff.jp/docbox/9/box9-2-e.html.

———. *Eiga no henkaku: Geijutsu teki rajikarizumu towa nani ka* [Transformation of cinema: What is artistic radicalism?]. Tokyo: San'ichi Shobō, 1972.

———. *Eizō no hakken: Avangyarudo to dokyumentarii* [Discovery of the image: Avant-garde and documentary]. Tokyo: San'ichi Shobō, 1963.

———. *Eizō no hakken: Avangyarudo to dokyumentarii* [Discovery of the image: Avant-Garde and documentary]. Reprint. Tokyo: Seiryū Shuppan, 2005.

———. "Ekusupandeddo shinema no tenbō" [An observation on expanded cinema]. *Eiga no henkaku: Geijutsu teki rajikarizumu towa nanika* [Transformation of cinema: What is artistic radicalism?], 163–82. Tokyo: San'ichi Shobō, 1972.

———. "Hōhō to imeeji" [Method and the image]. *Eizō no hakken: Avangyarudo to dokyumentarii* [Discovery of the image: Avant-garde and documentary], 57–65. Tokyo: San'ichi Shobō, 1963.

———. "Hyōgen keishiki no jikken." [Experiments in forms of expression]. *Gendai eiga jiten* [Contemporary encyclopedia of cinema], ed. Okada Susumu, Sasaki Kiichi, Satō Tadao, and Hani Susumu, 154–57. Tokyo: Bijutsu Shuppansha, 1967.

———. *Hyōgen no sekai* [The world of expression]. Tokyo: San'ichi Shobō, 1967.

———. "Kakusareta sekai no kiroku" [Record of the hidden world]. *Eizō no hakken: Avangyarudo to dokyumentarii* [Discovery of the image: Avant-garde and documentary], 79–93. Tokyo: San'ichi Shobō, 1963.

———. "Katachi ni naranai katachi e no mosaku" [Exploration of a form without form]. *Kiroku Eiga* [Documentary film] 54 (May 1963): 28–29.
———. *Matsumoto Toshio jikken eizōshū: 1961–1987* [Toshio Matsumoto experimental film works: 1961–1987]. DVD box set. Tokyo: Uplink, 2005.
———. "Mirai to mukiatte iru mono" [Those who face the future]. *Kikan Firumu* [Film quarterly] 2 (February 1969): 140–48.
———. "Ore tachi wa minna *Kichigai Piero* da" [We are all *Pierrot le fou*]. *Dezain Hihyō* [Design review] 6 (July 1968): 40–46.
———. "Purojekushon aato no kadai" [The task of projection arts]. *Eiga no henkaku: geijutsuteki rajikarizumu to wa nani ka* [Transformation of cinema: What is artistic radicalism?], 159–162. Tokyo: San'ichi Shobō, 1972.
———. "Saihan ni yosete" [For the reprint]. *Eizō no hakken: Avangyarudo to dokyumentarii* [Discovery of the image: Avant-garde and documentary], 242–46. Reprint. Tokyo: Seiryū Shuppan, 2005.
———. "Subete no zen'ei eiga no saizensen kara" [From the frontline of all avant-garde films]. *Andaaguraundo firumu aakaibusu* [Underground film archives], ed. Hirasawa Gō, 20–31. Tokyo: Kawade Shobō, 2001.
———. "Zen'ei kiroku eiga no hōhō ni tsuite" [On the method of avant-garde documentary film]. *Kiroku Eiga* [Documentary film] 1 (May 1958): 6–11.
———. "Zen'ei kiroku eiga ron" [A theory of avant-garde documentary film]. *Eizō no hakken: Avangyarudo to dokyumentarii* [Discovery of the image: Avant-garde and documentary], 47–56. Tokyo: San'ichi Shobō, 1963.
Matsumoto Productions. "Bara no sōretsu: Shinario" [Funeral parade of roses: Script]. *Art Theater* 70 (September 1969): 48–72.
McLuhan, Marshall. *Understanding Media: The Extensions of Man*. Cambridge: MIT Press, 1994.
———. "Address to Vision 65." *Essential McLuhan*, ed. Eric McLuhan and Frank Zingrone, 219–32. New York: Basic, 1995.
Metz, Christian. *Film Language: A Semiotics of the Cinema*. Translated by Michael Taylor. Chicago: University of Chicago Press, 1991.
Michelson, Annette. "Introduction." *Cinema, Censorship, and the State: The Writings of Nagisa Oshima*, by Oshima Nagisa, edited by Annette Michelson, translated by Dawn Lawson, 1–5. Cambridge: MIT Press, 1992.
Mishima, Yukio, and Oshima Nagisa. "Mishima Yukio / Oshima Nagisa: Fasisuto ka kakumeika ka" [Mishima Yukio / Oshima Nagisa: Fascist or revolutionary?]. *Eiga Geijutsu* [Film art] 16.1 (January 1968): 23–34.
Mitchell, W. J. T. "Imperial Landscape." *Landscape and Power*, ed. W. J. T. Mitchell, 5–34. Chicago: University of Chicago Press, 1994.
———. *Picture Theory: Essays on Verbal and Visual Representation*. Chicago: University of Chicago Press, 1994.
———. "What Is an Image?" *New Literary History* 15.3 (spring 1984): 503–37.
Mondzain, Marie-José. *Image, Icon, Economy: The Byzantine Origins of the Contem-*

porary Imaginary. Translated by Rico Franses. Stanford: Stanford University Press, 2005.

Monnet, Livia. "Towards the Feminine Sublime, or the Story of a 'Twinkling Monad, Shape-shifting across Dimension': Intermediality, Fantasy, and Special Effects in Cyberpunk Film and Animation." *Japan Forum* 14.2 (2002): 225–68.

Mraz, John. "Santiago Alvarez: From Dramatic Form to Direct Cinema." *The Social Documentary in Latin America*, ed. Julian Burton, 131–49. Pittsburgh: University of Pittsburgh, 1990.

Mulvey, Laura. *Death 24x a Second: Stillness and the Moving Image*. London: Reaktion Books, 2006.

———. "Visual Pleasure and Narrative Cinema." *Narrative, Apparatus, Ideology: A Film Theory Reader*, ed. Philip Rosen, 198–209. New York: Columbia University Press, 1986.

Musser, Charles. *The Emergence of Cinema: The American Screen to 1907*. Berkeley: University of California Press, 1990.

Nacos, Brigitte. *Mass-Mediated Terrorism: The Central Role of the Media in Terrorism and Counterterrorism*. Lanham: Rowman and Littlefield, 2007.

Nagae, Michitarō. *Eiga, hyōgen, keisei* [Cinema, expression, formation]. Edited by Makino Mamoru. Tokyo: Yumani Shobō, 2003.

Nakahira, Takuma. "Kiroku to iu gen'ei: Dokyumento kara monyumento e" [The document called illusion: From document to monument]. *Mitsuzukeru hate ni hi ga . . .* [Fire, at the horizon to which I gaze . . .], 222–46. Tokyo: Osiris, 2007.

———. *Mitsuzukeru hate ni hi ga . . .* [Fire, at the horizon to which I gaze . . .]. Tokyo: Osiris, 2007.

Nancy, Jean-Luc. *The Ground of the Image*. Translated by Jeff Fort. New York: Fordham University Press, 2005.

Noda, Shinkichi. "Higenjitsusei no akuchuaritii" [The actuality of nonreality]. *Kiroku Geijutsu* [Documentary art] 2.5 (May 1959): 30–34.

Noda, Shinkichi, Matsumoto Toshio, Teshigahara Hiroshi, and Hani Susumu. "Kiroku eiga to geki eiga: Dokyumentarii no hōhō o megutte" [Documentary film and fiction film: On the issue of the documentary method]. *Shin Nihon Bungaku* [New Japanese literature] 16.5 (May 1961): 125–37.

Nornes, Abé Mark. *Forest of Pressure: Ogawa Shinsuke and Postwar Japanese Documentary*. Minneapolis: University of Minnesota Press, 2007.

———. *Japanese Documentary Film: The Meiji Era through Hiroshima*. Minneapolis: University of Minnesota Press, 2003.

———. "Pōru Rūta: Paul Rotha and the Politics of Translation." *Cinema Journal* 38.3 (spring 1999): 91–108.

———. "The Postwar Documentary Trace: Groping in the Dark." *Positions* 10.1 (spring 2002): 39–78.

Obinata, Sumio. *Nihon kindai kokka no seiritsu to keisatsu* [The birth of the modern Japanese state and the police]. Tokyo: Azekura Shobō, 1992.

Ogawa, Shinsuke. *Eiga o toru: Dokyumentarii no shifuku o motomete* [Shooting films: Seeking bliss in the documentary]. Edited by Yamane Sadao. Tokyo: Satsuma Shobō, 1993.

Okada, Susumu. *Eiga gaku kara eizō gaku e* [From film studies to image studies]. Fukuoka: Kyūshū daigaku Shuppankai, 1987.

———. "Eizō no ronri to gengo no ronri" [The logic of image and the logic of language]. *Gendai geijutsu* [Contemporary art] 3 (1959): 100–105.

———. "Eizō to majutsu ni kansuru josetsu" [An introduction to the image and magic]. *Eizō to wa nanika* [What is an image?], ed. Itō Biichi, 5–23. Tokyo: Shashin Dōjinsha, 1966.

———. *Gendai eizō ron* [A contemporary theory of the image]. Tokyo: San'ichi Shobō, 1965.

Ōmae, Masaomi, Gōtō Kazuhiko, Satō Tsuyoshi, and Tōno Yoshiaki, eds. *McLuhan sono hito to riron* [McLuhan and his theory]. Tokyo: Daikōsha, 1967.

Oshima, Nagisa. *Cinema, Censorship, and the State: The Writings of Nagisa Oshima.* Edited by Annette Michelson. Translated by Dawn Lawson. Cambridge: MIT Press, 1992.

———. *Dōjidai sakka no hakken* [Discovery of contemporary auteurs]. Tokyo: San'ichi Shobō, 1978.

———. "Eiga zokusetsu e no chōsen" [A challenge to vulgar beliefs about cinema]. *Sengo eiga: Hakai to sōzō* [Postwar cinema: Destruction and creation], 75–81. Tokyo: San'ichi Shobō, 1963.

———. "'Ninja bugeichō' no kao" [The face of *Band of Ninja*]. *Art Theater* 47 (February 1967): 12–13.

———. "Ogawa Shinsuke: Tōsō to datsuraku" [Ogawa Shinsuke: Fighting and dropping out]. *Eiga Hihyō II* [Film criticism II] 1.3 (December 1970): 15–25.

———. *Oshima Nagisa: 1960*. Tokyo: Seidosha, 1993.

———. *Oshima Nagisa: 1968*. Tokyo: Seidosha, 2004.

———. "Seisaku nooto bassui" [Excerpts from production notes]. *Oshima Nagisa: 1968*, 7–14. Tokyo: Seidosha, 2004.

———. *Sengo eiga: Hakai to sōzō* [Postwar cinema: Destruction and creation]. Tokyo: San'ichi Shobō, 1963.

———. "Sengo nihon eiga no jōkyō to shutai" [Situation and subject in postwar Japanese cinema]. *Sengo eiga: Hakai to sōzō* [Postwar cinema: Destruction and creation], 185–212. Tokyo: San'ichi Shobō, 1963.

———. "Shinario ni tsuite" [About the script]. *Art Theater* 65 (February 1969): 20–21.

———. "Shura to shutai = Matsumoto Toshio." [Pandemonium and Subject = Matsumoto Toshio] *Dōjidai sakka no hakken* [Discovery of contemporary auteurs], 111–32. Tokyo: San'ichi Shobō, 1978.

———. *Taiken teki sengo eizō ron* [Theorizing postwar film from my experience]. Tokyo: Asahi Shinbunsha, 1975.
———. "Wakamatsu Kōji: Sabetsu to satsuriku" [Wakamatsu Kōji: Discrimination and carnage]. *Eiga Hihyō II* [Film criticism II] 1.1 (October 1970): 100–107.
Prashad, Vijay. *Darker Nations: A People's History of the Third World*. New York: New Press, 2007.
Project X: Osaka Banpaku shijō saidai no keibi sakusen [Project X: Osaka Expo: The biggest security operation in history]. DVD. Tokyo: NHK Enterprise, 2005.
Rancière, Jacques. *Disagreement: Politics and Philosophy*. Translated by Julie Rose. Minneapolis: University of Minnesota Press, 1999.
———. *The Emancipated Spectator*. Translated by Gregory Elliott. London: Verso, 2009.
———. *The Future of the Image*. Translated by Gregory Elliott. London: Verso, 2007.
———. *The Politics of Aesthetics*. Translated by Gabriel Rockhill. London: Continuum, 2004.
Reiko, Tomii. "*Geijutsu* on Their Minds: Memorable Words on Anti-Art." *Art, Anti-Art, Non-Art: Experimentations in the Public Sphere in Postwar Japan 1950–1970*, ed. Charles Merewether and Rika Iezumi Hiro, 35–62. Los Angeles: Getty Research Institute, 2007.
Renov, Michael. *The Subject of Documentary*. Minneapolis: University of Minnesota Press, 2004.
Richie, Donald. *A Hundred Years of Japanese Film: A Concise History, with a Selective Guide to Videos and DVDs*. Tokyo: Kodansha International, 2001.
———. *Viewed Sideways: Writings on Culture and Style in Contemporary Japan*. Berkeley: Stone Bridge Press, 2011.
Richman Kenneally, Rhona, and Johanne Sloan, eds. *Expo 67: Not Just a Souvenir*. Toronto: University of Toronto Press, 2010.
Ridgely, Steven C. *Japanese Counterculture: The Antiestablishment Art of Terayama Shūji*. Minnesota: University of Minnesota Press, 2010.
Rodowick, D. N. *The Crisis of Political Modernism: Criticism and Ideology in Contemporary Film Theory*. Berkeley: University of California Press, 1988.
Rosen, Philip. *Change Mummified: Cinema, Historicity, Theory*. Minneapolis: University of Minnesota Press, 2001.
Ross, Julian. "Projection-Performances: The Degree of Intermediality in the Japanese Expanded Cinema of the 1960s and 1970s." Paper presented at the symposium "Visual Underground: Theatre Scorpio and Japanese Experimental Cinema of the Sixties," Montreal, Canada, 17 September 2011.
Ross, Kristin. *May '68 and Its Afterlives*. Chicago: University of Chicago Press, 2002.
Rotha, Paul. *Documentary Film*. New York: Hastings House, 1952.

Saitō, Ayako. "Adachi eiga to feminizumu" [Adachi's films and feminism]. *Jōkyō* [Situations] 3.30 (June 2003): 164–67.

Sas, Miryam. *Fault Lines: Cultural Memory and Japanese Surrealism*. Stanford: Stanford University Press, 1999.

———. *Experimental Arts in Postwar Japan: Moments of Encounter, Engagement, and Imagined Return*. Cambridge: Harvard University Press, 2011.

Sasaki, Kiichi. *Geijutsuron nōto II* [Notes on theories of art II]. Tokyo: Gōdōshuppan, 1968.

Sasaki, Mamoru. "Fūkei ga kawaranakereba 'kakumei' wa dekinai" [We cannot have a "revolution" unless landscapes are changed]. *Oshima Nagisa: 1968*, by Oshima Nagisa, 284–304. Tokyo: Seidosha, 2004.

Satō, Tadao. ATG *eiga o yomu: 60 nendai ni hajimatta meisaku aakaibu* [Reading ATG films: An archive of classics that started in the 1960s]. Tokyo: Firumu Aato-sha, 1991.

Satō, Takumi. "Terebi ga utsushita 'hanran'" [The revolt captured on television]. *1968 nen ni nihon to sekai de okotta koto* [Events that took place in Japan and the world in 1968], ed. Mainichi Shinbunsha, 38–42. Tokyo: Mainichi Shinbunsha, 2009.

Sawaragi, Noi. *Sensō to banpaku* [The war and the Expo]. Tokyo: Bijutsu Shuppansha, 2005.

Schaefer, Eric. *"Bold! Daring! Shocking! True!": A History of Exploitation Films, 1919–1959*. Durham: Duke University Press, 1999.

Shigenobu, Fusako. "Eiga no senyū tachi" [Comrades in cinema]. *Jōkyō* [Situations] 4.6, special issue on Adachi Masao (June 2003): 6–20.

"Sōgetsu Aaato Sentaa no Kiroku." Kankō Iinkai, ed. *Kagayake 60 nendai: Sōgetsu Aaato Sentaa no zenkiroku* [The shining 1960s: A complete record of the Sōgetsu Art Center]. Tokyo: Firumu Aato-sha, 2002.

Solanas, Fernando, and Octavio Getino. "Towards a Third Cinema." *Movies and Methods: An Anthology*, ed. Bill Nichols, 44–64. Berkeley: University of California Press, 1976.

Stam, Robert. "Beyond Third Cinema: The Aesthetics of Hybridity." *Rethinking Third Cinema*, edited by Wimal Dissanayake and Anthony R. Guneratne, 31–48. London: Routledge, 2003.

Steinberg, Marc. *Anime's Media Mix: Franchising Toys and Characters in Japan*. Minneapolis: University of Minnesota Press, 2012.

Steinhoff, Patricia. "Student Conflict." *Conflict in Japan*, ed. Ellis S. Krauss, Thomas P. Rohlen, and Patricia G. Steinhoff, 174–213. Honolulu: University of Hawaii Press, 1984.

Sterritt, David, ed. *Jean-Luc Godard Interviews*. Jackson: University Press of Mississippi, 1998.

Sugiyama, Mitsunobu. "Media and Power in Japan." *De-Westernizing Media Studies*, ed. James Curran and Myung-Jin Park, 191–201. London: Routledge, 2000.

Suzuki, Yoshiaki. *Pinku eiga suikoden: Sono jūninen shi* [The saga of the pink film: Ten years of its history]. Tokyo: Seishinsha, 1983.

Takahashi, Tetsu. "Oshima eiga to bunseki kaunseringu" [Oshima and analytical counseling]. *Art Theater* 65 (February 1969): 13–15.

Taki, Kōji. *Kotoba no nai sikō: Jibutsu/kūkan/eizō ni tsuite no oboegaki* [Thought without words: A note on things/spaces/images]. Tokyo: Tabata Shoten, 1972.

Takiguchi, Shūzō. *Korekushon Takiguchi Shūzō* [Takiguchi Shūzō collection]. Vol. 1. Tokyo: Misuzu Shobō, 1991.

Tamai, Goichi. "Kiroku Geijutsu no Kai: Geijutsu undō shōkai I" [The Association for Documentary Art: Introductions of artistic movements I]. *Shin Nihon Bungaku* [New Japanese literature] 12.11 (October 1957): 120–27.

Tanaka, Tomohito. *Keibigyō no shakaigaku* [The sociology of the security-guard business]. Tokyo: Akashi Shoten, 2009.

Tarde, Gabriel. *L'opinion et la foule*. Paris: Presses Universitaires de France, 1989.

"Tokushū: Banpaku to Anpo/EXPOSE·1968 zenkiroku shūroku" [A special on Expo and Anpo: A complete record of "EXPOSE·1968"]. *Dezain Hihyō* [Design review] 6 (1969): 16–118.

Tomoda, Yoshiyuki. "Eizō ronsō aruiwa gengo to eizō ronsō" [The debate on the image or the debate on language and the image]. *Eizōgaku/Iconics* 82 (2009): 63–81.

Tosaka, Jun. "Ideorogii gairon" [General remarks on ideology]. *Tosaka Jun zenshū* [The collected works of Tosaka Jun], 2:95–222. Tokyo: Keisōsha, 1966.

———. "Jaanarizumu to tetsugaku no kōshō" [The encounter between journalism and philosophy]. *Tosaka Jun zenshū* [The collected works of Tosaka Jun], 4:145–52. Tokyo: Keisōsha, 1966.

———. *Nihon ideorogiiron* [On Japanese ideology]. Tokyo: Iwanami Shoten, 1977.

———. "Shinbun genshō no bunseki" [An analysis of the newspaper phenomenon]. *Tosaka Jun zenshū* [The collected works of Tosaka Jun], 3:118–44. Tokyo: Keisōsha, 1966.

———. *Tosaka Jun zenshū* [The collected works of Tosaka Jun]. 5 vols. Tokyo: Keisōsha, 1966–1967.

Tsivian, Yuri. "Introduction." *Lines of Resistance: Dziga Vertov and the Twenties*, ed. Yuri Tsivian, 1–28. Gemonda: Le Giornate del Cinema Muto, 2004.

Tsuchiyama, Kimie. *Kōdo seichōki "Toshi seisaku" no seiji katei* [Political process of "urban policy" in the high-growth era]. Tokyo: Nippon Hyōronsha, 2007.

Tsuji, Shun'ichirō. *Fōku songu undō: 25 nenme no sōkatsu* [The folk song movement: An overview after twenty-five years]. Tokyo: Shinpūsha, 2001.

Tsumura, Hideo. *Zoku eiga to hihyō* [Sequal: Film and criticism]. Tokyo: Koyama Shoten, 1940.

Turim, Maureen. *The Films of Oshima Nagisa: Images of a Japanese Iconoclast*. Berkeley: University of California Press, 1998.

Ushida, Ayami. ATG *Eiga + Shinjuku* [ATG films + Shinjuku]. Tokyo: D-bungaku Kenkyūkai, 2007.

Virilio, Paul. *Speed and Politics: An Essay on Dromology*. Translated by Mark Polizzotti. New York: Semiotext(e), 1986.

Wada, Yōichi. "Meiji/Taisho ki no jaanarizumuron" [Theories of journalism during the Meiji and Taisho periods]. *Shinbungaku Hyōron* [Newspaper studies review] 18 (March 1969): 70–75.

Wakamatsu, Kōji. *Jikō nashi* [No statute of limitations]. Edited by Koide Shinobu and Kakegawa Masayuki. Tokyo: Waizu Shuppan, 2004.

———. *Wakamatsu Kōji: Ore wa te o yogosu* [Wakamatsu Kōji: I dirty my hands]. Tokyo: Dagereo Shuppan, 1982.

Wakamatsu Production. "Sekigun-PFLP: Sekai sensō sengen" [The Red Army/PFLP: The declaration of world war]. *Eiga Hihyō II* [Film criticism II] 3.3 (March 1972): 12–25.

Waugh, Thomas. "Beyond *Vérité*: Emile de Antonio and the New Documentary of the Seventies." *Movies and Methods: An Anthology II*, ed. Bill Nichols, 233–59. Berkeley: University of California Press, 1985.

Weigel, Sigrid. *Body-and-Image Space: Re-reading Walter Benjamin*. New York: Routledge, 1996.

Weizman, Eyal. *Hollow Land: Israel's Architecture of Occupation*. London: Verso, 2007.

———. "Strategic Points, Flexible Lines, Tense Surfaces, Political Volumes: Ariel Sharon and the Geometry of Occupation." *Philosophical Forum* 35.2 (summer 2004): 221–44.

Williams, Linda. *Hard Core: Power, Pleasure and the "Frenzy of the Visible."* Berkeley: University of California Press, 1989.

Williams, Raymond. *Television: Technology and Cultural Form*. London: Fontana, 1974.

Wollen, Peter. "The Two Avant-Gardes." *Readings and Writings: Semiotic Counter-Strategies*, 92–104. London: Verso, 1982.

Yomota, Inuhiko. *Manga genron* [Principles of manga]. Tokyo: Chikuma Shobō, 1999.

———. *Paresuchina nau: Sensō, eiga, ningen* [Palestine now: War, cinema, and the human]. Tokyo: Sakuhinsha, 2006.

———. *Shirato Sanpei ron* [On Shirato Sanpei]. Tokyo: Sakuhinsha, 2004.

Yomota, Inuhiko, and Hirasawa Gō. "Wakamatsu Kōji intabyū" [Interview with Wakamatsu Kōji]. *Wakamatsu Kōji: Hankenryoku no shōzō* [Wakamatsu Kōji: A portrait of counter-power], ed. Yomota Inuhiko and Hirasawa Gō, 175–210. Tokyo: Sakuhinsha, 2007.

Yoshimoto, Mitsuhiro. "Japanese Cinema in Search of a Discipline." *Kurosawa: Film Studies and Japanese Cinema*, 8–49. Durham: Duke University Press, 2000.

———. *Kurosawa: Film Studies and Japanese Cinema*. Durham: Duke University Press, 2000.

Yoshimoto, Takaaki. *Jōkyō e no hatsugen* [Addressing the situation]. Tokyo: Tokuma Shoten, 1968.

———. "Sengo bungaku no genjitsusei: Akuchuaritii wa kanō ka" [The reality of postwar literature: Is actuality possible?]. *Bungei* [Literary art] 1.6 (August 1962): 210–20.

index

www.ingramcontent.com/pod-product-compliance
Lightning Source LLC
LaVergne TN
LVHW020507100826
845148LV00003B/717

* 9 7 8 0 8 2 2 3 5 5 0 4 5 *